IF YOU CAN'T STAND THE HEAT

ROBERT MEDINA

IF YOU CAN'T STAND THE HEAT

A NEW ORLEANS FIREFIGHTER'S COOKBOOK

TATE PUBLISHING & Enterprises

Published by Tate Publishing & Enterprises, LLC
127 E. Trade Center Terrace | Mustang, Oklahoma 73064 USA
1.888.361.9473 | www.tatepublishing.com

Tate Publishing is committed to excellence in the publishing industry. The company reflects the philosophy established by the founders, based on Psalm 68:11,
"The Lord gave the word and great was the company of those who published it."

Book design copyright © 2011 by Tate Publishing, LLC. All rights reserved.
Cover design by Bekah Garibay
Interior design by Nathan Harmony

Published in the United States of America

ISBN: 978-1-61777-168-2
1. Cooking / General
2. Cooking / Regional & Ethnic / Cajun & Creole
11.03.14

Other books by Robert Medina
Freefall (2002)

Dedication

For all of the guinea pigs ... you know who you are.

Acknowledgments

I would like to acknowledge everyone who put up with my constant and continuous taste testing. Thanks for being there for me.

Thanks to my family and friends for all of the support.

Thanks to all of the great guys I had the privilege of working and cooking with over the years.

Thanks to the photographers, Mari Darr-Welch and Marguerite Parker.

Thanks also to the members of the Destin Fire Control District for their help and cooperation.

Last but not least, I would like to thank the love of my life for everything good in my life.

For Lori.

Table of Contents

Introduction

I guess you could say that I come from a family of firefighters. My dad, my brother, my uncle, and I all worked for the New Orleans Fire Department. All of us were also firehouse cooks to one degree or another. I say cooks because none of us were trained in the culinary arts. We just liked to cook. It was a family thing, a firehouse thing … and a New Orleans thing.

My fascination with cooking started very early. When I was really young, my grandmother stood me up on a chair and handed me a wooden spoon. She told me to stir the roux and not to let it burn. What I remember most from that day wasn't all of the stirring. I remember the smelling. The aroma that was floating all around the room just smelled delicious. From that moment on, I was hooked. If there was any opportunity to help out in the kitchen, I took it. As I got older, those opportunities became few and far between, but I managed to make the most out of them when they came around.

New Orleans is a great training ground for people who like to cook, especially in our family. We were fortunate enough to have something we called "a camp." It was named the Ponderosa … maybe because it was so big. Basically, it was a huge four-bedroom house built out over the waters of Lake Pontchartrain. There were long piers to get out to it and even longer ones out back. That's where the crab nets were stacked, fishing poles were at the ready, and the boats were tied up. When we were kids, we spent a lot of summers out there. We fished, caught hard crabs, and harvested soft-shells. We had shrimp, oysters, and basically gathered in every type of seafood the lake had to offer. We were always boiling or frying or broiling something. Seafood was abundant and available for the grown-ups to cook. It was a great way for a kid to learn how to make the basics along with the classics.

We all loved going there, and it was great for as long as it lasted. Hurricane Camille blew it away, and it was never rebuilt. But, as after all disasters, life goes on. I grew up, and things went on as usual. I graduated from high school, joined the Navy, and eventually went on to join the New Orleans Fire Department. It was shortly thereafter that my cooking bug was reawakened. I didn't realize how much I missed putting together a big pot of something for the masses.

Because I spent a lot of time there as a kid, I was acquainted with the firehouse cooking etiquette. The way it worked was really simple. One guy was the cook. The others had their specialties, but for the most

If You Can't Stand the Heat

part, it was just the one guy. Like all great leaders (even in the kitchen), he was never chosen. It just came to be … grown out of the ranks, so to speak. That's the way it worked. So for many years, I felt like I was back in my grandmother's kitchen. I would help out, watch, and learn from the older master cooks.

Depending on how the manpower worked out for any given day, you could be sent to any engine house in the city. I liked it because they all had different styles of cooking. Some did Italian, others Cajun, and still others might have a fondness for Asian. Just like the fact that you never knew what would transpire on any given workday (fires, medical emergencies, and such), you never knew who was going to cook what. The diversity was there for the taking, and I took it all. After years of culling the talents of many cooks, I got to be stationed mainly at one house. I cooked a little here and there, and then I took over the role. Like those before me, it just sort of came to be.

Cooking for a bunch of firemen is kind of funny. Generally speaking, after a meal no one would say anything. That's the way it was. But every once in a while, every now and then, you would hear an admiring remark. You knew you did a good job if someone would nod their head. You also knew when you did a great job. Someone would look you in the eye and say, "That didn't suck." It was the ultimate firehouse cooking compliment! The perfect reward for putting together a good meal.

The other perk of preparing the food was that you didn't have to do the dishes. Score another one for the cook!

I worked at that engine house for many years until I was forced to retire. After nearly twenty-four years, I was done. I didn't want to go, but after sustaining an injury that couldn't be repaired, I had no choice. After that I wasn't sure what I would do with life. I was forty-eight and unemployable.

One day, after making a meal for a group of people, my wife suggested that I write down all of the things I have cooked and put them in book form. At the time it seemed like a good idea to me, especially since I was fresh out of ideas. The more I thought about it, the more I wanted to make a go of it. But if I was going to do this, I needed to go one step further. I needed to make what on the surface seems difficult seem easy. I wanted it to be unlike other cookbooks.

Don't you hate cookbooks that don't give enough details? Do I cover the pot? Leave it uncovered? Why use stock instead of water? Should the stock be cold or hot when I add it? They sometimes leave a little bit of info out that could change the way the dish comes out. I wanted to make sure that this book was loaded with little bits of information so that anyone could make anything in it. Hopefully, all of that info would remove any doubt from the mind of whoever would try to make any dish. That's why some recipes will seem rather lengthy. It's done on purpose. Cooking is all in the details.

Many people wanted me to add some firehouse anecdotes to this book to make it more "folksy." To be honest there is nothing folksy about being a firefighter in a big city. Sure, we had our moments of humor. But this is a serious job, and you deal with serious issues. It is difficult to be involved in someone else's tragedy firsthand, take what you have just experienced, and pretend like it didn't happen. Do this several times a day, and you begin to realize just how important the evening meal can be. Hopefully it becomes some quiet time to relax and enjoy something that makes you forget about the day, a time to partake in something that tastes so good that it makes you want to go back for seconds. In other words, it was important because it made things feel normal.

I promised that I would include one firehouse story. It doesn't make it folksy, but it's a good story:

Every Thanksgiving we would fry turkeys. If guys were off duty that day, they would bring their injected turkeys to the engine house where we would have several fryers going. They would come and "drop a turkey," hang out, and shoot the breeze while their bird would finish frying. That was the generally accepted "rule," if you will. You stayed with your turkey.

One Thanksgiving our friend K.P. was in a hurry. He rushed in and asked if we could fry his turkey, and he would be back to pick it up. We balked at first, but finally relented. He took off to places unknown and left us with the possibility of messing with him big time. Besides firefighting, we excelled at that!

One of the other guys decided to teach him a lesson. We took a small chicken and fried it along with his turkey. We put this tiny chicken in his giant turkey pan and covered it up. When he came back, we asked him where he got that turkey. He asked why, and we told him that it was full of water, and when it cooked, it shrank up. When he opened the lid, he nearly fell over. "I've got to feed ten people with that!" We milked it for all it was worth then let him off the hook. Needless to say, he never left his turkey unattended again.

So that's it. That is how this book came about. I hope you will enjoy it. I also hope that it sparks the cooking flame inside of you; no pun intended.

I will leave you with just one final thought. A very famous chef once said that everything she learned about cooking, she learned after she got out of culinary school. You don't have to be a chef to cook great dishes. You just need to know the right steps to take, and I hope they are all in this book.

Enjoy!

Read This First

Flashover Seasoning and Roux

The first thing you need to know is that you will see the letters FOS indicated in the ingredients throughout this book. The very first recipe in the book is for flashover seasoning. That is FOS. It's easy to put together, and you might find it useful to have on hand to add to many of your own dishes.

The second thing you need to know is how to make a roux. Roux can be made in many different ways. Basically it is flour and oil. Sometimes it is flour and butter, depending on what you are cooking. The thing about a roux is that you never want to leave it. Once you get started, you have to stir the roux until it's done so that it doesn't burn. If that happens, you have to start over. Not fun!

A roux takes time to develop. Don't crank up the fire and expect it to happen faster. That will only make it burn faster. Take your time; do it right. A roux is equal amounts of flour and whatever oil you are using. Equal amounts!

Once the ingredients are in the pot, you mix them, and use a low heat. Now, start scraping the bottom of the pot. Slowly, the flour will start to turn colors. First, there is a white or blond roux. Next, there is a golden brown roux. After that comes a peanut butter roux. Then there is the light brown, followed by the rust colored (sometimes referred to as a red roux), then the dark brown (sometimes referred to as a chocolate roux), and it ends with a black roux. The black roux is difficult to achieve without burning it, but it has the most flavor you can get from a roux.

If you look at a recipe, which indicates using a peanut butter roux, just stir it until it becomes the color of peanut butter. It's that simple. If you need a dark brown roux, just continue to cook it and scrape it until it turns that color.

The darker the roux, the more intense the flavor. So just give it a try. Go out and cook something great!

Sauces, Stocks, and Seasonings

Firehouse Flashover Seasoning

If you take a look around, you'll find that there are literally dozens and dozens of Cajun spice mixes out there. Everybody usually makes up one of his or her own and then puts it out on the market for public consumption. But to my taste, they all seem to be pretty close with a few minor exceptions. This seasoning mixture is an amalgam of many flavorings that I like. I tried quite a few combinations and ultimately ended up with this one. I start with FOS as a base spice to which I add other ingredients for different dishes.

2 tablespoons of kosher salt
1 tablespoon of packaged (not fresh-ground) black pepper
1 tablespoon of white pepper
1 tablespoon of cayenne pepper
2 tablespoons of garlic powder
2 tablespoons of onion powder
2 tablespoons of dried oregano
1 tablespoon of sweet basil
1 tablespoon of ground thyme
2 tablespoons of paprika

If you want a Mexican flavor, leave out the oregano, basil, and thyme; then add cumin, chili powder, and smoked paprika. Experiment with something of your own. That is what's fun about cooking. There is no right or wrong. There is only what tastes good or bad. If you like the way it tastes, run with it. Chances are you won't be alone.

Note: For the ingredient listings in the rest of this book, flashover seasoning will be referred to as FOS. I gave a recipe to someone that included FOS, and he thought it meant French Onion Soup. Don't go there.

If You Can't Stand the Heat

Homemade Mayonnaise

1 large egg
1 tablespoon of fresh lemon juice
1/2 teaspoon of yellow mustard
1/2 teaspoon of salt
1 cup of vegetable oil

Anyone can go to the grocery store and buy a jar of mayonnaise. It may be easy. It may be practical. But it doesn't have the flavor or the freshness of homemade.

This recipe is so simple to prepare that…well…even I can do it. Once you learn how, you will find that you will use it in all sorts of dishes instead of the store-bought variety.

First, break the egg into your blender. Add the lemon juice, mustard, and salt. Put the top back on and remove the little plastic piece in the center. Put your blender on mix and slowly drizzle the oil through the top. Slowly! It will soon turn into a thick emulsion. You will know when this happens because you will not only see it—you will hear it. The blender will change in pitch because it no longer has a lot of liquid in it. Kill the motor.

Once the emulsion is made, stop adding oil. You don't necessarily have to use all of the oil in your measuring cup. Sometimes it will take a little more than half or three-quarters of the oil to turn into mayo. If you try to force more oil into it, the mayo will break and get runny.

This should yield approximately one cup—maybe a little less. If you need more, it's easy to make more. Just start over.

Note: Be sure to shield the opening with your other hand while you are drizzling in the oil. It has a tendency to spray back at you through that little hole. You don't want to wear the mayo. You just want to eat it.

P.S. Thanks to Phyllis Moore for turning me on to this over thirty years ago. I never went back to store-bought.

Hollandaise Sauce

4 egg yolks
1 tablespoon of chicken stock
2 tablespoons of lemon juice
1/2 teaspoon of salt
Pinch of cayenne
Pinch of white pepper
1 cup of Clarified Butter (see recipe)

Ladies and gentlemen, get your wrists ready for some action. There is a lot of whisking to this, but it is worth the wait—and the whisking!

Put about an inch of water in a pot and heat it up until it is simmering. Place the egg yolks and the chicken stock in a metal bowl and begin to whisk them vigorously. Place the bowl over the pan of water and keep whisking. The yolks will start to froth up. Do not let the bowl touch the water. You don't want to cook the eggs. If the eggs get too hot, take the bowl away from the heat and keep whisking. Once it cools down, you can go back to the heat. It should be smooth and creamy when done.

Take the bowl away from the heat and slowly add the butter while continuing to whisk. Once all of the butter is incorporated, you should have a nice thick yellow sauce. If it gets too thick, just add a little more chicken stock to the pan. Now whisk in the lemon, salt, cayenne, and white pepper.

This sauce will not hold up for long, so be ready to serve it immediately.

Note: I have never done this, but I have heard that people will keep this sauce in a thermos for a while and that it will stay warm and hold together. In my case, the guys usually ate the stuff too quickly and never gave it time to cool off.

If You Can't Stand the Heat

Choron Sauce

1/3 cup of white wine
1/3 cup of tarragon vinegar
1 shallot (finely chopped)
8 peppercorns (crushed)
1/2 cup of Roma tomatoes (peeled, chopped, and seeded)
1/2 teaspoon of tomato paste
1/4 pound of butter (clarified and warm) (see recipe for Clarified Butter)
3 egg yolks
1 teaspoon of lemon juice
Fresh-ground pepper
Salt

This sauce goes well over practically anything. It was invented by a French chef named—you guessed it—Choron. One day he got the bright idea to mix hollandaise with a tomato puree and ended up with this sauce. So he named it after himself. Those French people are so clever.

In a sauce pan, heat up the wine, vinegar, shallots, and peppercorns until they reduce down to a couple of tablespoons of thick liquid among the shallots. Add the tomatoes and the tomato paste and cook until almost all of the liquid is gone. Set the pot aside for now.

Over a double boiler or a pot of simmering water (not boiling), put the lemon juice and the egg yolks into a metal bowl. Using a metal whisk, start to whisk vigorously. Keep your bowl out of the water. You don't want to cook the eggs. If they start to scramble, take the bowl away from the heat. Regulate the temperature in that way until your whisking has produced a foamy mixture. Now, slowly whisk in the clarified butter a little at a time. Once it has emulsified, pour in the tomato mixture. Add a pinch of salt and fresh-ground pepper to the bowl and mix everything together. Now, strain the mixture and keep it warm.

Note: I know it sounds tough, but it really isn't that hard to do. It's worth it in the end. Try putting this over a couple of fried soft shell crabs. Try it on fish. Try it on any seafood. Just try it!

Cocktail Sauce

1 cup of ketchup
2 tablespoons of cream style horseradish
Juice from one half lemon
2 tablespoons of Creole mustard

There are so many different recipes for this sauce—it isn't even funny. This is the basic sauce. You can then change it as you like. Some like to add hot sauce. Some like to add Worcestershire sauce. I just like it as is.

This is relatively straightforward. Mix all of the ingredients and let it sit in the fridge for at least an hour. The flavors get better with time.

Use this on all sorts of seafood dishes: boiled shrimp, marinated crab claws, fried fish, the works. If you are having boiled crawfish, you can add one-quarter cup of mayo to the cocktail sauce for something to dip the tails in. That is, if you have time. In most cases at the firehouse, the crawfish were gone as soon as they hit the table.

If You Can't Stand the Heat

Béchamel Sauce

1 cup of milk
1 cup of whipping cream
2 tablespoons of butter
2 tablespoons of flour
Pinch of nutmeg
Pinch of white pepper

This is a handy little sauce that is easy to make. It is one of the mother sauces that can be used as a base to form other sauces. I don't believe my mother ever made a mother sauce. That's okay. She made enough other sauces that would make mother sauces envious.

Put the milk and the whipping cream in a saucepan and heat to a simmer. Put it out of the way over a very low fire. You want to keep it warm (but not boiling).

In another pan, melt the butter and then add the flour. Stir constantly until you have a golden brown roux. Slowly, whisk in the heated milk a little at a time until fully incorporated. Now, add the nutmeg and white pepper. Cook it for a few minutes and stir occasionally. It will thicken up. That's it. Easy, right?

For the cheese lovers in the family, add one cup of grated Parmigiano-Reggiano to create a Mornay sauce.

Creole Crab Sauce

3/4 cup of vegetable oil
1 tablespoon of fresh lemon juice
1 clove of garlic (chopped)
1 tablespoon of Creole mustard
1 large egg
1 tablespoon of fresh-ground horseradish
1 tablespoon of Pickapeppa sauce
1 tablespoon of ketchup
1/2 teaspoon of Tabasco sauce
1/2 teaspoon of fresh-ground pepper
1/2 teaspoon of sea salt

This sauce is one that you don't refrigerate after making. Most sauces get better after the flavors have time to get friendly with each other. Not this one. This is the lone wolf of sauces!

Put all of the ingredients (except the oil) into a blender. Turn on the mix setting and slowly drizzle in the oil until it is all incorporated. That's it. Quick, clean, and simple.

Note: Remember—no matter whether you are serving this with fish, shrimp, or even a seafood martini—serve immediately after making it. The flavor changes after it gets cold. Not that it tastes bad or anything even close to that; it just isn't the taste you initially wanted. Just serve it freshly made, and you will achieve your crab sauce goal for the day.

Wendy's Smoky Honey BBQ Sauce

2 tablespoons of white vinegar
4 tablespoons of dark brown sugar
4 tablespoons of lemon juice
1 cup of ketchup
4 tablespoons of Worcestershire sauce
1/2 teaspoon of yellow mustard
4 teaspoons of tomato paste
1 teaspoon of garlic powder
1 1/2 teaspoons of Karo dark syrup
4 tablespoons of honey
3 tablespoons of pineapple juice
5 tablespoons of molasses
1 tablespoon of liquid smoke
2 tablespoons of butter
1 cup of onions (finely chopped)

Barbeque sauce is something I use sparingly. I find it takes away from the taste of the meat. Some of the guys like to slather it on thick. I guess it's all a matter of taste. They like to taste the sauce, and I don't.

Melt the butter in a small pot and then add the onions. Cook on a low fire until the onions are translucent. Add all other ingredients and simmer uncovered for one hour. After it cools, pour it into a covered container and place in the fridge overnight.

Note: This recipe came from our friend Wendy whose mother made it and handed it on down the line. Wendy improved on it, and after I tasted it, I just knew it was the best I had ever tasted. Maybe I'll have to slather it on after all.

Tomato Sauce for Lasagna

6 medium-sized Creole tomatoes (chopped)
5 cloves of garlic (finely chopped)
2 tablespoons of carrots (finely chopped)
2 medium onions (chopped)
1/2 dozen fresh basil leaves (chopped)
1 teaspoon of dried oregano
1 teaspoon of dried thyme
1/2 teaspoon of sugar
15-ounce can of tomato sauce
6-ounce can of tomato paste
1/2 cup of olive oil
14 ounces of chicken broth
Salt and fresh-ground pepper

If you are going to make lasagna, you need the sauce. Sure, you can go out and buy tomato sauce from a store, but why? Use this recipe and everyone will wonder why your lasagna is so superior. You can tell them that you have a sauce that has been handed down to you for generations. Okay, so it's one generation, but who's counting?

Over medium/high heat, heat the olive oil in a pot and sauté the onions, garlic, and carrots until the onions are translucent (approximately ten minutes). Lower heat to medium and add the oregano, thyme, and basil leaves. Cook for an additional three minutes. Stir often so it doesn't stick. Lower the temperature to med/low and add the tomato paste. Stir and scrape the pan for another ten minutes. If it gets to a rusty brown color before the ten minutes is up, move on to the next step. Just don't let it burn. Add the tomato sauce and blend in. Cook for another ten minutes. Add the tomatoes, chicken broth, and sugar. Incorporate everything and mix well. This is the time to adjust the seasonings of salt and fresh-ground pepper to taste.

Cover the pot and simmer for three hours, stirring occasionally. This should make about six to eight cups of Tomato Sauce for Lasagna.

Note: Sometimes I go a bit further. After about two hours of cooking time, I like to use my submersible hand blender and smooth out the sauce. Some people like it chunky, some don't. In either case, it will taste the same. It's just the texture that will be different. It's up to you. The only problem with smoothing it out with a blender is that people will hound you for the brand name of the sauce. They will think you bought it in a specialty store and will want to get some for themselves. Just make up a name. They'll look for it everywhere and forever.

Twenty-Megaton Tartar Sauce

1/4 cup of garlic (finely chopped)
1/4 cup of dill pickles (finely chopped)
3/4 cup of mayonnaise
Fresh-ground pepper to taste

This is a recipe I got from my friend Richard "Maddog" Hughes. We worked together at Engine 40 for years. He made this simple little tartar sauce for us, and it rocked!

Combine all of the ingredients in a bowl. Mix together and, if possible, refrigerate overnight. I say "if possible" because we would make it at work and only had part of the day to chill. Later, I discovered that overnight cooling in the fridge really brings out the maximum amount of garlic flavor.

You'll find that you are not just lightly dipping your fried fish into this tartar sauce, but rather slathering it all over the fish. You won't be able to help yourself. But it's all right; there's no need to be embarrassed by your behavior. Everybody else at the table will be doing the same thing.

Note: Oh, and by the way, if you have problems with vampires in your area, you need not worry about them after you eat this. There is enough garlic in there that you'll have a good two or three days of vampire-free activity coming your way.

If You Can't Stand the Heat

Remoulade Sauce

2/3 cup of Homemade Mayonnaise (see recipe)
1/3 cup of Hellman's mayonnaise
1/3 cup of Zatarain's Creole mustard
1 teaspoon of Pickapeppa sauce
3 cloves of garlic (finely chopped)
1 teaspoon of fresh lemon juice
1/2 teaspoon of Worcestershire sauce
2 teaspoons of ketchup
Dash of Tabasco
Dash of fresh-ground black pepper
Dash of white pepper

This sauce is so good that I put it on shrimp, salads, crawfish, and many other things. It is the ultimate creamy sauce. If it were possible to put this sauce on another sauce, I swear it would make that sauce taste better.

Mix everything in a bowl and refrigerate overnight (or at least until it's chilled really well). You need time for all of those flavors to come together. Spoon it over some boiled shrimp that are sitting on a bed of shredded romaine lettuce and garnish with a few Creole tomato slices.

After all of that mixing and chopping, it's time for your hands to rest and your mouth to have some fun!

Note: This sauce will stay good for five days if refrigerated. The best part is that it will taste better the longer all of the ingredients hang around and get to know each other.

Pot Sticker Dipping Sauce

1 teaspoon of fresh ginger (grated)
1 tablespoon of garlic (finely chopped)
1/4 cup of soy sauce

If you are going to go through the simple process of making pot stickers, you need to go through the simple process of making a pot sticker sauce. I know that sounds repetitive, but I love saying the words *pot stickers*. It sounds so—filling! Sorry about the pun. Just go eat.

Mix all of the ingredients in a bowl and refrigerate overnight to let the flavors marry. If you can't manage overnight, a couple of hours will suffice. The flavors may not be totally married, but at least they will have dated for a while.

Serve as a dipping sauce for the Pot Stickers (see recipe).

Pizza Sauce #1 Tomato

28-ounce can of San Marzano tomatoes
2 cloves of garlic (chopped)
1 cup of onions (chopped)
1/4 cup of olive oil
1 teaspoon of dried Italian seasoning
3 tablespoons of fresh basil (chopped)
2 teaspoons of fresh oregano (chopped)
2 teaspoons of fresh thyme (chopped)
Fresh-ground pepper and salt to taste

We have two kinds of sauces that we use for pizzas. One is red (this one), and the other is white (see Pizza Sauce #2 Garlic recipe). The red is more traditional, and the white is more—let's just say, "garlicky." If that isn't a real word, it is now.

Put the olive oil in a pot and heat it up. Add the onions, a pinch of salt and fresh-ground pepper, and cook until the onions are translucent. Add the garlic and cook for one minute. Add the dried Italian seasoning. Mix it in and cook for one minute. Add the tomatoes and the fresh herbs. Bring it back up to a simmer and cook covered on a low fire for one hour. Remove from the fire, uncover, and let it cool.

Now comes the part where you will have to choose your preferred thickness. Put the sauce into a food processor. If you want your sauce to be chunky, just pulse it until it reaches the desired thickness. I personally like to just turn it on and let it puree until I end up with a smooth sauce. Either way, you can spoon it on, and it will be good. I promise. I pizza promise!

Note: If you don't want to use a food processor, you can also use a submersible hand blender. They work just as well and are easier to clean up afterward.

Pizza Sauce #2 Garlic

1 whole head of Roasted Garlic (see recipe)
2 cups of olive oil
Pinch of kosher salt

This is the second version of the pizza sauces we use. The other is a red version (see recipe for Pizza Sauce #1). It's more traditional, but being a nontraditional guy, I prefer the garlic sauce. I guess it's all a matter of taste … the kind of taste that's in your mouth.

Remove the roasted garlic from the pods and put them into a blender. Pour in the olive oil and mix for sixty seconds. Pour it into a bowl, add the salt, and mix together. Cover and let it sit for at least one hour.

When you are ready to make pizzas, spoon this onto your pizza dough instead of the tomato sauce (or you can even combine it with the tomato sauce). Make sure you stir it well before you spoon it on. Things may settle to the bottom.

Note: This is especially good if you top your pizza with Italian sausage and mozzarella cheese.

If You Can't Stand the Heat

Your Basic Tomato Gravy

4 pounds of Roma tomatoes
10 cloves of garlic (chopped)
2 large red onions (chopped)
15-ounce can of tomato sauce
6-ounce can of tomato paste
4 teaspoons of dried Italian seasoning
4 cups of chicken stock
2 teaspoons of sugar
1 cup of olive oil
4 tablespoons of fresh basil (chopped)
Salt (to taste)
Fresh-ground pepper (to taste)

This is just your basic gravy for your basic pasta dish. There is nothing basic about the taste, though. I guess, basically, that's about it!

Parboil the tomatoes in hot water for a few minutes. You will see the skins begin to crack on some of the tomatoes. When that happens, take them out and put them in a bath of ice water. After a few minutes, the peels will come right off. Some people also seed them at this point. They say seeds make the sauce taste bitter. I have never found that to be the case, so I leave them in. After peeling, squeeze them in your hands and break them up into a bowl and set aside.

Put the olive oil in a large pot and heat it up. Sauté the onions over medium heat until they are translucent. Lower the heat and then add the garlic. Cook for two minutes. Next, add the tomato paste and cook for five to ten minutes or until it slightly browns. Add the tomato sauce and half of the dried Italian seasonings. Let it cook for ten minutes, stirring frequently over a low fire. Mix in the crushed Roma tomatoes and cook for ten minutes. Add the other ingredients (including the other half of the dry seasonings, but not the basil), and simmer on a low fire uncovered for ninety minutes. It's at this point that I like to introduce a submersible blender into the pot. It helps to break up the larger pieces that have not fallen apart. It isn't necessary, but I do it because I don't like my sauce chunky.

Now add the basil. Cook for an additional twenty to thirty minutes uncovered, check for salt, and then remove from the fire and cover. Let it sit for at least one hour before serving. This will give you about three quarts of sauce. If you don't need three quarts, either cut the recipe in half or freeze the rest for another time.

Note: It will also keep well in the freezer.

If You Can't Stand the Heat

Fresh Basil Pesto

3 ounces of fresh basil leaves (rinsed and patted dry)
5 cloves of garlic (peeled)
1/2 cup of pine nuts
1 cup of grated Parmigiano-Reggiano cheese
2/3 cup of extra virgin olive oil
Pinch of salt and fresh-ground pepper

Quick, easy, and great. What could be better? Put all of the ingredients in a food processor except the cheese, salt, and fresh-ground pepper. Turn the processor on, and let it run for about two minutes. Turn it off and add the cheese, salt, and fresh-ground pepper; pulse until incorporated.

This can be used for pesto bread, pasta dishes, and just so many things. Make up something of your own. Trust me; it's gonna taste good!

Note: If you happen to be at home and have little or no time to fix something to eat, try this: Heat up some crusty bread. Break off a big piece, and butter it. Now spread some pesto on top and sprinkle on a little Parmigiano-Reggiano. That's it. Enjoy that with a good glass of wine, and you won't need anything else. It is a meal in itself…and a good one at that!

Balsamic Vinaigrette

1/4 cup of balsamic vinegar
1 cup of olive oil
2 teaspoons of fresh basil (chopped)
1/2 teaspoon of Zatarain's Creole mustard
1 clove of garlic (finely chopped)
Salt and fresh-ground pepper

If you want a quick and tasty salad, this is the one. It's fresh. It's fast. It's really good. I suppose it could be good for you too, but that is just a hunch. I'm not a nutritionist; I'm just a cook.

Put the vinegar, salt, fresh-ground pepper, basil, garlic, and mustard into a bowl. Slowly whisk in the olive oil until incorporated. That's about it. Now get together some salad greens, cherry tomatoes, and a handful of sliced red onions. Drizzle the vinaigrette on top and toss to cover veggies with the vinaigrette.

Note: If you use an inexpensive balsamic vinegar, add about one-half teaspoon of sugar to the vinaigrette. I personally like to use the good stuff. That's why they make it. Besides, using inferior products is just a way of cheating yourself and whomever you are feeding. Oh, and by the way, don't try using cheap stuff on firemen … they can smell a cheapskate a mile away!

If You Can't Stand the Heat

Horseradish Cream

1 cup of Homemade Mayonnaise (see recipe)
1/2 teaspoon of tomato paste
5 tablespoons of ground horseradish (from the jar)
1 tablespoon of garlic (finely chopped)
1/2 teaspoon of Worcestershire sauce
1 teaspoon of ketchup
1/2 teaspoon of Tabasco
Fresh-ground pepper to taste

Start out by making some Homemade Mayo (see recipe), but with a twist. Before you begin to add the oil, add the one-half teaspoon of tomato paste along with the other mayo ingredients. Place the finished mayo in a bowl and add all of the other ingredients from the list above. Whisk together and place in the refrigerator covered for a couple of hours for the flavors to become close personal friends.

Get some bread—any bread—and spread a little horseradish cream on it. Now put on some brisket, and heads will turn. That's right. They'll want some too. It's a good thing you made five pounds of brisket isn't it?

Note: If you happen to be in New Orleans, stop off at Tujagues's Restaurant. They make the best version of brisket and horseradish cream in the city. I'd go so far as to say anywhere on the planet. If you happen to be there during the French Quarter Festival, they usually have a booth set up, so you can sample it. Lucky you—always in the right place at the right time!

Chipotle Remoulade

1 cup of Homemade Mayonnaise (see recipe)
4 teaspoons of chipotle peppers in adobo sauce
1 tablespoon of garlic (finely chopped)
1 teaspoon of fresh lemon juice
1/3 cup of Creole mustard
1/2 teaspoon of Worcestershire sauce
Dash of Tabasco

When you make the homemade mayo, the recipe will show that you will be making it in a blender. While you are in the process of making the Homemade Mayo (see recipe), add the chipotle pepper and adobo sauce to the other ingredients in the mayo. They are kind of chunky, and the blender does the job of finely chopping and incorporating them into the mayo so you don't have to do it by hand.

Once you have made the mayo/chipotle, put it in a bowl, and then mix in all of the other ingredients above and cover. Let this sit in the fridge overnight or as long as you can that particular day. The longer they hang out with each other, the better. All of those flavors will get together, and then they will want to go out and find a crab cake to really party with!

Note: I also use this as a sauce to dip fried shrimp, fried fish, and even boiled crawfish. Putting that chipotle in there gives it a little kick. Find something for yourself to dip into this sauce. Try some fried artichoke hearts. Try it on anything fried, really.

Crabmeat Dressing

1/2 pound of white lump crabmeat (picked over for shells)
1 cup of plain breadcrumbs
2/3 cup of yellow onions (finely chopped)
1/2 cup of green onion tops (chopped)
1/4 cup of celery (finely chopped)
2 cloves of garlic (finely chopped)
1 stick of unsalted butter (one quarter pound)
1/2 cup of white wine
3 teaspoons of flashover seasoning

This is one of the most versatile things you can make. It is used in many dishes where a stuffing is required. I swear that if you stuffed this into an old tennis shoe it would make that shoe taste great.

In a frying pan, melt the butter until it slightly browns. Now add in the onions, green onions, celery, and one teaspoon of the FOS. Cook for two to three minutes; then add the garlic. Cook for one minute and then add the white wine and then another teaspoon of FOS. Cook for two to three minutes more and then take it off of the fire. Next you add in the breadcrumbs. Mix well with the butter and wine sauce. Now fold in the crabmeat and the last teaspoon of FOS. You should now have a big ball of crabmeat dressing ready to go into ramekins or even to stuff a flounder.

Note: Stuffed crabs are really good too, but that's another recipe. I guess that's about it … unless you happen to have an old tennis shoe hanging around.

Cilantro Dressing

1 bunch of fresh cilantro as sold in the grocery tied together with a band, approximately 12 ounces (rinsed and spin dried)
3 cloves of garlic
1/2 cup of olive oil
1/2 cup of Homemade Mayonnaise (see recipe)
1 tablespoon of Worcestershire sauce
1 tablespoon of lime juice

The basic idea for this came from our friend Cheri. I experimented with it a bit. I embellished it a bit. I even went so far as tweaking it a bit.

I promise you that this is a great dressing. I also promise you that it's easy to make. I refer to this as our Mexican dressing because of all of the cilantro. I put it on all kinds of things besides salads, such as grilled chicken or grilled shrimp. Experiment with it and see what else you might like it on.

Put the cilantro, garlic, mayo, Worcestershire, and lime juice in a food processor. Turn on and process for thirty seconds. Now slowly drizzle in the olive oil. That's about it. Quick isn't it? Just like I promised.

Note: If you were making cilantro infused coleslaw for fish tacos, you would add the chipotles and the crema after the dressing itself is made in the food processor (see recipe for Fish Tacos). Process for another twenty seconds, put it into a bowl, and mix with the shredded red cabbage. Make it ahead of time if you are going to make fish tacos. That way the dressing has time to permeate the cabbage and give it an awesome flavor.

Clarified Butter

1/2 pound of unsalted butter
1 pot
1 stove

If you clarify butter, you can use it to do things in cooking that you couldn't do before. All you are basically doing is removing the milk solids from the butterfat. The solids are the parts in butter that will burn when you try to cook with butter at high temperatures. Once it is clarified, you can use it to make dishes containing butter and that also need to be cooked at a higher heat.

You don't really have to use a half-pound of butter. You can use as much as you want to clarify. Just keep in mind that you are going to lose some of the butter when you go through this process. So if you want a half-pound of clarified butter, start out with three-quarters of a pound of butter to make up for the difference that removing the solids will take.

Put the cold butter in a pot and heat it up very slowly. Don't stir it up. Keep it on a low fire for ten minutes. That should be enough time to melt all of the butter. Turn off the pot. Skim off any foam that is on the top then let the pot sit for five minutes or so. You are letting the solids sink to the bottom.

Very carefully (not stirring the pot), pour the clarified butter into a container and leave the solids in the bottom of the pot. Cover it tight and keep it in the fridge until you need it.

Now that wasn't so hard was it?

Roasted Garlic Butter

1 stick of softened salted butter
1 head of Roasted Garlic (see recipe)
1 teaspoon of fresh parsley (chopped)

This is a simple thing to make. I always like to keep some handy in the fridge at home and at work. You never know when you might feel like some garlic toast.

Place all of the ingredients in a food processor and blend until smooth or until all of the ingredients are combined. Scoop it out and put it into a bowl. Cover and chill in the fridge until the butter is hard again. That's it. It should stay good for about a week.

Note: I'm not sure who first thought of making roasted garlic butter, but I'd like to shake his hand. Some brilliant individual figured out how to make butter better. What a guy!

If You Can't Stand the Heat

Roasted Garlic

1 whole head of garlic
2 tablespoons of olive oil
Kosher salt
Fresh-ground pepper

As soon as you walked into the engine house, you knew when someone was roasting garlic. It has such a wonderful aroma. I especially liked it when that smell got into my clothes. I walked around all day smelling like I just came out of the oven.

Preheat the oven to 350 degrees. Cut the head of garlic in half to expose the insides of the pods and pour a tablespoon of olive oil over each half. Sprinkle a little salt and fresh-ground pepper on each. Wrap them in a pouch of aluminum foil. Try to make a hollow pocket and make sure that you close the ends really tight. You'll create a sort of steam chamber that will roast them perfectly. Put it in the oven and bake it for about forty minutes. Take your little foil package out and let it cool without opening it. When it does cool, open it up and squeeze out the soft roasted garlic pods into a small bowl. Cover until ready for use.

Note: We use this to make garlic butter, garlic toast, garlic mashed potatoes, and garlic bread sticks. I suppose you could put it on a regular stick if you wanted to. I'm certain that it would make the stick taste sensational. I haven't tried it myself yet, mostly because I haven't figured out how to cook a stick. Just give me some time; I'm working on it.

Miles' Mexican Biz

3 ounces of dried chipotle chilies
2 cups of olive oil
1 tablespoon of cayenne pepper
1 tablespoon of salt

One night a few of us went to a Mexican place with a friend of ours named Miles. We tried this sauce on our chips that just about blew our socks off. Miles looked at me and said, "What's this biz?" That was that. Soon after, we made our own version of it and called it Biz.

Open up the pack of chilies and remove the stems from the peppers. Break up the chilies into three-quarter to one-inch pieces. Place them in a small saucepan. I actually break them up over the pot so all of the seeds and small pieces will fall right in. And by the way, don't accidentally reach up and rub your eyes right after this. Ouch!

Cover with two cups of olive oil. Heat on medium and, once it comes up to a simmer, cook them uncovered for five minutes. Add the salt and cayenne to let the salt dissolve. Remove from the heat and allow it to cool.

Next, pour it all into a food processor. Grind for at least three minutes or until it all turns into a thin, oily mixture. Remove it from the processor and pour it into a glass container for storage. I use something with a spout and a cork so I can pour it out onto whatever I am going to eat and keep it bottled up when I'm not. If it has been sitting for a while, make sure you shake it up before you use it, as most of the mixture will settle on the bottom.

This concoction will yield a very spicy blend that goes great with tacos, Pico de Gallo, or just on some tortilla chips. I also add it to other dishes to give them some smoky chili zip.

This stuff can be pretty hot, so watch it. You can't control how hot the dried peppers are, but if you want less heat, cut back on the cayenne. I don't know why you'd want to do that, but I guess some people are funny that way.

If You Can't Stand the Heat

Fish Stock

3 fish carcasses (bones and heads)
1 celery stalk (roughly chopped)
1 carrot (roughly chopped)
1 yellow onion (quartered)
1 tablespoon of black peppercorns
1 bay leaf
4 quarts of water

If you are going to make a fish dish, you need to use stock instead of water. It just tastes better. I'd bet that if you could ask a fish, they would prefer to swim in stock rather than plain water.

Put all of the ingredients into a stockpot. Bring it to a boil uncovered. Cut the fire down to a simmer. Skim off any foam that might accumulate. Let this cook for ninety minutes and then strain. This should yield about two quarts of stock and maybe just a tad more. Let it cool and settle. There will be some sediment on the bottom that you will discard when you use the final product.

It's oh-so simple, but it adds a richer flavor to any seafood dish as opposed to using just water. The biggest thing is to get the fish bones and heads. If I haven't caught the fish myself, I have no problem asking the fish cleaner at the market for some bones. Trust me; they are glad to get rid of them.

Note: Make sure you rinse them well and clean out any place where there may be a pocket of blood left over from the initial filleting (especially in the heads).

Shrimp/Seafood Stock

3 quarts of water
1 large onion (cut in half)
1 head of garlic (cut in half)
1/4 cup of celery (roughly chopped)
1/2 teaspoon of kosher salt
1 tablespoon of black peppercorns
1 bay leaf
3 gumbo crabs
Shells from two pounds of peeled shrimp (heads too if they are head-on shrimp)

Using stock instead of just plain water is important. It gives any dish added dimensions of flavor that water can't give. I'll bet you didn't know that water has no dimensions. Although, I sometimes wonder about the water we get from the Mississippi River. I think it might have dimensions no one has even thought of before.

Put all ingredients into a stockpot and simmer uncovered for one hour or until the liquid is reduced by almost a third. Strain, save the liquid, and discard everything else. This should give you about two quarts of stock. Let it settle and discard whatever dregs settle to the bottom.

Note: This is a Shrimp/Seafood Stock. If you want to have a strictly shrimp stock, leave out the crabs. If you should decide to do that—not invite the crabs—they won't mind. Tomorrow they are invited to the seafood gumbo party we are having.

If You Can't Stand the Heat

Soups, Salads, and Sandwiches

Alligator and Andouille Sauce Piquante

2 pounds of alligator meat (cut up into 1/2 inch pieces)
24 ounces of andouille sausage (cut up into small pieces)
1/2 cup of unsalted butter
1/2 cup of flour
4 cups of onion (diced)
1/4 cup of celery (diced)
1/2 cup of bell pepper (diced)
1 tablespoon of tomato paste
2 tablespoons of garlic (finely chopped)
2 twenty-eight ounce cans of diced tomatoes and chilies (drained)
3 teaspoons of flashover seasoning
2 bay leaves
1 teaspoon of sugar
64 ounces of chicken stock
Salt to taste

Not everybody is into eating gator meat. If you happen to be one of those that are, this recipe for the big critters just might bite you back!

Start by putting the butter in a pot and melting it. Add the flour and make a dark roux the color of chocolate. Once you have reached that point, add the celery, onions, bell pepper, and a teaspoon of FOS. Cook these veggies until they are soft and the onions are translucent. Add the tomato paste and mix it in well. Cook until the paste turns a rust color. It will not take long, so keep an eye on it. Now add the garlic. Cook for one minute; then add the diced tomato and chilies and another teaspoon of the FOS. Once that is mixed well, cook it for five minutes. Now add the stock (a little at a time), sugar, bay leaves, and the last teaspoon of FOS. Mix it all well. Cook for ninety minutes uncovered on a low fire.

If You Can't Stand the Heat

Add the meats and cook covered on a low fire for another hour or until the alligator is tender. Taste for salt and serve over cooked white rice.

Note: If you buy the alligator meat packaged or fresh, make sure you clean away all of the fat and sinew that you find on the meat. Alligator fat is not very tasty, and the sinew is tough. Also make sure that you rinse any packaged gator meat really well under cool water. It was probably marinated, and you want to rinse it off as much as you possibly can.

Triple Creamed Maque Choux

1/2 pound of applewood smoked bacon
2 cups of onions (finely chopped)
1 cup of red bell pepper (finely chopped)
3 cloves of garlic (finely chopped)
4 Roma tomatoes (chopped)
4 large ears of corn (corn removed from husk and scraped for milk)
1 teaspoon of sugar
2 cups of whipping cream
1 teaspoon of flashover seasoning
1/2 cup of green onion tops (cut fine)
Salt and fresh-ground pepper to taste

This is a traditional dish that came from a combination of Cajun and Native American cooking techniques. Although the word *choux* is French for cabbage, there will be no cabbage in this one. For me, that is just something to help stretch the dish if more people are showing up than you expected. When I wrote this recipe, I was only expecting four. Fortunately, only four showed up, thus, no cabbage.

I called this "triple" for a reason. You can actually use this dish in three separate ways. If you cook it as per the instructions, you will have something akin to a creamed corn consistency. That is great for a side dish. If you don't cook it quite as long, leaving more of the moisture in, it can be used as a soup. If you cook it all of the way through (as per instructions) and then add one pound of headless shrimp, it can be used as an entrée. If you should opt for an entrée version, you can eat it as is or put it over your favorite pasta. Three for one … triple. Either way it's really a homerun!

Fry the bacon down until it is crisp and then put it aside to drain on paper towels. Using three tablespoons of the bacon fat left over, render down the onions, bell pepper, and a teaspoon of FOS until the onions are translucent. Now add the garlic and cook for one minute.

When you cut the corn from the cob you'll want to use the back of the knife to scrape the milk from the cobs after the corn is off.

Now put the corn, its milk, tomatoes, sugar, salt, and fresh-ground pepper into the pot. Cook covered on a low fire until the liquid begins to come out of the corn (about fifteen minutes). Break up the bacon into small pieces and put it back into the pan. Next, add the cream and green onion tops and cook uncovered until almost all of the liquid is gone. This will take about an hour. That would be for the side dish recipe. Leave more liquid by not cooking it as long, and you have a soup. Add fresh shrimp, and their fluid will release and make it moist and creamy for an entrée. Your choice. Just pick one!

Note: If you have the time, let the cooked maque choux sit for a while covered after cooking. This will really bring out the flavors. Also be careful with the salt. The bacon has salt in it, so taste it before you add salt.

Turtle Soup

3 to 4 pounds of turtle meat (on the bone and cleaned of all fat)
64 ounces of beef stock
1 1/3 stick of butter
1/3 cup of flour
4 cups of onion (chopped)
1/2 cup of bell pepper (chopped)
1/4 cup of celery (chopped)
2 tablespoons of garlic (chopped)
1 teaspoon of flashover seasoning
1 tablespoon of tomato paste
1 pound of tomatoes (peeled, seeded, and chopped)
1 tablespoon of dried Italian seasoning
1 teaspoon of lemon juice
1 tablespoon of Worcestershire sauce
3 bay leaves
3 eggs (hardboiled, peeled, and chopped up into small pieces)
1 tablespoon of sherry (per individual)
1/2 cup of fresh parsley (finely chopped)
Salt and fresh-ground pepper to taste
Lemon wedges

You can find turtle soup on the menus of just about every fine dining restaurant in New Orleans. You generally don't find it on the tables of your everyday New Orleanian. Locals don't go out looking for turtles to eat on a regular basis. That wasn't always the case, but in today's world, it's become more of a delicacy.

If You Can't Stand the Heat

If I want to prepare this soup, I am usually able to find commercially caught turtle meat at a local seafood or specialty store. It's in the frozen section right next to the rabbit. The tortoise and the hare, together again!

Put the beef stock into a pot and add the turtle meat and a little salt and fresh-ground pepper. Cook for one hour covered. During this time, remove the cover once in a while and skim off any foam that may have come to the top and discard. After an hour, take the meat out and allow it to cool. Save the stock. Once the meat is cool enough to handle, remove the meat from the bones. Put the meat in a food processor and pulse until the meat is ground up fine. Allow the stock to come to room temperature. Strain the stock. You should have about two quarts left. Even though you have strained the stock, once it cools down there will be some sediment on the bottom. Do not put this sediment into the cooking pot. If you need to, just use a bit more of the beef stock or a little water to make up the difference.

Put one stick of butter into a pot and melt it down. Now add the turtle meat to the pot. The meat will absorb the butter pretty fast, but that's all right. Over a medium heat, brown the turtle meat. It will be hard to see it turning brown since it is slightly brown already. What you really want is to have a little brown color form on the bottom of the pot. This will not take long. That's what you are looking for. Don't overdo it. You don't want it to burn.

Once that is done, remove the meat from the pot. Now add the other one-third stick of butter. Melt it down, and then add the flour. Scrape the bottom of the pan to release all of the tasty brown bits into the roux. You don't want them to burn. Turn down the heat and stir constantly until you have a peanut butter colored roux. Now add the celery, onions, and bell pepper along with the teaspoon of FOS. Cook until all of the veggies are wilted and soft.

Now add the tomato paste. Mix it in well, and it will start to turn a rust color. It will not take long. Once you have browned the tomato paste, add the garlic and cook for one minute. Put in the tomatoes and mix well. Now pour in the stock a little at a time until it is all blended together. It's at this point that I like to introduce an immersion blender. Put it in the pot and blend as much of the soup as you can. Now add the bay leaf, Worcestershire sauce, lemon juice, and the Italian seasonings. Cover and put on a low fire for ninety minutes. Remove the cover and stir it around and see if there are any chunks of tomato left in the soup. If there are, use the immersion blender again, but first remove the bay leaves.

Once it is smooth, add the turtle meat and cook for one hour uncovered on a low fire. Now mix in two of the chopped eggs. Check the taste for salt and fresh-ground pepper, and that's it.

To serve, put into individual soup bowls topped with a tablespoon of sherry, just a bit more of the chopped egg, a pinch of finely chopped parsley, and a wedge of lemon.

Note: I say a tablespoon of sherry per bowl, but it really depends on the size of the bowl you serve the soup in. If you only serve a cup of soup, use less sherry. Adjust it accordingly.

If You Can't Stand the Heat

Crawfish Etouffee

2 one-pound bags of crawfish tails (with fat)
1 stick of unsalted butter
1/4 cup of flour
1 medium onion (finely chopped)
1/2 cup of bell pepper (finely chopped)
1/4 cup of celery (finely chopped)
1 tablespoon of tomato paste
2 cloves of garlic (finely chopped)
3 cups of Shrimp Stock with three tablespoons reserved (see Shrimp/Seafood Stock recipe)
2 bay leaves
2 teaspoons of dried parsley flakes
1 tablespoon of flashover seasoning
3 tablespoons of sherry
1/2 cup of green onion tops (finely chopped)
Salt and fresh-ground pepper to taste

Like so many dishes from Louisiana, there are about 947,000 versions of this one. My mother has a version. So does my sister … and my uncle and his mother (that would be the proverbial grandmother). This is the firehouse version that has been handed down to me. It has been a closely guarded secret that is only known by 6,902. Now it will be 6,903, but who's counting?

Put the stick of butter into a pot and melt it. Now add the flour and whisk it until you have made a peanut butter colored roux. Once that is done, add the onion, bell pepper, celery, and half of a tablespoon of the FOS. Cook until the onions are translucent. Next add the tomato paste and cook it until it starts to brown slightly. Now add the garlic and cook for one minute.

Slowly begin to add the (room temperature) stock. Just put in a little at a time and incorporate it. Once it is all in there, toss in the bay leaves, the sherry, and the other half-tablespoon of FOS. Once you have it all in, let it cook uncovered on a low fire for thirty to forty-five minutes or until it reduces by half.

Now put the crawfish into the pot and any fat in the bags. Also add the parsley flakes. Use the reserved three tablespoons of stock by putting it into the crawfish bag. Shake it around in there to try to gather any of the fat that remained behind when you poured out the crawfish. Use that same liquid to do the same thing with the other bag. Now pour it into the pot. Once it comes back up to heat and starts to bubble, cook for fifteen minutes and then taste for salt and fresh-ground pepper. Add the green onion tops and stir in. Cover and let it sit for thirty minutes. Warm it up again, remove the bay leaves, and serve over cooked white rice.

Note: French bread and butter on the side is a welcome addition. Even if it is an unwelcome addition, put it on the table anyway. I promise you it will disappear!

Shrimp Creole

3 pounds of head on shrimp
1/2 cup of flour
1/2 cup of vegetable oil
3 cups of onion (finely chopped)
1/2 cup of celery (finely chopped)
1 cup of bell pepper (finely chopped)
3 cloves of garlic (finely chopped)
8 ounces of tomato sauce
2 cups of Creole tomatoes (peeled, seeded, and chopped)
4 teaspoons of flashover seasoning
4 cups of shrimp stock (See Shrimp/Seafood Stock recipe)
1 cup of green onion tops (finely chopped)
1 teaspoon of fresh lemon juice

Shrimp Creole is one of the most popular dishes in New Orleans. It is similar in a way to shrimp etouffee. The real difference is that in an etouffee, you are smothering the dish down in veggies that are smothered in butter. Here it's more of a tomato base.

Peel and rinse your shrimp. If they are large enough, you can butterfly and devein them. Put them on the side for now. You can use the peelings to make your stock. Do that before you make the rest of the dish. You'll want the stock to be room temperature when you begin.

Make your roux out of the oil and flour. You want it to be the color of peanut butter when you are done. Now add all of the veggies except the garlic. Also put in one teaspoon of the FOS. This will stop the roux from cooking any more. Put the pot on a very low fire. Cook until the onions are translucent. Now add the garlic to the pot along with another teaspoon of the FOS. Cook this for two minutes. Now add the tomato sauce and cook for five minutes. Add the tomatoes and cook for two more minutes.

Slowly blend in the shrimp stock. Make sure it is room temperature and not hot. As always, if you add hot stock to hot roux, disaster may follow. The roux could break, and you will have little pieces of congealed flour floating in your pot.

Once the stock is in and blended, put on a low fire, add the rest of the FOS, and cover the pot. Cook for one hour. Now uncover and cook for another hour on a low fire. At this point, taste it and check for salt and fresh-ground pepper. If you need more, add it.

When that is done, add the shrimp, green onion tops, and the teaspoon of lemon juice. Cook uncovered for another fifteen minutes. Take the pot off of the fire and cover it. Let it sit for one hour covered before you serve it over cooked white rice.

Note: This is classic stuff, people! It should be served with classic French bread and butter on the side. You will need something to dip into the sauce. Did I say that this is classic? If your answer is yes, congrats. You have paid attention, and I'm certain that your dish will be an instant classic!

Gondrella's Goulash

1 pound of ground beef
2 medium-sized tomatoes (diced)
1 small eggplant (peeled and diced)
1 small cucumber (peeled and diced)
5-ounce bottle of Pickapeppa sauce
Salt and fresh-ground pepper to taste

One of the guys I used to work with by the name of Pete Gondrella used to make this dish. He and his father had a vegetable market down in the French Quarter for a gazillion years. Pete would often bring in fresh veggies and fruit from the stand. One day he was making this, and I sort of adopted it from him. I think he was just using up whatever he had on hand, but then again maybe there was a method to it. He would never tell.

Fry off the ground beef until browned in a medium-sized pot. Now add the veggies and the Pickapeppa sauce. Stir it around to blend it really well and let it cook covered over a low fire for about an hour. It may take a little more time or maybe a little less. The eggplant is the last thing that will break down. You want the eggplant to be soft and not still crunchy to the bite. Don't worry in the beginning if it seems like there isn't enough liquid to do the trick. The veggies will make plenty after a while. Give it a stir about every ten minutes or so. When done, salt and fresh-ground pepper to taste. That's all there is to it.

My wife and I eat it like a soup. Pete used to eat this over pasta. Either way, it is a killer little dish. Thanks, Pete!

Smoked Duck, Chicken, and Andouille Gumbo

For the Stock:
1 large chicken (reserve bones)
1 large duck (reserve bones)
4 quarts of water
1 small onion (quartered)
1 stalk of celery
2 tablespoons of black peppercorns
1 teaspoon of kosher salt
4 cloves of garlic
For the Gumbo:
Meat from duck and chicken broken into small pieces
2 pounds of andouille sausage (diced)
4 large onions (finely chopped)
1 cup of green bell pepper (finely chopped)
5 cloves of garlic (finely chopped)
1/2 cup of celery (finely chopped)
1/2 cup of vegetable oil
1/2 cup of flour
4 quarts of stock (see above)
2 tablespoons of flashover seasoning
Salt
Fresh-ground pepper
1 cup of green onion tops (finely chopped)

This is something you can do a day or even two days ahead of time. The longer those flavors linger together, the more they become buddies and taste even better than they would when they were strangers.

If You Can't Stand the Heat

The first thing you need to do is to put the chicken and the duck on an indirect smoker. Using a smoker with the firebox on the side, you can slow smoke them half of the day. I usually will leave them on for about three hours. Use a meat thermometer, and when the center of a breast is about 180 degrees, take them off of the smoker. My personal choice of wood to smoke with is pecan, but if you can't find it, hickory or mesquite will do nicely. Once the birds are fully cooked, remove them from the smoker and allow them to cool. When they are cool enough to handle, remove the meat from both birds. While you are doing this, break the meat up into bite-sized pieces. Place all of the meat in a bowl and cover for later use.

Now take all of the bones and the smoked skins and put them in a stockpot along with the other ingredients listed for the stock. Bring this to a simmer. Cook covered for two hours and allow the stock to cool. Strain into a container you can cover and let it sit to settle for thirty minutes. There should be some sediment at the bottom afterward. You want to only keep the pure stock and not the dregs. Put that stock into a container and let it come to room temperature. There will be a lot of fat that floats to the top. Skim off as much as you can. I like to use a little of it when making the roux. Gives it a little extra smoky duck flavor.

Now the fun begins. In a large Dutch oven, pour in the oil and the flour and make a dark roux. It should be as dark as you can get it without burning it. If you reach the color of dark chocolate, congrats. You made it. Add the onion, bell pepper, celery, and mix with the roux. Wilt down the veggies until the onions are translucent. Next, add the garlic and a tablespoon of FOS. Cook for another minute or two. Now add the stock a little at a time until it is all blended well. Bring it up to a simmer and then cook covered on a low fire for ninety minutes. Now uncover and add the other tablespoon of FOS. Cook another ninety minutes uncovered. Next add all of the meats, including the andouille. Cook for another hour uncovered; then add the green onion tops. Mix them in well and remove the pot from the fire. Taste for salt and fresh-ground pepper and adjust if necessary. Let the pot sit covered for at least an hour. Serve over cooked white rice.

Note: As unusual as it might sound, we sometimes use Smashed Potato Salad (see recipe) instead of rice with gumbo. When I tell people who are from distant places, let's say Texas for instance, that we do this in Louisiana, they usually have this really odd look on their faces. That is until they taste it. Once you've had it this way, you'll never go back to rice.

Smoked Corn and Crab/Shrimp Soup

4 fresh ears of yellow corn
1 Cameron stovetop smoker
2 tablespoons of applewood smoke chips
2 pounds of head on shrimp or one and one half pounds of white lump crabmeat picked over for shells
1 tablespoon of peppercorns
1 teaspoon of salt
1 small onion
1 stalk of celery
3 quarts of water
2 quarts of stock
3 cups of onions (finely chopped)
1/2 cup of celery (finely chopped)
1/2 cup of bell pepper (finely chopped)
4 cloves of garlic (finely chopped)
1 stick of butter
1/2 cup of flour
2 tablespoons of flashover seasoning
1 cup of whipping cream
1 cup of green onion tops (chopped)
Salt and fresh-ground pepper to taste

This little gem of a dish can either be done with crab or with shrimp. Use one or the other, or even use both if you like. If you use the shrimp, use the shells along with the corncobs for your stock. If you use crab, get some gumbo crabs and use them along with the corncobs for a stock. Either way, it's a winner.

If You Can't Stand the Heat

The first step to this is to smoke your corn. Place the cleaned ears of corn in the smoker and follow the instructions that come with the smoker. It should take about twenty minutes to finish. Once they are done, let them cool and then cut the corn from the cob. Put the cobs into a stockpot. Save the corn on the side.

The second step is to peel your shrimp and clean them well. Place them in some cold water and set aside. Put the shrimp peelings into the stockpot with the corncobs. Now add the peppercorns, celery, salt, onions, and water to the stockpot. Heat up the pot and let it cook until it is reduced by a third. That should leave you with two quarts of stock. Strain and let it settle and cool to room temperature. There should be some non-liquid leftovers from the stock that settles to the bottom. You will want to discard that from the dish. Just pour off the clear stock and throw out the dregs. If you are doing a smoked corn and crab dish, use gumbo crabs along with the corncobs. They are inexpensive and will impart the crab flavor into the stock without you having to use expensive crabmeat for flavor.

Next you put the butter into a large pot. Melt the butter and then add all of the vegetables with the exception of the garlic. Cook until the onions are translucent and then add a tablespoon of the FOS. Now add the garlic and cook for another two minutes. Sprinkle in the flour and mix in. Cook on a low fire for about ten minutes; keep cooking and scraping the bottom of your pan. You want to cook the raw taste of the flour out of the pan. This will give you a wilted veggie and golden roux mixture. Add the other tablespoon of FOS and blend in. Now slowly pour in the two quarts of stock little by little and blend it all together. When it comes to a simmer, cover and put over a low fire for one hour.

Remove the cover and add the smoked corn kernels. Cook uncovered on a low fire for another hour while stirring often. It's at this point, if you like, you could add a touch of sherry. I choose that option occasionally just for a change.

Stir in the whipping cream a little at a time. Cook uncovered on a low fire for another hour. Once again, stir a lot. Add the shrimp or crabmeat and cook until the shrimp are pink or the crabmeat is heated through. Now add the green onion tops. Salt and fresh-ground pepper to taste. Mix it all together really well and get your mouth ready for something special. Serve with some crunchy French bread and butter.

Note: If you do decide to go with both the shrimp and the crab, use one pound of shrimp and one pound of crabmeat. If you want to use more or less of either, do it. There is no way you can go wrong … unless you serve it all to others and not get some for yourself. In New Orleans, that would not only be wrong, but I believe it would be a criminal offense.

Venison Chili/Beef Chili

4 pounds of ground venison or ground beef
2 pounds of Vidalia onions (chopped)
1 cup of roasted red peppers (chopped)
6 cloves of garlic (chopped)
28-ounce can of crushed tomatoes
1/2 pound of bacon
1 bottle of Abita dark beer
32 ounces of beef stock
1/2 cup of chipotle in adobo sauce (chopped)
4 teaspoons of tomato paste
2 tablespoons of brown sugar
2 tablespoons of southwest chipotle seasoning
2 tablespoons of Miles' Mexican Biz (see recipe)
1 tablespoon of flashover seasoning
1 tablespoon of cumin
1 tablespoon of chili powder
1 teaspoon of kosher salt

Let's see a show of hands. How many of you out there have a recipe for chili? Wow. That's a lot of hands. Well I had my hand up too, and my recipe is pretty good. Maybe not as good as yours, I'm sure, but still pretty good. You can do this with venison or with lean ground beef. Either way, it's still chili! Oh … I almost forgot. You can put your hands down now.

In a large pot, fry down the bacon until crisp. Remove the bacon, but leave in the rendered down bacon fat. When the bacon is cool, crush it in your hands to make bacon bits and set aside. There is very little fat in venison, so you will need the bacon fat to help brown the meat. Now add the meat, the FOS, and slowly cook in the bacon fat until browned.

  If You Can't Stand the Heat

After it is browned, remove the meat to a separate container. Now put the onions and the Biz into the big pot and cook until the onions are translucent. Add the tomato paste and cook for a few minutes until it starts to get a rusty brown color. Add the garlic and the roasted red peppers and cook another two minutes. Now put in the crushed tomatoes, chipotles with adobo sauce, southwest seasoning, salt, cumin, and the chili powder. Mix well and cook for another two to three minutes.

Next, put in the brown sugar and the beer. Cook for another five minutes; then add the browned venison (or beef) and the bacon bits. Mix well; then stir in the beef stock. Simmer uncovered on a low fire for two and one half to three hours, depending upon how thick you want it to be. The more moisture that cooks out of it, the thicker it will be. Stir often and make sure that it doesn't stick to the bottom of the pot. That's about it. Invite a lot of friends. Eat!

Note: I usually serve it without beans, but if you have to stretch it a little, add a couple of cans of kidney beans. Also try making this with lean ground beef. It will still have a low fat content and will be extremely tasty.

Shrimp Etouffee

3 pounds of shrimp (headless, peeled, and cleaned)
6 cups of onions (chopped)
1/2 cup of celery (chopped)
1/2 cup of bell pepper (chopped)
4 cloves of garlic (chopped)
2 sticks of unsalted butter
2 tablespoons of tomato sauce
1 tablespoon of sherry
1/2 cup of green onion tops (chopped)
1/3 cup of flour
1/3 cup of vegetable oil
6 cups of Shrimp/Seafood Stock (see recipe)
Crabmeat from the crabs used to make the stock
2 tablespoons of flashover seasoning
1 teaspoon of sea salt

You start this dish by making the stock and keeping it warm on the side. The next thing you need to do is to make a roux with the flour and oil that is the color of dark brown chocolate. After you are finished, set it aside and let it cool.

In a Dutch oven, melt the butter and cook over medium heat until it begins to slightly brown. Add the onions, bell pepper, and celery and add one tablespoon of FOS. Cook until the onions are translucent, almost to the point of being caramelized. This may take awhile because the onions will excrete a lot of fluid. You want to cook it until almost all of that fluid is gone and then add the garlic. Cook for another two minutes. Next, add the tomato sauce and cook for another two minutes. Now add the stock, and blend everything together while you are bringing the dish up to a simmer. Next you want to slowly add the roux a spoonful at a time until all of the roux is incorporated. After all is blended, add

If You Can't Stand the Heat

the sea salt and the last tablespoon of FOS. Simmer one hour with the lid on. Now take the lid off and simmer for another hour. Stir often.

At this point it is time to add the shrimp and cook uncovered for another fifteen to twenty minutes. They will excrete a lot of fluid, so it will help with the fact that it was getting rather thick. Add the green onion tops, the sherry, and the crabmeat and cook for five more minutes. Remove from the heat. Cover and let sit for one hour before serving over cooked white rice.

Note: I've seen some people make etouffee recipes that are cooked uncovered. Etouffee means, "To cook smothered." How can you take a shortcut and call it etouffee? You have to smother it for at least a little while. Also true is that the original etouffees were cooked with butter and a blond roux, but the recipe that I use comes from an old Cajun grandmother. She liked to combine butter and dark roux. It had something to do with the flavors being more intense with butter and roux together. And if you never learn anything in your life, learn this: never argue with an old Cajun grandmother!

Black Bean Soup (and/or Refried Beans)

1 pound of black beans
32 ounces of chicken stock
2 cups of water
2 tablespoons of garlic (chopped fine)
2 cups of onions (chopped)
1 tablespoon of olive oil
3 tablespoons of bacon fat
1 tablespoon of cumin
Salt and fresh-ground pepper to taste
Red onion (chopped)
Mexican melting cheese (grated)

This recipe will cover either black bean soup or refried beans. It's another two for one deal. Sometimes I will make the soup and save half, then continue on with the other half to make refried beans. I also sometimes wonder why they are called refried. They're not even fried once.

Rinse the beans well; then check them to make sure there are no stones in the beans. Put them in a pot and cover the beans with the chicken stock and water. Add the olive oil, cover, and simmer for an hour. While that is happening, sauté the onions in the bacon fat until the onions are translucent. Now put in the garlic and cook for two minutes. Add the cumin and the fresh-ground pepper to taste, cook for one minute and then add it all to the beans. Do not add the salt in the early stages. The bacon fat will have enough salt that you may not have to add any. You'll have to check for the salt taste toward the end.

Somewhere between three and three and a half hours later (stirring often), you will find that they have become a semi-creamy and soup-like consistency. Those three and one-half hours do not include the first hour that it simmered. That is black bean soup!

Add some fresh chopped red onions and some Mexican melting cheese on top and serve.

If you want refried beans, cook for four hours (after the initial hour of simmering), strain (reserving the liquid), mash the beans, and then add the strained liquid back into it.

Be sure to stir often and scrape the sides. If it gets too thick, add more stock as needed. Also serve with a little chopped red onion and Mexican melting cheese on top.

Note: There are times when I have made these and it took longer than the three to four hours that I needed to cook them. It sometimes depends upon the beans themselves. Some are harder than others. If you should get to the end of the time allowed and they are still hard, just keep cooking them until they come to that semi-creamy consistency that makes the bean soup so special.

Every once in a while you can get a bag of beans that just won't cooperate. They never quite soften up enough no matter how long you cook them. In that case you skip the soup and go right to the refried version. They will still taste great, and no one will know you spent half the day cooking impossible beans.

White Beans and Venison Sausage

2 pounds of Camellia white beans
6 14-ounce cans of chicken stock
1 1/2 quarts of water
1 pound of smoked ham hocks
2 pounds of venison sausage (smoked or otherwise cured and diced)
1 pound of pickled pork (diced)
1/2 cup of bell pepper (chopped)
1/2 cup of celery (chopped)
3 cloves of garlic (finely chopped)
4 cups of onions (chopped)
1/2 cup of green onions (chopped)
3 bay leaves
Fresh-ground pepper to taste
Tabasco

At the firehouse, we made white beans served with fried rabbit. We made them served with pork chops. And we made them with venison. Guess which one this is.

In a large pot, rinse the beans thoroughly. Set the pot of beans aside.

Take the ham hocks and place them in the bottom of a separate pot. Cover them with the six cans of chicken stock (or eighty-four ounces of stock). Bring to a simmer and cook uncovered for approximately one hour or until the ham hocks are tender enough so that what meat is on them will start falling off of the bone. Remove the ham hocks and let cool. Transfer the broth from the ham hocks into the large pot containing the beans. Bring your bean pot up to a slow simmer. Once the ham hocks are cooled enough to touch, remove any meat from them and add that meat to the beans.

In a large frying pan, place the pork and the sausage and bring them up to temperature. Cook until the pickled pork is cooked through. Because the sausage is already fully cooked, you will just be extract-

If You Can't Stand the Heat

ing some flavor from it. Once the meat is cooked, use a slotted spoon and remove the meat. Put it in the pot with the beans. Now add all of the vegetables to the meat frying pan. Mix with the meat juices and cook until the onions are translucent. Pour all of it into the bean pot. Add fresh-ground pepper. Do not add any salt. There is enough salt in the meats and the stock to compensate for any salt you may feel like you need to add. Now put in a few drops of Tabasco and the bay leaves. Mix together and add the one and one half quarts of water. Cook covered on a low fire for two hours. Stir often. Remove the cover and cook another hour. The cooking time will really vary a bit. Some beans are harder than others and naturally will take longer to cook. It will also depend on how creamy you want your beans to be. Your choice. But be sure to taste them and see if they are cooked all the way through. If any salt is needed, now is the time to add it; otherwise you are good to go. Serve over some cooked white rice and with a big chunk of French bread. If you have any venison sausage left over, fry it up and serve it on the side.

Both Right and Lite Red Beans and Rice

Growing up I'd always heard stories about when and why this dish is served. Everybody and their mama will tell you that red beans and rice is always served on Monday.

The story goes that Monday was washday, and the women would put on a pot of beans over a low fire. That way the beans would cook all day while the wash was getting done. When the laundry was finished, the supper would be ready. At least that's the way I heard it. The way things were in our house, it never happened like that. We had so many people living in that apartment that every day was a laundry day. But being traditional people, we still stuck with tradition and only ate red beans and rice on Mondays.

I'm going to give you two versions of this dish. The first one is the get down serious way to make red beans. It has all of the good stuff. The second is the lite version. This is just in case you want the flavor of a good plate of red beans and rice but don't want all of the fat.

Red Beans the Right Way

2 pounds of dried kidney beans

4 large onions (diced)

1/2 cup of celery (diced)

6 cloves of garlic (finely chopped)

3 32-ounce containers of chicken stock

6 cups of water

1 pound of pickle meat (diced)

1 pound of hot smoked andouille sausage (cut into small pieces)

4 small smoked ham hocks

1/4 cup of fresh parsley (chopped)

1 cup of green onions (chopped small)

2 whole bay leaves

Fresh-ground pepper

Dash or two of Tabasco

Cooked white rice

Before you start, there are a few ground rules. First, you will notice that there is no salt in this dish. That's because there is so much salt in all of the meats and the stock that any more would be too much. Second, check and stir them often … maybe even more than often. They like to be cooked over a low fire and really slow. Did I mention stirring? Don't burn the beans.

  If You Can't Stand the Heat

And last but not least, people like their beans different ways. Some like them runny, and some like them thick. If you're a thick bean person, here's what you do: In the last half hour or so during the cooking process, mash a few beans along the inside of the pot with the back of a spoon. Scrape them off of the sides and mix them in. The more you mash, the thicker the beans will get. Just don't mash them all and wind up with bean soup. Remember the bean mantra. Low and slow!

People will tell you that you need to soak your beans overnight. This is supposed to help them expand by absorbing water and make the beans cook faster. I almost never do that. (Navy beans are my exception.) When the guys in the engine house would decide to eat beans, it was usually on the morning of that same day, so there was no time to soak. All you really need to do is to make sure that you rinse them really well before you start to cook them. Before I go any further, I want to go on record again by saying that you should not, under any circumstances, add salt to this dish. Besides, individuals can always add salt to their own taste requirements after they are cooked.

The first thing to do is to put all of the chicken stock in a large pot along with the ham hocks. Let that simmer uncovered until the meat is ready to fall off the bone. This may take awhile, so be prepared. It may take from an hour to ninety minutes, depending upon the ham hocks, so begin it as early as you can. When done, remove the ham hocks to a plate to cool and save the stock. Add the beans to the hot stock and bring to a boil; then turn it down to a simmer.

The next step is to put your sausage and pickle meat in a non-stick frying pan and turn up the heat. You want to render some of the meat flavors and juices into the skillet. When the pickle meat is cooked through, remove both meats from the pan and add them to the bean pot.

Put your onions, parsley, green onions, and celery into the frying pan with the meat juices and cook them until the onions become translucent. Add the garlic and fresh-ground pepper. Two minutes after you add the garlic and fresh-ground pepper, pour the mixture into the pot with the beans.

Break the meat from the ham hocks into bite-size pieces and put it all in the pot along with the six cups of water. Add bay leaves and a good shot of Tabasco.

Turn the fire down low and cover. Stir the beans often and make sure they don't stick to the bottom of the pan. Like I said before, don't burn the beans. If you burn the beans, you'll have to throw them out and start over. Nothing tastes worse than burned beans.

Once all of the ingredients are in the pot, cooking time is usually about two and a half to three hours. After the first two hours, you will want to smash some of the now softened beans against the side of the pot and mix them back in. This will help to make the beans creamy and thick.

I hate to be redundant, but … stir a lot.

After the allotted time has passed, the beans should be very soft. If not, cook them a while longer until they are. If they get too thick, add more water. Some dried beans are just harder than others and take longer to break down. Once you have cooked them for a while, you will be able to judge how thick you want them. Just try a couple of beans to make sure they are all cooked through and soft; then mash or don't mash to get your proper thickness.

When they are done, serve over cooked white rice. I'm sure that almost everyone would like to have a generous portion of French bread and butter to compliment the meal.

Note: We used to say that this recipe is enough to feed eight to ten normal people or six firemen. If we had extra men and we needed to stretch the meal at the engine house, we'd serve the beans and rice with a side order of fried pork chops.

If there are any beans left over, they freeze really well. Believe it or not, beans taste even better the second time around.

Red Beans the Lite Way

1 pound of dried red beans
64 ounces of fat free low sodium chicken broth (reserve one half cup on the side)
1 14-ounce pack of lean turkey smoked sausage (sliced into small pieces)
1 four ounce pack of turkey tasso (cut into small pieces)
1 8-ounce pack of ninety-five percent fat-free cubed ham

1/2 medium bell pepper (diced)
3 large onions (diced)
1/2 cup of celery (diced)
4 cloves of garlic (finely chopped)
Fresh-ground pepper
2 bay leaves
Dash of Tabasco
Cooked rice

If You Can't Stand the Heat

These red beans are more or less the same as the original, but with a few modifications. Start by heating up all but a half of a cup of the chicken broth. You'll need that a little later. Rinse the beans and add them to a large pot with the chicken broth (except for the reserved 1/2 cup).

Place your cut up tasso, sausage, and ham into a frying pan and heat it up. Once again, you just need to extract some of the meat flavor, so don't go overboard and burn the meat. There will be very little fat that will come out of the meat, as it is all pretty close to fat free already. Next, spoon the meat into the pot with the beans, making sure to leave behind any meat bits and juices left in the pan. Sauté your vegetables in the frying pan with what juice you have leftover from sautéing the meat. Put everything in but the garlic. When the onions are translucent, add the garlic and cook for another two minutes. Use the leftover half cup of chicken stock to get everything unstuck from the pan. Now add it all to the beans pot.

Fresh-ground pepper, the Tabasco, and the two bay leaves go in next. Just as in the original, put it on a low fire and cover. Stir often. Don't let them stick to the bottom. Also as in the original, do not add salt at any time, but do feel free to taste it often to see if the beans have softened. Cooking time depends upon how soon the beans get soft and how much of a creamy consistency you want them to be. If you mash some beans against the side of the pot when they are partially softened, the beans will get thicker. Generally speaking, about two and a half hours after everything is in the pot, they are done.

Serve over cooked white rice. Enjoy a lot. These are low fat, people. Go after them!

Note: If you can't find turkey tasso, just add a little more turkey sausage. No one will know! You will also notice that the cooking time is shorter than the original. That is because you are only cooking one pound of beans as opposed to two. You know what that means. It will feed less people than the original. I knew you would figure it out. You're so good at math!

Louisiana Creole Seafood Gumbo

Once again, ask a hundred people, get a hundred different recipes for gumbo. These are the ingredients and the steps I follow to make this type of gumbo. It takes some time to make a good gumbo, but it's worth the trouble. As an older, wiser, and better cook than I once said, "You can make it quick, or you can make it right."

Step 1: Make Shrimp/Seafood Stock (see recipe).

Step 2: Make okra and tomato mixture from:
12 ounces of andouille sausage (sliced into one-eighth-inch-thick pieces)
4 medium Creole tomatoes (peeled, seeded, and chopped)
16 ounces of frozen, chopped okra
1 small onion (finely chopped)
2 teaspoons of flashover seasoning
1 1/2 teaspoons of white vinegar
2 cups of Shrimp/Seafood Stock

Step 3: Make roux from:
1/2 cup of vegetable oil
1/2 cup of all-purpose flour

Step 4: Vegetables
3 medium onions (chopped)
1/2 cup of celery (chopped)
1/2 cup of green bell pepper (chopped)
3 cloves of garlic (finely chopped)
1 tablespoon of flashover seasoning

If You Can't Stand the Heat

Step 5: Assembly of the gumbo
1 1/2 quarts of Shrimp/Seafood Stock (see recipe)
Cooked veggies
6 gumbo crabs (cleaned and broken in half)
2 bay leaves
Tomato and okra Mixture

Step 6: The big finish (putting it all together)
3 pounds of peeled shrimp
3 dozen oysters and their liquor
1 tablespoon of flashover seasoning
1 cup of green onion tops (finely chopped)
Cooked white rice

As in all gumbos, there are as many variations as there are people who make them. This particular one is a seafood gumbo. I like to put a bit of sausage into mine. Some folks would never dare to put meat in a seafood gumbo. To them I say, "Write your own book, and you can leave out the sausage." Also, this may look like a daunting recipe to try, but it's really not. I just broke it down as much as I possibly could to make it easier to do and understand.

Step 1: Stock

Go to Shrimp/Seafood Stock recipe and follow it. Strain and let it sit until it comes to room temperature. If you make it a day ahead of time and put it in the fridge overnight, take it out the next day and let it come to room temperature before you use it. Mixing cold stock and hot roux does not work. You will have lots of flour lumps floating around, and that makes for a bad gumbo. You will need one and one-half quarts for the final assembly plus two cups for the tomato okra mixture.

Step 2: Tomato and okra mixture

Over a medium heat and in a pot that you can cover, fry the andouille down until it starts to brown a bit and releases some of its oil; then stir in the chopped onions. Next add the FOS and stir it in thoroughly. Cook the onions until they are translucent. Now add the tomatoes and cook for five minutes. Add the stock; then mix well. Cook another five minutes. Next add the okra and the vinegar. Mix well and bring up to a simmer. Cover and cook over a low fire for thirty minutes. Remove it from the fire and set aside.

I know there is enough acid in the tomatoes to break down the "rope" in the okra, but somewhere along the way I was told to add a pinch of vinegar to the dish to help out. The rope refers to the sticky substance that is in the cut okra that some refer to as "the slime." We prefer to call it rope. Go figure!

Also, this little concoction can be eaten all by itself. It's almost like a soup. Try to resist eating it, and make sure that it makes it into the gumbo pot.

Step 3: Make roux

Heat up the oil in your black iron pot or whatever you will be making the gumbo in; then add the flour. I use a big black iron Dutch oven like my family did. Just make sure you have a pot that really conducts heat well and is large enough to accommodate all of the ingredients.

Cook over a medium heat until you have achieved a dark roux. It should be a very dark rusty color. Not quite chocolate but close.

Step 4: Vegetables

Add the veggies to the cooked roux (except the garlic). This will keep the roux from cooking any further. Now add the FOS and mix in. Cook until the veggies are wilted and the onions are translucent. Now add the garlic and cook for two minutes.

Step 5: Assembly

Start adding your room temperature stock a little at a time into the roux/veggie pot. Do this until all of the stock is incorporated. Now add the bay leaves and bring it to a simmer. Cook covered on a low heat for sixty minutes. Uncover and add the okra and tomato mixture. Also add the gumbo crabs at this stage. Stir to incorporate well. Cook for ninety minutes uncovered. Stir it often.

Step 6: The big finish

Now add the shrimp, oysters and their liquor, green onions, and one last tablespoon of FOS. Cook uncovered for about ten minutes and then check for salt. When you dump all of that cold seafood in, it will dramatically reduce the temperature. Turn the heat up a bit to get it cooking and then continue to cook. By the time it comes back up to a simmer, the ten minutes will be up. Cover, remove from the fire, and let sit covered for at least one half hour.

Serve over cooked white rice, and keep a little bottle of file on the side for those who might want some. And that's not a "file" like a nail file. *File* (pronounced fee-lay) is ground sassafras leaves. You've heard of file gumbo haven't you? Like in the song.

Note: As I said in the beginning, I know that looking at this recipe might be rather daunting. It really isn't. It appears to be long only because I have included every detail I could think of so that anyone can cook an authentic Louisiana seafood gumbo. I hate it when people give you instructions and then leave out the details. Don't you?

Cobia Courtbouillion

3 pounds of cobia fish filets (cut into bite-sized cubes)
3 quarts of Fish Stock (see recipe)
1 cup of bell pepper (chopped)
1/2 cup of celery (chopped)
5 cups of onions (chopped)
4 cloves of garlic (finely chopped)
8-ounce can of tomato sauce
2 cans of diced tomatoes and chilies (ten ounces each)
1/2 cup of vegetable oil
1/2 cup of all-purpose flour
4 tablespoons of butter
3 tablespoons of flashover seasoning
1 teaspoon of sea salt
Few drops of Tabasco
4 lemon slices
1/2 cup of fresh parsley
1 cup of green onion tops (chopped)
2 bay leaves

This is a takeoff of redfish courtbouillion. You can use redfish instead if you like. I just happened to write this recipe when I came back from Florida with an ice chest full of cobia.

I usually break up the time it takes to make this dish by making my stock ahead of time (see Fish Stock recipe). Use the half-cup of oil and the half-cup of flour to make a dark brown roux, also ahead of time. Make it the color of dark chocolate. Once it is done, remove it from the pot and set it aside to cool. This will save you time when it is time to put this together. Not to be redundant, but do you think I used the word *time* enough times? If you don't have that kind of time (sorry), this dish can be done

If You Can't Stand the Heat

all in the same day. Also on that day, cut up the fish into bite-sized chunks, and put them in a Zip-lock bag. Add one tablespoon of FOS, sprinkled over the fish, and let it marinate for at least one hour (or preferably overnight).

With those three things out of the way, when you are ready to cook, get out your big Dutch oven and melt the butter on medium heat. It may seem like an odd way to go about making a courtbouillion, but I have my reasons. Traditionally you would make the roux, then wilt down the veggies in it, then add the stock. I like mine with a little buttery taste, so I make the roux ahead and add it later.

Once the butter is melted, add the bell pepper, celery, and onions. Cook them until the veggies are wilted and the onions are translucent. Lower the fire and then add the garlic, one tablespoon of the FOS, and cook for about three minutes. Now add the tomato sauce, and cook for five minutes. Stir to keep it from sticking. Add the diced tomatoes and chilies and the last tablespoon of FOS, and cook for another five minutes.

Pour in your room temperature stock and one half-teaspoon of sea salt. Right about now is a good time to put in a few drops of Tabasco. Bring the mixture up to a simmer.

Next, you slowly add your roux, one tablespoon at a time, until it is all incorporated. Now, toss in the two bay leaves and turn the fire down to low. Cook covered for one hour and uncovered for two hours. Stir often. Some people will tell you that you can cook this in half the time, and they are right. But I like to do the first hour covered to let the flavors marry and uncovered for two hours to evaporate and concentrate the flavors even more. I think the flavors are more intense that way.

When the time is up, add the fish, green onions, and parsley. Kick up the fire and cook it for ten minutes; then turn off the fire. Now, check for salt to taste and add the other half-teaspoon of salt if needed. Toss in the lemon slices. Let it sit covered for about an hour before you serve it over cooked white rice.

Note: You can always make this dish the normal way. Like I said, just the roux, veggies, and stock, and leave out the butter. It will still be great, but you will lose an opportunity to use butter in a dish. What's wrong with you?

Crawfish Bisque

Boil:
2 gallons of water (to boil the live crawfish)
5 pounds of crawfish (fresh, live, and rinsed clean)

Stock:
3 quarts of water (for the stock)
Crawfish peelings and claws

Stuffing:
1/2 of the peeled crawfish tails (with their fat) and 6 ounces of a 12-ounce pack of frozen crawfish tails (with their fat)
(All of the crawfish tails will be put into a food processor together, and half will be used in the stuffing, the other half in the bisque.)
4 tablespoons of butter
1 cup of onions (chopped)
1/4 cup of bell pepper (chopped)
1/4 cup of celery (chopped)
1 large clove of garlic (chopped)
2 teaspoons of flashover seasoning
3/4 cup of plain breadcrumbs
1 cup of flour
50 to 60 crawfish shell backs

If You Can't Stand the Heat

Bisque:

1/2 cup of vegetable oil

1/2 cup of flour

4 cups of onions (finely chopped)

1/2 cup of celery (finely chopped)

1/2 cup of bell pepper (finely chopped)

3 cloves of garlic (finely chopped)

1 heaping tablespoon of tomato paste

2 quarts of crawfish stock

1/2 of the peeled crawfish tails (with their fat) and 6 ounces of a 12-ounce pack of frozen crawfish tails (with fat) (The other half of the food processed crawfish tails.)

1 tablespoon of flashover seasoning

1 teaspoon of salt

Salt and fresh-ground pepper to taste (at the end)

1 cup of green onion tops (finely chopped)

Before you begin, you have to know that this is a time-consuming dish. It's worth it in the end, but know that this is not something you will just throw together.

Boil: First, get a big pot and put in two gallons of water. Bring it up to a boil, and then add the live crawfish. That will stop the boil, but when they come back to a simmer, let them cook for ten to fifteen minutes (depending upon their size), and then drain. Allow them to cool before you peel them.

I like to set up a sort of assembly line on the counter for this next part. Four bowls with four different uses. Once I start peeling the crawfish, I put the tail meat and fat in one bowl. The second bowl I use for the tail peelings and the claws. There is meat in the claws and the peelings that will help flavor the stock. Now for the slightly tricky part. From the leftover head you need to break off the front piece, which includes the eyes and antennae. Discard this piece. All you really want to keep is the shell of the back. This is the part you will stuff. These shells go into the third bowl. You will only need about fifty to sixty shells to stuff. You may have more shells at your disposal, but you won't need them because you will run out of stuffing. The fourth bowl is for everything else that is leftover. That would be the trash bowl. Use your fingers to clean out the back shell. Rinse the shells in cold water several times. You want them to be empty, clean, and eventually dry.

Stock: Put the tail peelings and the claws into a stockpot and add the three quarts of water. Bring it up to a simmer and cook it uncovered for forty-five minutes. It will reduce down, and after you strain it there should be about two quarts left. Let it cool down to room temperature before you use it. Adding hot stock to hot roux is a no-no in my book. Also, it will settle, and there will be some sediment that collects on the bottom. Do not use this sediment in the dish. Just use the crawfish stock and discard the settled particles. If there is not enough stock, just add a little water to it to bring it up to two quarts.

Note: You are going to be processing all of the crawfish tails that you peeled together with a twelve-ounce pack of frozen tails. Half of them will go into the stuffing and half will go into the gravy.

Stuffing: Take all of the crawfish tails and their fat and put them in a food processor. This includes the ones you peeled and a twelve-ounce pack of frozen tails. There should be some water in the tails that comes from thawing out the frozen tails. That will give them a little moisture when you chop them. Just pulse them about ten times to chop them up. You don't want a paste, just a rough chop. Now put those tails in a bowl and set aside.

Heat up the butter in a sauté pan; then put the onions, celery, bell pepper, and one teaspoon of the FOS in with it. Cook until the onions are translucent, then add the garlic. Cook for one minute and then remove it from the fire. Allow it to cool.

Once it is cool, add the sautéed seasonings and the other teaspoon of FOS to half of the processed crawfish tails. Remember, the second half is for the gravy. Put in the breadcrumbs and mix. You don't want anything that is runny, but you also don't want it to be too bread-like. It should cake together when you roll it into a ball without being sticky or mushy. If it's too sticky, add a little more breadcrumbs. This comprises your stuffing.

Take each crawfish shell back that you saved and dried, and fill it with the mixture. Pack it in and smooth out the top with your fingers. There should be enough filling to do about fifty to sixty shells depending on their size. Once they are all stuffed, you will put them in a bowl and sprinkle the flour on them. Mix them around and try to cover them all with a light coating of flour. As some people like to say, just dust them with flour. Place them on an oven tray and bake them at 375 degrees for about twenty-five or thirty minutes. It may take a little more time or a little less time depending on your particular oven. You are just trying to brown the flour slightly. I like to shake them up a couple of times during the baking process, move them around a bit to make sure they are evenly browning. Remove the tray from the oven and set aside for the moment.

Bisque: This is actually the gravy portion of the program. Heat up the oil in a Dutch oven and then add the flour. Stir slowly until you have made a brown roux. That would be just past the peanut butter colored roux but not quite chocolate colored. Now add the onions, celery, bell pepper, and a tablespoon of FOS. Cook until the onions are translucent and then add the garlic. Cook for one minute and then add the tomato paste. Mix it in well and cook until the tomato paste starts to brown slightly. When that happens, start adding the stock (room temperature) a little at a time until you incorporate it all. Now add the other half of your processed crawfish tails that you didn't use for the stuffing along with the teaspoon of salt.

Cook uncovered on a low fire for ninety minutes. Stir it occasionally to make sure nothing is sticking. After that, add the stuffed crawfish shells to the pot. Check it now for salt and fresh-ground pepper and amend it to your own taste. Add the chopped green onions, and when the mixture comes back up to a simmer, cook uncovered on a low fire for fifteen minutes. Turn off the fire and cover. Let it sit for one hour before serving. That helps to let the gravy absorb into the stuffed shells. Serve over cooked white rice with a healthy portion of French bread and butter.

Another note: I will usually get the bisque gravy started and then bake the stuffed shells in the oven. That way they don't have to sit around for very long after they come out of the oven.

I also like to serve this with a little sherry on the side. It will be your guest's choice as to whether or not they want to enhance the dish with a touch of warm sherry goodness.

Some people in today's world don't like to hassle with cleaning and stuffing the heads. The will, instead, roll the stuffing into jawbreaker-sized balls called boulettes. They will then dust them with flour. They bake them in the oven just as they would the stuffed shells, just until slightly brown. I happen to prefer the old-fashioned way so I stuff the shells. But that's just me. I don't take shortcuts unless I'm driving somewhere. Never in cooking! Besides, to me they look like crawfish meatballs, and there is something about that that just isn't right.

And just for clarification, you eat the stuffing out of the shells, not the shells themselves. I only mention it because someone asked me if they should eat the shells too. He wasn't invited back.

Smoked Chicken Salad Sandwich

1 5-to-6-pound roasting hen (smoked)
1 cup of Homemade Mayonnaise (see recipe)
6 hardboiled eggs (peeled and rough chopped)
Salt and fresh-ground pepper (to taste)
Smoked paprika (a little to sprinkle on top)
Kaiser rolls (with poppy seeds)

Sometimes it gets rather busy at the firehouse. You don't have time to prepare anything elaborate. So if we had some leftover smoked chicken, this would be easy to throw together. Without the chicken we'd just make egg salad. The way I look at it, egg, chicken, it's the same thing. The only difference is that it's really hard to smoke an egg.

Clean your chicken and pat it dry with paper towels. Place it in your smoker, and cook it until the internal meat temperature is 180 degrees. I like to use mesquite, but whatever wood you choose is still going to work. Your hen may have one of those little red top thermometers already in it that pops out when done, but I prefer to use a meat thermometer to be sure. Besides, those things aren't really that accurate.

Once it is done, remove from the smoker and let it cool off until it is easy to handle with your bare hands. Remove the meat from the bones and break it up into small pieces. Put those pieces into a bowl and either discard the bones or use them to make a smoked chicken stock for another time. Add the hardboiled eggs, homemade mayo, and salt and fresh-ground pepper to taste. Mix it all together and sprinkle the smoked paprika on top. Cover until you are ready to serve. Toast the rolls and spread a generous amount of chicken salad on each.

Note: Sometimes I put on lettuce and tomatoes, but usually I will serve it just like it is. If you want it to seem a bit fancier, use the lettuce and tomatoes. I'm sure the chicken will enjoy being dressed up for dinner.

Also, if you are really pressed for time, some stores have smoked chicken already done. You can use the rotisserie chicken if you have to, but smoked is 100 percent better.

Smashed Potato Salad

6 medium potatoes (diced into 1-inch cubes)
6 hardboiled eggs (diced into one 1/2-inch pieces)
2 cups of Homemade Mayonnaise (one and a half cups now and one half cup for later) (see recipe)
Salt (to taste)
Fresh-ground pepper (to taste)

This particular recipe is for six people. That's one egg and one potato per person. If you want to have more potato salad, just double up on all of the ingredients. That would be a lot of potato salad! Just how hungry are you?

I know that it seems like a rather simple recipe (no onions, celery, etc.), but by using the homemade mayo, it tastes different from any potato salad you've ever had. It is made to eat warm and preferably right away. We eat this as a side for ribs, chicken, and the like. We also use this with gumbo. Put a scoop in your bowl instead of rice, and you won't believe how good it is.

Boil the potatoes until they are fork tender; then drain completely. Put those in a bowl and add fresh-ground pepper and salt to taste. Now put in the eggs and one and a half cups of the homemade mayo. *Do not use store-bought mayo.* It will not work in the same way.

Once the mayo is in the bowl, blend it in by making a chopping motion with the side of a large spoon over and over again. What you are trying to do is to mix it all together, but at the same time, break up some of (not all of) the potatoes. There will be chunks of potatoes, chunks of eggs blended with a smooth mixture, sort of like a lumpy mashed potatoes. Now taste for any additional salt and fresh-ground pepper you might want.

Cover and keep aside until ready to serve. When you are ready to eat (it's about time), mix in the other half-cup of mayo right before you serve.

Note: I know it seems like it might not have much in the taste area, but I bet that once you try it, you will never serve potato salad any other way. Any takers? I'm ready to put my money where my mouth is. Literally!

Caesar Salad and Dressing

1 cup of Parmigiano-Reggiano cheese (grated)
1/4 teaspoon of kosher salt
3/4 teaspoon of fresh-ground pepper
1 teaspoon of anchovy paste
4 cloves of garlic (three chopped up fine and one whole clove)
1 tablespoon of Creole mustard
1 tablespoon of lemon juice
1 tablespoon of red wine vinegar
Splash of Worcestershire sauce
1 coddled egg
4 tablespoons of olive oil
10 ounces of romaine hearts (torn into small pieces)

This is a cool recipe. It involves coddling. I rarely ever coddle, so this is a unique opportunity. I did say coddle and not cuddle. That would be creepy (unless you are a chicken)!

The first thing you need to do is coddle the egg (not cuddle). Put an egg, in the shell, into boiling water for forty-five seconds. Take it out and immediately put it in an ice water bath to keep it from cooking anymore. When cool, set it aside for the moment.

Take the whole clove of garlic and rub it on the inside of a wooden bowl. Throw away the clove when done. Add salt and fresh-ground pepper to the bowl, and using the back of a spoon, mash them together in the bowl. Now add the cut up garlic cloves, and mash them into the seasonings to make a paste. Put in the anchovy paste and mustard; again mash into the paste. Crack open the coddled egg; add it to the bowl along with the Worcestershire and the lemon juice. Incorporate it into the mixture. Using a whisk, blend in the vinegar. Now slowly drizzle in the olive oil and whisk until an emulsion forms. Mix in the cheese, and you are done with the dressing.

If You Can't Stand the Heat

Mix the dressing with romaine lettuce. This is your basic Caesar salad. Some folks like to add extra anchovies. Some like to add bacon bits. Try it with some grilled shrimp or grilled chicken. Toss in some croutons if you have them. Either way, it's some good stuff!

Parmesan Cheese Cup Caesar Salad

30 heaping tablespoons of shredded Parmesan cheese
Caesar Salad and Dressing (see recipe)
A short list of ingredients, but long on taste.

You are about to make some bowls that you can eat. This gets into something I've always thought of doing. Why not make edible tableware? No dishes to clean at all!

Spray a large baking sheet with Pam, and heat the oven to 375 degrees. Place five tablespoons of cheese on the sheet in the form of a six-inch round. Repeat with remaining cheese. You should have six rounds when finished. I usually do two to three at a time depending on how big of an oven sheet I have.

Bake in the oven for about ten minutes or until golden brown. Remove the tray from the oven and let cool only until the rounds can be handled without you burning yourself. This won't be all too long. Lay each one over the top of an inverted small bowl. Mold the warm cheeses to take that shape and allow them to cool completely. Now you have small bowls which you can fill (and eat) with fresh-made Caesar salad.

Note: You can make the bowls ahead of time and keep the salad on the side until you are ready to serve. If you do this, serve right away because the dressing may make the cheese bowl a little soggy if you wait too long to serve the salad. Also, if you were serving another dish that you feel would go well with a golden cheese round, don't make them into bowls, just leave them flat. It would be like a little cheesy cookie for a garnish. If you love cheese, you gotta love this!

If You Can't Stand the Heat

Crabmeat Salad Vinaigrette

1/2 pound of white lump crabmeat (picked over for shells)

16 ounces of triple hearts salad mix (pre cut and cleaned in bags from the store: romaine hearts, Greenleaf, and sweet butter)

2 cups of Parmigiano-Reggiano cheese (freshly grated)

1 cup of olive oil

1/2 cup of red wine vinegar

1 teaspoon of balsamic vinegar

1 shallot (finely chopped)

1/4 cup of fresh basil and fresh oregano (mixed, very finely chopped)

Salt and fresh-ground pepper to taste

2 ounces of toasted pine nuts

If you like crabmeat, you will love this salad. Vinaigrette and crab seemed at first to be an odd pairing, but it turns out that they are excellent together. Also, this is a recipe for a lot of salad. This is really an entrée-sized salad as opposed to a normal side salad. One of these will feed anyone, except for a fireman, naturally.

Pour all of your salad greens into a large salad-mixing bowl. Set aside in the fridge to chill.

Whisk together your olive oil, the two vinegars, shallots, fresh herbs, and your salt and fresh-ground pepper. Cover, and set aside to let flavors marry for at least thirty minutes. While that is happening, gently toast your pine nuts in a pan. I do mean gently. They will burn really easily so watch them closely. Set them aside when done.

When you are ready to serve, pour your cheese into the vinaigrette and mix well. Now pour it over the salad mixture and toss well to cover. You may not have to use it all. Just use an amount that suits your personal taste. Now mix in the pine nuts.

Like I said earlier, this recipe will make a lot of salad. Use as much or as little as you like. As always, this is enough to feed six regular people or four firemen.

In four salad plates (or six?), divide the salad. Now do the same with the crabmeat. I like to fold the crabmeat into each individual salad, but some people like it to sit on top with a little drizzle of vinaigrette on the crabmeat. That's about it. Simple and delicious.

Fried Shrimp Salad with Pickapeppa Dressing

Shrimp:
1 pound of headless shrimp (peeled, deveined, and butterflied)
Peanut oil
1 egg
1 cup of milk
1 teaspoon of flashover seasoning (plus a pinch after frying)
2 cups of fish fry

Pickapeppa Dressing:
1 egg
1/4 cup of ketchup
1/4 cup of Creole mustard
4 small cloves of garlic
The juice of one half of a medium sized lemon
1 tablespoon of Pickapeppa sauce
1/2 teaspoon of flashover seasoning (and a little for the fried shrimp)
1 tablespoon of fresh-ground horseradish
A pinch of salt
3/4 cup of vegetable oil

Assembly:
2 cups of shredded lettuce
4 lemon wedges

Start out by making your dressing. Put everything on the dressing list (except the oil) into a food processor. Start it up and let all the ingredients combine. Now slowly drizzle in the oil. This will make an emulsion. That's pretty much it. Put your dressing into a covered bowl and refrigerate.

Next is the shrimp portion. Mix the egg, milk, and the FOS in a bowl. Put in the shrimp and give them a bath.

Put enough peanut oil into a pot or a pan that will cover the shrimp once they are frying. How much oil you use will depend on the size of the pan you are frying in. At the most, only go about halfway up whatever pot or pan that you are frying in to avoid overspill. If you use any more than that, once you add the shrimp it will overflow, and you will have a minor catastrophe on your hands. Don't overload the pot. If you do too many at a time, you will have greasy shrimp. Take the shrimp out of the milk bath and put them into the fish fry. Shake off the excess and begin frying in small batches. Once the shrimp are fried to a golden brown, remove them from the oil, and place onto a plate with paper towels to drain the excess oil. Sprinkle a little FOS on them immediately after they come out of the oil.

Take four plates and divide the lettuce evenly among them. Now, evenly distribute the fried shrimp on the lettuce and spoon on however much dressing you like. Garnish with lemon wedges. You might want to add a few cherry tomatoes on the side just for color. After all, it is a salad. Serve immediately.

If You Can't Stand the Heat

Cold Smoked Duck Salad with Fig Vinaigrette

4 ounces of cold smoked duck breast (and layer of duck fat)
8 ounces of fresh figs
4 ounces of fresh greens (I use bagged mixed salad greens)
1/4 cup of shallots (finely diced)
1 small red onion (julienned)
1/2 cup of chicken stock
1/4 cup of red wine vinegar
1/2 cup of grape seed oil
1/2 cup of brown sugar
Pinch of salt
Pinch of fresh-ground pepper
2 tablespoons of butter

The first thing you need to find is the duck. Nueske's makes a really fine pre-done smoked duck breast. It will come with a layer of fat attached to the meat that will come in handy. I can find it here easily, but if you can't find it where you are, Nueske's has an online store that delivers!

Remove the stems and clean the figs under cold water. Cut them in half and put them aside.

Remove the layer of fat from the breast and place it in a small saucepan. Heat it up and render down the fat until you have about two tablespoons of duck fat. Remove the layer of duck fat you started with and discard. Now add the shallots to the leftover fat and wilt down for a minute or two. Next add the figs, chicken stock, and the brown sugar. Cook for five minutes or until the sugar dissolves, and remove from the fire.

Put this in a food processor and run for one minute. Now add the vinegar, salt, and fresh-ground pepper, and pulse a few times to incorporate. Now turn the processor on again, and slowly drizzle in the grape seed oil. Once it is incorporated, remove and keep warm.

In a small frying pan, add the butter and bring up to heat on a low fire. Put the red onions in the butter and cook until wilted. This will caramelize the onions and make them nice and sweet. Keep them warm.

Place equal amounts of the greens on four plates. Using a mandoline (or something similar) to shave the smoked duck into four equal servings on top of the greens. You want thin shavings so as not to have thick pieces of meat. Now divide your caramelized onions onto the salads, and then spoon on your dressing.

That's about it. Now just eat and smile really big!

Creole Caprese Salad

1 very ripe, large Creole tomato
1/2 pound of fresh mozzarella cheese
Fresh basil (chopped chiffonade style)
Salt
Fresh-ground pepper
Olive oil
Balsamic vinegar

Caprese is a wonderful Italian salad. Simple and elegant. I "Creoled" it up a smidge. Why should the Italians have it all to themselves? We should share.

Cut the tomato into one-half-inch thick slices. Do the same with the mozzarella. Sprinkle a bit of salt and fresh-ground pepper on the tomato slices. On a plate, place a section of tomato and, on top of it, a section of cheese. Repeat. I like to fan them out with tomato, cheese, tomato, and cheese in a curve. Now sprinkle a bit of the chopped up basil on the fanned out slices. Drizzle some olive oil on top. Take the balsamic vinegar and pour it into a small bowl below the tomato and cheese fan. This is for sprinkling on the salad or for dipping.

This is such a simple, tasty, and really fresh appetizer. You'll love it. And if you don't, call me. I'll come eat it for you.

Note: If you don't want to serve it community style, or you just don't want to share the dip, serve one slice of tomato, mozzarella on top, salt, fresh-ground pepper, basil, and then drizzle a little balsamic vinegar and olive oil on top of each individual serving. You would make it just like any other caprese. The only difference is that you are using Creole tomatoes, and it adds a whole lot of flavor that a regular tomato would not give you. But why would you not want to share? You greedy little thing… kind of reminds me of me!

Olive Salad

1 quart of extra virgin olive oil
2 6-ounce cans of large black pitted olives (drained and roughly chopped)
1 10-ounce jar of sliced green salad olives (some come sliced in the jar)
2 3/4-ounce jars of capers (drained)
2 cups of carrots (chopped)
2 heads of garlic (chopped)
4 medium to large onions (chopped)
1 cup of celery (chopped)
1 cup of cauliflower (chopped)
Vinegar (enough to top off the jar)
1 gallon glass jar with lid

Every once in a while the guys would have a hankering for a big muffuletta sandwich. We would always keep a jar of this olive salad on hand for those days. One of the firefighters at Engine 17 named Hoppy would eat it right out of the jar like it was a regular salad. That is one reason why we were always making more.

In the gallon glass jar, pour in the olive oil and then add all other ingredients above, except the vinegar. Once everything is inside, you want to fill the jar to the top with the vinegar (approximately twenty ounces). Cover the top with some aluminum foil and then screw the cap on. Shake it up a bit, and then let it marinate for a couple of days before you eat it. Some people like to use it right away. They claim that the fresher, the better. I like to wait a couple of days to let the veggies soften a bit. Either way this stuff is killer!

Note: I don't blame Hoppy for eating it right out of the jar. If I had a nickel for every time I dipped into the jar without anyone noticing, I'd have … well … a lot of nickels.

If You Can't Stand the Heat

London Broil Sandwich with Horseradish Mayo (Recipe Enough for Two Sandwiches)

Meat:
1 1/4 pounds of London broil
1 tablespoon of olive oil
1 tablespoon of flashover seasoning

Onions:
1 large red onion (cut up julienne style)
4 tablespoons of butter
Salt and fresh-ground pepper (to taste)

Horseradish Mayo:
1/2 cup of Homemade Mayo (see recipe)
2 tablespoons of fresh-ground horseradish
1 teaspoon of Creole mustard

Sandwich:
2 loaves of Easy Herbed Bread (see recipe)
1/4 pound of gruyere cheese (grated)

There are so many versions of this sandwich out there that they all seem to crossover each other in one way or another. Some with onions, some without. Cheese or no cheese. This version has everything. It's also enough for a lot of people to snack on.

Start out by rubbing the olive oil all over the meat. After that, rub in the FOS all over the meat, and then put it in a Ziploc bag. Keep it in the fridge for three to four hours.

Put the three ingredients for the mayo together and cover. Keep in the fridge for three to four hours. Do you see a pattern here?

Melt the butter in a pan. Put the onions in and salt and fresh-ground pepper. Cook them on a low fire until they are wilted, soft, and caramelized. Put aside for now. Make sure that you have your Easy Herbed Bread (see recipe) ready to go. That means cooked and waiting in the wings.

When you are ready to eat, turn on the broiler to high. Place the meat on a cooking tray. Now we cook with the rule of five. The meat goes under the broiler for five minutes on each side and five inches from the flame. When done, let the meat rest for five minutes. Cut the meat on a bias and across the grain in really thin slices. Now it's time to put it all together.

Cut your bread down the middle lengthways. Put half of the meat on the bread, half of the cheese and half of the onions on top of the meat. Put it in a warm oven for just long enough for the cheese to slightly melt. When that is done, remove and put half of the mayo on the inside of the top half. Put that on top of your sandwich, and cut the sandwich up into three- to four-inch-wide pieces. Repeat with second loaf.

Grab the first piece for yourself before it all disappears!

If You Can't Stand the Heat

Easy Herbed Bread

11 ounces of Pillsbury crusty French loaf
1 1/2 teaspoons of dry Italian seasonings

It's called easy for a reason. There were many times at the firehouse where we didn't have time to make fresh dough. It's not really something one does every day, unless you are a baker of course. This was the alternate choice, but still a good one.

Unroll the dough. Use half of the seasoning on the inside. Roll it back up, and use the other half of the seasoning on the outside. When you roll it back up, it will elongate by quite a few inches. That's all right. Just fold it back like you were closing a jackknife. It will look like two skinny versions of its original shape. When you fold it back, line them up side by side, and pat them together to form one loaf. Be sure to form them together or it will separate when it's baking. Cook at 350 degrees for thirty minutes.

Note: This bread is great for sandwiches. It's also good if you use it to dip in some infused olive oil. After you taste it, I'm sure you will find other good things to do with it!

Crawfish Bread with Crawfish Butter

1/2 loaf of French bread (cut in half lengthwise)
2 sticks and a tablespoon of butter
1 pound and 4 ounces of crawfish tails
8 slices of smoked provolone cheese
2 teaspoons of flashover seasoning
1 small onion (finely chopped)
1 clove of garlic (finely chopped)
1/2 cup of green onion tops (finely chopped)

It seems the only time I ever see crawfish bread is during Jazz Fest. I don't know why that is. It's like turkeys with Thanksgiving. There are turkeys all year round, but you rarely cook them until a holiday comes around. It's up to you to break that cycle. Make some crawfish bread today…even if it is only Wednesday.

Crawfish butter:

Put the two sticks of butter in a pan, and cook until the butter solids start to turn slightly brown. Remove the pan from the fire. Add the four ounces of crawfish and one teaspoon of FOS and mix in. Let it cool. Once it has, put in food processor and turn it on. Process it for one minute. Transfer the mixture to a bowl and put it in the fridge. Do this ahead of time so the butter has a chance to harden in the fridge.

Bread:

Using the tablespoon of butter, heat it up in a pan and add the onions, one teaspoon of FOS, and the green onions. Sauté until the onions are translucent. Add the garlic and cook for one minute. Now add the one pound of crawfish tails and heat it up. Incorporate it all together, and let it cook until all of the liquid is gone. Let it cool. While it is cooling, take the crawfish butter from the fridge and let it soften.

Cut the bread into four equal pieces. In the top halves, spread some of the crawfish butter. Bottom halves, spoon out some of the crawfish mixture onto the bread. Now top each of the bottom pieces with two slices of cheese. Continue until you have done all four pieces. Put the tops over the bottoms and wrap each piece in aluminum foil. This can be done early so that when you are ready to eat, most of the work is finished.

Heat the oven to 325 degrees. Put the foil packets into the oven and heat them up for fifteen to twenty minutes. Remove from the oven and then open up the foil. If I have to tell you what to do next …

Pesto Cheese Bread

1 loaf of Italian bread (still warm)
Thin slices of Parmigiano-Reggiano cheese
Fresh Basil Pesto (see recipe)
Butter (room temperature)

The first thing you will notice is that the only increment I put on anything was the loaf of bread. As you will see, the rest is a matter of personal taste.

We love to go to a great restaurant in the French Quarter called Maximo's. They make homemade, fresh Italian bread every day. Their pesto is made in house as well as their sausage. They have an herb garden on the roof, so everything is fresh. All of their olive oil, wine, and cheese are procured by constant visits to Italy to retrieve them. I guess you've figured out by now that everything is authentic and fresh.

One of our favorite things to do there is to rip off a chunk of the warm bread and slather on some butter. Next, we spread on some pesto, and then top it off with thin slices of Parmigiano-Reggiano cheese. That is it. Now put it in your mouth and savor the flavor.

Note: If you have a bottle of your favorite Italian wine and a few friends over, it doesn't get any better than this. No need for any other food. It quite literally becomes a meal in itself! And if you ever go down to New Orleans, try Maximo's if you want Italian with a New Orleans twist. It's the best.

If You Can't Stand the Heat

Box of Napkins Sloppy Roast Beef
and Swiss Cheese Po'boy

6-to-7-pound chuck roast
10 cloves of garlic
1 teaspoon of kosher salt
1 teaspoon of fresh-ground pepper
4 teaspoons of flashover seasoning
1/3 cup of vegetable oil
26-ounce can of cream of chicken soup
1 10 3/4-ounce can of cream of onion soup
4 cups of low sodium beef broth
1 10 3/4-ounce can of beef gravy
1 loaf of French bread
2 tomatoes (sliced)
2 cups of lettuce (shredded)
8 slices of Swiss cheese
Mayo to taste

Is there anything better than a good old sloppy roast beef sandwich? I don't think so! If you find something better, let me know. It's called "box of napkins" for a reason. When we would shop for the ingredients to make this, we made sure somebody had a box of napkins in hand. We needed them. In the meantime, let's build perfection.

Preheat your oven to 350 degrees. Peel all of the garlic and then make small slits in the roast. Push a clove of garlic into each slit. Spread them around as much as you can.

Now mix the FOS, salt, and fresh-ground pepper together and rub all over the meat.

I like to use a large black iron Dutch oven for this, but a pot big enough to hold it all and one that is a heavy gauge pot will do. You need something that will conduct the heat all around the meat. Don't use a thin aluminum pot; it just won't work. Also make sure it is a pot with a tight lid.

Place the oil in the pot and bring it up to heat. Now put the roast in and brown it on all sides. Once you have done that, remove the roast and place it aside for now.

Deglaze the pot with the beef broth. Once you've scraped all of the tasty brown bits from the bottom, cook the broth until it begins to simmer. Now add the beef gravy and soups to the pot. Once that starts to simmer, put the roast back into the pot. Cover, place in the oven, and cook for three hours.

Now carefully remove the pot from the oven and take out the meat. Put it on a cutting board and slice or break up the roast into thin slices or pieces. Put the meat back into the gravy and then put the pot back into the oven. Cook covered for another thirty minutes. When it's done, you should be able to pull the beef apart with a fork. You want the meat to be broken completely apart and immersed in rich gravy.

Now on to the sandwiches!

Cut your French bread into four pieces, and then slice them down the middle.

Cover the bottom piece of bread with a generous portion of roast beef and gravy. Place slices of Swiss cheese on top of the meat. Next is a little of the shredded lettuce, a row of tomatoes, and mayonnaise inside of the top piece of bread.

You have just built the perfect sloppy roast beef sandwich. I wasn't kidding about the napkin part. Keep plenty on the table. You'll need them! You know you have a good sandwich when the gravy runs down your arms.

Note: Unless you are gluttons, you will not use all of the beef. This recipe is for four, but you will have meat and gravy left over. Either freeze it (still good) or invite more people.

Another note: If you come down to New Orleans (or Destin), you have to go to Acme Oyster House (one of my favorite places to eat). Not only do they have great oysters, but they serve something called Boo Fries. They take French fries, sprinkle cheese on top, and then cover them in the roast beef gravy. Awesome!

If you want to make it heartier, next time you make Debris (see recipe under Chuck Pot Roast/Debris and Gravy) you can put it on the fries instead of just using the gravy.

If You Can't Stand the Heat

Pizza/Calzone Dough

1 cup of warm water (100–110 degrees)
1 1/4-ounce packet of yeast (Check the date to make sure it's still good)
3 cups of "OO" farina flour
1 tablespoon of olive oil
1/2 teaspoon of salt
Corn meal

I have made this dough over and over again, and I have used two methods to do so. Some firehouses have really good equipment, and some don't. I guess the same could be said for people houses. In other words, if you have the equipment, do this the easy way. If not, I guess you're stuck with the hard way. It's not really that hard … just not as easy.

The hard way:

Put the yeast into the warm water and let it dissolve. Wait about five to ten minutes for the yeast to activate. When it starts to foam up, it is ready to go.

Get a big bowl and pour in the flour. Make a little hole in the center and add the salt and olive oil in the middle. Now, pour the water with the yeast in it into the center, and mix in the flour with your hands, drawing it from the sides to the center a little at a time.

Mix well until you have a ball of dough that doesn't stick to your hands anymore. You may have to add a bit more flour to the mix to accomplish this. You may have to add a little more water. It's never the same every time. Knead for five minutes, and stretch and fold it over itself often.

The easy way:

Put the oil and the salt into the bowl of a Kitchen Aid Mixer with a dough hook attached. Pour in the water with the activated yeast and turn the mixer on very low. Slowly add the flour. It will start to incorporate and wrap itself around the dough hook. When it doesn't stick to the side of the bowl and all of it is incorporated into the dough ball, increase the speed, but still keep it slow. You don't want your dough to fly out of the bowl. Let it knead for five minutes. Remove from the dough hook.

Either way:

Use a little olive oil to oil a bowl that will hold twice the size of your dough. Place the dough ball inside and cover with plastic wrap. Let it sit for at least ninety minutes in a warm and dry area. It should double in size. Push it down and roll it out onto a flat surface. Sprinkle some corn meal on that surface to keep it from sticking. Now make it into either your pizzas or your calzones.

    Note: If you are making pizza, save me a slice. If you are making calzones, save me two.

If You Can't Stand the Heat

Crepes

1 3/4 cups of flour
1/3 cup of water
1 cup of milk
4 tablespoons of melted unsalted butter
4 eggs
1/2 teaspoon of salt
Butter (for the cooking of the crepe, not to be put in the blender)

Crepes are wonderful things. You can use them for sweet dishes or for savory ones. You can stuff them with strawberries and whipped cream or stuff them with fresh seafood or meats. They are versatile. The other good thing is that you can make them ahead of time and keep them in the fridge. Genius!

Just mix all of the ingredients in a blender (except the butter for cooking the crepes). Don't blend it for too long. Just pulse it enough to mix it all well. If you blend it too much, the crepes will be a little rubbery. I also like to let it sit for about twenty minutes to a half an hour after blending to let some of the bubbles settle before I make the crepes.

Use a crepe pan if you have one. If not, just use a non-stick frying pan. Put a little butter in the pan and heat it up. That would be enough butter to lightly cover the bottom of the pan. Now pour about half of a cup of the crepe mix into the pan. Swirl it around to make a very thin coating on the bottom of the pan. Try to get it as even and as round as possible. Heat it on one side for about two minutes. Lift up an edge and check it. If it is golden brown, turn it over, and cook the other side. That's all there is to it. Simple and easy, and if you serve both savory crepes and dessert crepes in one meal, you'll look like even more of a genius.

Note: Usually, being the lazy guy I am prone to be, I will just heat up the crepe pan and then peel back the paper on a stick of butter. I rub the butter on the pan and then remove the pan from the fire. I pour in the crepe mix and swirl it around until it is spread out. Then I put it back on the fire to cook. It works pretty well this way, and you will find that once you get the hang of it you will be whipping out crepes like some cool mad French chef. Like I said, you'll look like a genius.

Garlic Bread

1 loaf of French bread
Roasted Garlic Butter (See Recipe)
2 cups of Parmigiano-Reggiano cheese (grated)
Olive oil (just enough to lightly brush on the French bread)

Garlic bread goes well with just about anything. Even if you make it just to eat by itself, it's worth the effort. Sometimes we made it just to munch on.

Preheat oven to 375 degrees. Cut loaf of French bread down the center length ways. Brush olive oil on both sides. Spread the garlic butter on both sides to your liking. So what if you use it all. You only live once. Sprinkle cheese on both sides … also to your liking. If you use all of the cheese, so be it. I won't tell. Bake the bread in the oven on a tray for about eight to ten minutes.

Since some ovens are hotter than others, keep an eye on it. You want it to be crispy, not burned. Unless you like it burned, then don't keep an eye on it. Just wait for the smoke alarms to go off. You'll know it's done!

Note: Of course it goes without saying that you will have to cut the loaf of French bread into smaller pieces to fit it in an oven. That is unless you have a really big and long oven. Then I suppose you can put a whole loaf in all at once. Aren't you special!

If You Can't Stand the Heat

Appetizers, Sides, and Snacks

Fish Beignets and Remoulade Tartar Sauce

Beignets:
1 pound of fresh tilapia
2 tablespoons of olive oil
4 teaspoons of flashover seasoning
2 eggs (beaten)
1/8 cup of bell pepper (chopped fine)
1/4 cup of green onions (finely chopped)
1/4 cup of yellow onions (finely chopped)
1 1/2 cups of flour
1/2 cup of milk
1 teaspoon of baking powder
Peanut oil (for frying)

Remoulade Tartar Sauce:
1 egg
1 tablespoon of fresh lemon juice
1 tablespoon of Creole mustard
1 tablespoon of ketchup
4 teaspoons of dill relish
1/2 teaspoon of kosher salt
1 teaspoon of flashover seasoning
1 large clove of garlic (chopped)
1/4 teaspoon of Tabasco
1 cup of vegetable oil

If You Can't Stand the Heat

I have always lived by the rule that if two things taste good separately, try putting them together and see how it tastes. Remoulade is great with fish and so is tartar sauce. Why not meld them together and use them with fish beignets? Hopefully you will agree with this rule too.

Sauce:

Start by making the sauce ahead of time so the flavors will party together. Put the egg into a blender along with everything else on the remoulade/tartar sauce list except for the oil and two of the teaspoons of the dill relish. Turn on mix and slowly drizzle the oil into the top of the blender. It will thicken up into an emulsion. You may not use all of the oil, and that's all right. Better to start with too much than to not have enough. Remove from the blender, put it into a bowl, add the last two teaspoons of dill relish, cover, and put into the fridge for hopefully overnight but at least four hours.

Beignet:

Heat up a tablespoon of olive oil in a frying pan and add the fish. Sprinkle on a teaspoon of FOS. Let it cook on one side until it cooks half way through. Flip it over and cook the other side until it is cooked through. Remove from the fire and allow to cool completely. Once that is done, remove from the pan and break it up into small pieces. Put into a bowl.

Put the other tablespoon of olive oil into the same pan and heat it up. Put in the bell pepper and yellow onions and cook until the onions are translucent. Remove from the fire and allow them to cool.

Put the eggs into the bowl with the broken up fish. Add the onion and bell pepper mixture, green onions, flour, milk, baking powder, and two teaspoons of the FOS. Mix this well and have your frying oil prepared ahead of time.

Heat the peanut oil to 375 degrees. When it reaches that temperature, you will be using two metal tablespoons and a cup of warm water. It sounds weird, but I will explain. Wet a tablespoon and scoop up a big heaping tablespoon of batter. Use the other spoon to push it off into the hot oil. The warm water will make it slide off easily, but watch out for splatter from the oil.

Don't overload the pan. Do a few at a time. Cook until golden brown all the way around. You may have to flip them over with a spoon to do both sides. When you have finished, put them on a paper towel to drain. Sprinkle the last teaspoon of FOS on the finished beignets. Some people want to call them fritters or hush puppies, but I like to call them beignets. You can make them bigger by using a larger spoon or keep them smaller to make them bite-sized.

Serve this with the combo remoulade/tartar sauce.

Note: You can also do this with shrimp and with crawfish…or both. Mix and match. Remember, the only rule in cooking is whether or not you think it tastes good.

If You Can't Stand the Heat

Shrimp and Crab Au Gratin Appetizers

1 pound of shrimp (peeled, deveined, and rinsed well)
8 ounces of fresh white lump crab meat (picked over for shells)
16 ounces of whipping cream
4 tablespoons of butter
4 tablespoons of flour
2 cloves of garlic (finely chopped)
1/4 cup of onions (finely chopped)
Pinch of sea salt
Pinch of white pepper
2 teaspoons of dried Italian seasoning
8 ounces of grated mozzarella cheese
4 lemon wedges

Everybody tells me that this is too big to be an appetizer and should be considered a meal in itself. That's if I serve it in sixteen-ounce ramekins. If I use twelve-ounce ramekins, the bowl is smaller, but the contents are the same. They just think it's smaller portions. You can trick the eye but not the belly!

Melt the butter in a frying pan and then add the flour. Cook over a low fire until you have made a light golden butter roux. After a few minutes it should look like the color of vanilla pudding. Now add the onions. Cook over a low fire and sauté the onions for two minutes. Stir it a lot. Add the garlic and the Italian seasoning. Cook for one minute.

Now whisk in the white pepper, salt, and the cream to the pan. It should thicken up pretty quickly. Now add the shrimp and cook until they are cooked all the way through. They should release some water to help thin it out a bit, but you really do want the sauce to be pretty thick and not runny. Taste once again for salt and put in more if needed.

Using twelve-ounce ramekins (or sixteen if you like plenty of room), divide the crabmeat into four equal parts in the bottom of the ramekins. Now equally spoon in the shrimp into the four ramekins.

Spoon the leftover sauce equally into the ramekins to cover the shrimp and crabmeat. Now put two ounces of cheese into each bowl to top the sauce. Heat up the broiler and place the ramekins under the broiler. Cook them until the cheese is melted and slightly browned, and then remove them from the broiler to cool for a bit. Serve with a lemon wedge on the side. We also like to serve this with some French bread crostinis for dipping or just plain French bread slices.

Note: You can cut up the shrimp into tiny pieces, mix in the cheese, then put it in the sauce. Bake it all for ten minutes in a single casserole dish. Use this as a dip with the crostinis or just some small French bread slices.

Another Note: Never use canned or pasteurized crabmeat with this dish. Only use fresh white lump crabmeat. If you use anything else it will taste fishy and totally ruin what is supposed to be a great little (or big) appetizer. Besides, who wants crab that tastes like fish?

　　If You Can't Stand the Heat

Chinese Pork Ribs

3 pounds of boneless pork ribs
2 tablespoons of soy sauce
2 tablespoons of Hoisin sauce
1/2 teaspoon of five-spice powder
3 tablespoons of dark cane syrup
1 tablespoon of dry sherry
1/2 teaspoon of red food coloring
2 tablespoons of water

I usually make these so that I can cut them up and put them into Fried Rice (see recipe). But I must admit that sometimes I make them and just eat them before they see any rice. So if you are making Fried Rice (see recipe), try to avoid the temptation to just eat them all right out of the oven. Just kidding.

Whisk together the ingredients (except the meat), and pour it into the Ziploc bag. Make sure the meat is cut into rib strips. It usually comes that way from the grocer, but sometimes they don't cut it all the way through. You want them to be individual boneless pork rib strips. Now, put the meat into the bag, and move the bag around enough to cover all of the pork with the mixture. Put it in the fridge to marinate overnight. I also like to put the bag into a bowl just in case of a leak. Otherwise you could have what we lovingly called "red fridge disease." Not easy to clean.

Put four cups of water into an oven pan. I use the twelve-by-sixteen-inch pan that came with my oven. Place a wire rack over the pan. I use a mesh rack that is for cooling cookies. As long as it covers the pan and keeps the meat above the water, it doesn't matter what rack you use.

Put the meat on top of the rack. Save the marinade for basting. No water should touch the meat. Set the oven to 300 degrees and bake for one hour and forty-five minutes. Flip the meat over about halfway through. Baste every fifteen minutes. That's about it. Now go out there and make Fried Rice (see recipe) the way it was meant to be!

I'm sure that you realize that I was really was just kidding about eating them all before they reach the Fried Rice. You just cooked three pounds of ribs! The Fried Rice only takes eight ounces. Unless you are going to break the world record for making Fried Rice in one day, you will have plenty to enjoy and still save enough for that rice.

Note: If you want the ribs to be sweeter, for your last basting use dark cane syrup instead of the marinade. Also, the ribs freeze well, so you can make Fried Rice this week and make it again the next week without going through the rib cooking process again.

Also try marinating them and then throw them on the grill instead of cooking them in the oven. Barbequed Chinese pork ribs are sensational!

If You Can't Stand the Heat

Artichoke Tapenade Crostini

12 ounces of marinated artichoke hearts (drained)
1/2 cup of olive oil
1/4 cup of fresh Italian parsley
4 leaves of fresh basil
2 cloves of garlic
Pinch of kosher salt
Pinch of fresh-ground pepper
1 cup of grated Parmigiano-Reggiano cheese (more if you like)
4 slices of pancetta
Balsamic vinegar
8 slices of French bread

In New Orleans, we eat a lot of dishes that contain artichokes. This recipe is just another excuse to eat artichokes. I know that you don't need an excuse to eat them, but now, if anybody ever asks, you have one.

Fry the pancetta in a pan until crispy. Remove and place on paper towels to drain and cool. Once cool, break up into little bits and set aside for now.

In a food processor, combine the drained artichoke hearts, olive oil, parsley, basil, garlic, salt, and fresh-ground pepper. Turn on the processor and let it run until you have a smooth paste. Remove from the processor and put into a bowl. There will be more than enough for the eight slices of bread. There will be enough left over to experiment with your own tastes. Try a different type of bread, a different cheese, or some tomato on top. Make more than eight crostini. It's your ball, so run with it.

When you are ready to eat, heat up your oven to 325 degrees. Slice the French bread into one-inch-thick, round pieces. Place the bread slices on a baking tray and put them into the oven. You just want to slightly toast them on both sides. If you have a toaster that will do the same thing, use it. Whatever is easier so long as the bread is toasted. Once that is done, remove them from the oven (or toaster). Once they are cool enough to handle, spread some of the artichoke paste on each of them. Now sprinkle some of the pancetta bits on top. Place some of the cheese on top of each. Put them under the broiler for just enough time to slightly melt the cheese. Remove and sprinkle a little bit of balsamic vinegar on each. Serve while warm.

Note: For an added twist, make this dish and eat it all before your guests arrive. They'll never know.

Oysters Algiers

4 ounces of pancetta (cut up small like bacon bit pieces)
1 cup of onions (chopped fine)
Pinch of fresh-ground pepper
1/2 cup of green onion tops (chopped fine)
2 cloves of garlic (chopped fine)
Creamed Spinach (see recipe)
1 pint of oysters (fresh shucked)
1/2 cup of Italian breadcrumbs
1/2 cup of Parmigiano-Reggiano cheese

This is called Oysters Algiers because that's where I lived. I could have called it Oysters Saint Thomas Housing Project because I also used to live there once, but that just didn't sound right.

Put the pancetta into a frying pan and cook on a low fire until it turns slightly crispy. Now add the onions, the fresh-ground pepper, and cook until the onions are translucent. Add the garlic and green onion tops. Cook for two minutes; then add the creamed spinach. (You will use the entire amount that comes with the finished Creamed Spinach recipe.) Mix well to incorporate.

I like to use ramekins that I use for crème brûlée. They are about one-inch deep, and four and one-half inches across. Drain the oysters of their liquor and save it for whenever you are making a seafood gumbo or something. Don't throw it away … it's good stuff!

Line the bottom of the four ramekins with equal amounts of oysters. Spoon the creamed spinach and pancetta mix on top until it's about one-quarter of an inch from the top. You need to save room for the breadcrumb and cheese topping. Put them into a 350-degree oven for twenty minutes. Remove them from the oven and turn on your broiler. Top each of the dishes with equal amounts of breadcrumbs. Now sprinkle some cheese on each and put them under the broiler until they are slightly toasted. Serve immediately if not sooner.

Note: Don't you just hate it when people say "if not sooner"? It would mean that I'd have to serve them in the oven wouldn't it?

Shrimp Patty Cakes with Asian Aioli

Patty:
1 pound of headless shrimp (peeled and deveined)
1 cup of panko crumbs
3 tablespoons of Creole mustard
2 tablespoons of sesame seed oil
1/2 cup of onions (finely chopped)
1/4 cup of bell pepper (finely chopped)
1/4 cup of celery (finely chopped)
1 teaspoon of flashover seasoning

To cook:
2 eggs
1 cup of milk
1 cup of flour
1 cup of panko crumbs
1 teaspoon of flashover seasoning
1/4 cup of vegetable oil

Sauce:
1 egg
1/2 teaspoon of lemon zest
1 tablespoon of lemon juice
3 tablespoons of Thai chili sauce
1 clove of garlic
1/2 teaspoon of salt
Fresh-ground pepper (to taste)
2 tablespoons of fresh parsley
1/2 cup of vegetable oil

If You Can't Stand the Heat

I've seen crab cakes and lobster cakes and lots of other cakes, but never a shrimp cake. Why not shrimp? So we made up this dish because shrimp are plentiful here, and because we didn't want them to feel left out.

This part needs to be done ahead of time, so be prepared. Chop up the shrimp into little pieces. Heat the sesame oil in a pan, and add the chopped onion, bell pepper, celery, and a teaspoon of the FOS. Cook until the onions are translucent. Add the shrimp and cook until shrimp are pink and cooked through. Let this mixture cool. There will be some juice in there, and that's all right. It will help you to recover the tasty bits left in the bottom of the pan after you have cooked the veggies. Once it is cool, mix in mustard and then panko crumbs. Get your hands in there and mix it all up really well. Now form four equal patties, cover, and refrigerate.

When it's time to cook, remove the patties from the fridge and let them come almost to room temperature. You want them to be barely chilled but not cold. Assemble three bowls side by side. Have the flour and a teaspoon of FOS in one, beat the eggs and milk together in the second, and have the panko crumbs in the third.

Cover a patty in flour and shake off the excess. Put your patty into the milk and egg wash. Remove, let excess drip off, and then put into the panko. Let excess fall off and place back on the plate. Repeat until all four are done. If one should start to break up, just reform the patty with your hands, and it will hold together.

Heat up the vegetable oil in a frying pan on medium. Place two of the patties in the oil and fry to a golden brown on one side. Flip them over, and do the same to the other side. Repeat with the last two. Put them on paper towels to drain.

Serve with a drizzle of the sauce on top.

Sauce:

Put all of the ingredients into a blender except for the oil. Pulse it until everything is chopped and mixed well. Slowly drizzle in the oil while the blender is on mix. That is your sauce. I like to make it a little ahead of time to be sure that the flavors have a chance to blend.

Note: You can do the same dish using lobster or crab. I've even done it using fish. Experiment. Have some fun with it.

Bruschetta Caprese

Roma tomatoes (thinly sliced)
Fresh mozzarella (sliced, one or two for each piece of bread)
2 tablespoons of fresh basil (chopped)
Olive oil
Salt and fresh-ground pepper
Balsamic vinegar
French bread (3x3-inch, round slices and 1/2-inch thick)

This is a seriously awesome appetizer. Sometimes we start to eat these, and we can't stop. In that case, tonight's dinner entrée is now tomorrow's leftovers before we even take off the lid!

Toast the bread on both sides under the broiler at 500 degrees until golden brown. If you have a toaster that will accommodate the bread, then by all means use it. Remove the bread from the oven (or toaster), and brush olive oil on each piece. Now put the tomato slices, then the mozzarella slices, and then some basil on each. Drizzle additional olive oil on top of each and then a little salt and fresh-ground pepper. Follow that up with a drizzle of Balsamic vinegar on each. Put back into the oven under the broiler for just a few seconds just to warm it all up. Serve immediately.

Note: There are no listed amounts of individual ingredients to this dish. Use your own judgment. Some people like a little more cheese or a little less tomato, etc. Basically they will all have bread, tomato, cheese, and toppings. The quantity of ingredients you use will also depend on how many you are making. I usually serve these as an appetizer, and everybody will just get one. They may beg for more, but they only get one. Okay, maybe give them two, but only if they beg (and they will)!

Eggplant Napoleon

6 eggplant rounds
1 cup of flour
1 cup of milk
1 egg
2 teaspoons of flashover seasoning (and a pinch or two on the side)
1 cup of Zatarain's fish fry
1 quart of peanut oil
1/2 cup of white lump crabmeat (picked over for shells)
1/2 cup of Choron Sauce (see recipe)
1 tablespoon of green onion tops (chopped fine)

This recipe is for two appetizer servings. If you want more, just repeat the process and double up on the ingredients until you have enough to feed your crew.

You can put just about anything on top of fried eggplant, and it will taste good. You can do this same dish using crawfish tails instead of crabmeat. You can use hollandaise sauce or even remoulade sauce if you like. Experiment a little bit and see what combo you like best. This is the one we picked out for this book, and we find it works pretty well.

The first thing you want to do is to try to find a small eggplant. This is an appetizer, so rounds of fried eggplant that are six inches across are not what you want to use. You want your eggplant to be peeled and cut about a half-inch thick. It should be about three inches across.

Put the flour in one bowl, followed by the egg and milk whisked together in the second bowl. Follow that with a bowl of the fish fry. Put one teaspoon of FOS into the flour and mix together. Do the same to the fish fry. Get your peanut oil up to 375 degrees, and you are ready.

Dip the eggplant into the flour and then shake off the excess. You just need a thin coating. Now dip into the egg and milk mixture. Let the excess drip off, and then put it into the fish fry. Shake off the excess of that and put into the hot oil. Cook until golden brown and remove to a paper towel to drain.

Do this with three pieces of eggplant for one serving. Sprinkle on a pinch of FOS right after they come out of the oil. Be very liberal with the sprinkle because the eggplant is relatively bland. Repeat with the other three.

Put three of them on a plate and spoon on one-quarter of a cup of crabmeat on top of them. On top of that, spoon on one quarter of a cup of Choron Sauce (see recipe). Sprinkle on the green onions. Repeat with plate two. If you have some extra sauce left over, pour it on; it can only make it better. Serve immediately if not sooner.

Note: And by the way…whatever you do, try not to snack on the crabmeat while you are cooking. You know who you are out there. Save it for the dish!

Smothered Okra and Tomato with Shrimp

2 pounds of shrimp (peeled and rinsed)

2 pounds of fresh okra (cut into one-inch pieces with stems and tips removed)

4 Creole tomatoes (cut up into one-inch pieces)

1 large onion (coarsely chopped)

1 cup of bell pepper (finely chopped)

1/4 cup of celery (finely chopped)

2 cloves of garlic (finely chopped)

1 quart of Shrimp/Seafood Stock (see recipe)

1 teaspoon of Tabasco sauce

4 strips of applewood smoked bacon

2 teaspoons and one tablespoon of flashover seasoning

I've often wondered if this should be called a side dish, a soup, or an appetizer. Like many things in New Orleans, it is unique unto itself. So feel free to use it in any or all of the ways above.

The first thing you need to do is, in a good-sized pot, fry down the bacon until it is crispy. Remove the strips from the pot and transfer them to a paper towel to drain.

Use the bacon drippings to begin sautéing the onions, bell pepper, celery, and one teaspoon of the FOS. Once they have cooked until the onions are translucent, add the garlic. Cook for one minute and then add the okra and tomatoes to the pot. Mix well. You will see that, as always, the okra gets what we call rather "ropey." The acid in the tomatoes will help to counteract that to some extent, but some will also remain in the okra to help thicken the dish.

Now add the Shrimp/Seafood Stock (see recipe) and the other teaspoon of the FOS. Crumble up the bacon strips and put them into the pot. Now cook this covered on a low fire for one hour. Stir occasionally. Once that is done, uncover and add the shrimp, Tabasco, and the tablespoon of FOS. Cook this until the shrimp are pink. Taste it and check it for salt content. I like to let it sit covered for an hour before I serve it. Serve by itself or over a little cooked white rice.

Note: Since this is as close to being a gumbo as possible without actually making a roux, put a bottle of file powder on the table. Plenty of French bread and butter is also a nice touch. That way whoever is eating it will have choices, and they will decide for themselves if it is a soup, side dish, or an appetizer. You don't even have to know!

Italian Marinated Crab Claws

1 pound of crab claws
1/4 cup of Italian red wine vinegar
1 clove of garlic (finely chopped)
1 tablespoon of Creole mustard
1 teaspoon of sea salt
1/2 teaspoon of fresh-ground pepper
1/2 tablespoon of lemon juice
1 tablespoon of dried Italian herbs
1/2 teaspoon of balsamic vinegar
3/4 cup of extra virgin olive oil

Crab claws are a delicacy in New Orleans. You will not find them on many menus. It is probably because of the expense. I guess it takes time to crack and peel all of those little suckers, and you have to pay dearly for it. But every once in a while you just have to splurge and do something nice for yourself. This is one of those times.

Combine all of the ingredients in a bowl with the exception of the crab claws and the olive oil. Now take a whisk and slowly drizzle in the olive oil until it is all incorporated. Next, put in the crab claws, and very gingerly fold them into the marinade. You don't want to break the meat off of the claws. Cover the bowl and let sit in the fridge overnight. Serve chilled.

Sometimes I just marinate half of the claws. I keep the other half for dipping into a Cocktail Sauce (see recipe). That way you get two different taste experiences from one pound of claws.

Note: You can also remove the crab claws from the marinade and set on the side. You then make a bed with some spring mix salad greens. Warm up the marinade and use it as a salad dressing for your greens. Put some crab claws on top. Do this as individual servings, and use it as a salad/appetizer.

Hot Tamale Boulettes

Boulettes:
1 pound of ground beef
1 pound of Jimmy Dean hot sausage
46-ounce can of V8 juice (Just use three-quarters cup for boulettes, and the rest is for the gravy.)
1 1/2 cups of yellow cornmeal
2 teaspoons of cumin
2 teaspoons of chili powder
1 teaspoon of garlic powder
1 teaspoon of kosher salt
1 teaspoon of cayenne pepper
1/2 cup of flour
6 tablespoons of olive oil

Gravy:
The rest of the 48-ounce can of V8 juice (after using three-quarters cup for the boulettes)
2 teaspoons of cumin
2 teaspoons of chili powder
2 teaspoons of kosher salt
1 teaspoon of chipotle chile pepper powder
1 teaspoon of smoked paprika
2 cups of chicken stock

A great fireman from Ladder 6 by the name of Cliff gave me this recipe. Although he is no longer with us, he was a pretty good cook as well being one of the best guys I ever worked with. It's very simple to do and keeps you from having to deal with the cornhusks as you would in normal tamale making.

Mix all of the top ingredients (boulettes) except for the olive oil together in a big bowl (make sure you only use three-quarters of a cup of the V8). Now, using your hands, roll out a ton of little tamale balls (not really a ton, but it will make a lot of balls). Try to make them each about one to one and one half inches in diameter.

Put half of the olive oil into a pan and heat it up. Now put some of the tamale balls into the pan and fry them. You will have to do this a bunch at a time, so don't try to cram them all in at once. What you are trying to accomplish is to brown them slightly on all sides to seal them and keep them from coming apart in the gravy. Roll them around in the pan to get the maximum coverage during the frying process.

Take out the first batch and continue with some more. The rest of the olive oil is to be used a little at a time as you fry the balls. The oil will disappear as you fry, and you will need to add some for future batches of tamale ball frying. If you should happen to need more olive oil than listed, it's all right. Just use what you need to get the job done.

Once they are all finished frying, get a large pot and mix the gravy ingredients together. Now put the tamale balls into the gravy, and once they come up to a simmer, let them cook for forty-five minutes uncovered. After that, cover the pot and let them sit for one half hour. Eat.

Cliff would be proud!

Asian Marinated Fried Shrimp

Marinade:
1 pound of headless shrimp (peeled, cleaned, and butterflied)
1/2 cup of chicken stock
1 tablespoon of wasabi powder
1/2 teaspoon of soy sauce
1/2 teaspoon of oyster sauce
1/2 teaspoon of fish sauce
1/2 teaspoon of fresh-ground ginger
1/2 teaspoon Chinese five spice

Pre-Batter:
1 egg
1 cup of milk
1/2 cup of the marinade

For Frying:
Peanut oil
2 cups of panko breadcrumbs
1 tablespoon of flashover seasoning

Dipping Sauce:
2 tablespoons of plum sauce
1 tablespoon of Thai chili sauce
1/2 teaspoon of soy sauce

If You Can't Stand the Heat

I call this Asian shrimp because they have a little Thai, a little Japanese, and a little Chinese. Thus … Asian! I know. Brilliant. But let's hold down the applause until after we're finished cooking.

Mix together all of the marinade ingredients in a large bowl. Whisk until they are all combined. Put the shrimp into the marinade and place in the fridge. I like to keep them bathing overnight but a couple of hours will do.

Before you get started with the rest of it, you may want to get your oil going. Decide which pot or pan you will use for frying. Only put enough of the peanut oil into the pot so that the shrimp are just barely covered. Don't overfill, or you may need the services of your local fire department once you add the shrimp and it overflows. Heat it until the oil reaches 365 degrees. Use a thermometer.

Drain off the marinade from the shrimp and reserve. Beat together the egg, milk, and one half cup of the marinade to form the pre-batter. Take the shrimp and place them into the pre-batter a few at a time. Take them from the pre-batter and let the excess drip off back into the bowl. Now put them into the panko breadcrumbs. Shake until they are covered with the panko, and then let excess fall back into the bowl. Put them into the oil and fry until they are golden brown. Fry them in small batches. Don't overload the pot or the temperature will drop and you will have soggy shrimp. Yuck! Remove to a paper towel to drain the excess oil. Sprinkle a little FOS on them immediately after they come out of the oil.

Mix the three ingredients of the sauce into a small bowl. Dip the fried shrimp into the sauce and eat.

Note: Chopsticks are optional.

Shrimp and Crab Dressing Appetizer Italian

8 very large shrimp (ten count to a pound would be great)
1/2 cup of Crabmeat Dressing (see recipe)
8 slices of prosciutto (thin)

This is one of the never-ending Creole Italian types of dishes that we like to serve here in New Orleans. Creole food is great. Italian food is great. Together they are spectacular.

Peel and remove the vein from the shrimp. Now butterfly them so they will lay flat on a cutting board. Using equal amounts, place some Crabmeat Dressing (see recipe) in the middle of the shrimp lengthways. Now fold the shrimp over and place it on the end of one of the slices of prosciutto. Roll it down so that the shrimp is encased in the prosciutto. Once you have done all of the shrimp, put them all on the grill for about five minutes or until the shrimp has cooked through. Let them cool for a minute or two and then eat.

Note: Do not taste one before you serve them. If you do (trust the voice of experience), I can personally assure you that they will not make it to the table.

Shrimp and Crab Martini

16 large boiled shrimp (see Snappy Spicy Boiled Shrimp recipe)
1/2 pound of fresh white lump crabmeat (picked over for shells)
1/4 cup of Creole Crab Sauce (see recipe) (plus four tablespoons more for the end of this recipe)
4 lemon wedges
1 1/2 cups of baby romaine mix (torn into small pieces)
Salt
Fresh-ground pepper

First you need four big martini glasses. You can serve this in a bowl if you want to, but then it would be a shrimp and crab bowl (not a martini). Where's the fun in that?

Put the glasses in the fridge and get them good and cold.

Boil the shrimp following the Snappy Spicy Boiled Shrimp recipe, and then peel them. Put them in a Ziploc and into the fridge to chill.

In a bowl, put in the crabmeat and Creole Crab Sauce (see recipe), and fold together. Now get your cold martini glasses out of the fridge. Build a nest of romaine in the bottom of each glass using one-quarter cup in each. Now you spoon in equal portions of the crab mixture on top of the nest. Put four shrimp in each glass standing on their sides and hooked over the edge of the glass if you can. Sprinkle a bit more of the romaine in each then drizzle a tablespoon of Creole Crab Sauce on top of the shrimp and lettuce. A pinch of salt and fresh-ground pepper in each glass, and that should be it. Serve with a little wedge of lemon on the rim of each glass.

Remember that you should serve this immediately after making the Creole Crab Sauce. Don't refrigerate the sauce for any length of time before making this dish. It will affect the overall taste.

Note: No vodka was bruised or harmed in any way while making these martinis.

Stuffed Crabs

6 large boiled blue crabs (boiled in Zatarain's crab boil)
1 teaspoon of flashover seasoning
1 full recipe of Crabmeat Dressing (see recipe)
2 tablespoons of melted butter
12 lemon wedges

We would often boil crabs at the firehouse, and I would save and freeze the empty shells. It probably sounds a little weird, but as you will see, it is for a purpose. Not much goes to waste here. We try to use everything. Besides, once again, it's something to stuff.

Depending upon where you live, pre-boiled crabs may be hard to come by. In New Orleans they are readily available just about everywhere. If you can find them, pick the spicy crabmeat from them and put it aside. Since you already have the crabmeat required for this dish in the Crabmeat Dressing itself (see recipe), you have this spicy picked crabmeat as lagniappe. (I don't like to use spicy boiled crabmeat in this dish because the seasonings can be overpowering to the stuffing. You will usually taste a lot of the liquid crab boil.) Use this picked crabmeat in a salad or in a Crabmeat Martini (see recipe). Since it has the seasonings that are in the boiled shrimp potion of the martini, it will blend in nicely. Just don't use it in this dish.

The next part is important. The reason you want the fresh crabs is for the shells. You are going to stuff the dressing back into the shells, so you need to keep the top shells of your crabs. They will form a little bowl for you to stuff. Clean them out as much as you possibly can, and then place them aside for now.

Just make the Crabmeat Dressing (see recipe), and then stuff it equally back into the six shells. Now brush the butter over the stuffing and sprinkle some FOS on each. Put them under the broiler until the tops begin to brown, and that's it. Squeeze a lemon wedge over each as soon as they come out of the oven. Place another lemon wedge on the side and serve.

Note: If you can't find fresh boiled crabs (for the shells), they do sell these little aluminum faux crab shells. I've seen them in restaurants and in grocery stores. You can stuff them as you would a real shell, but the visual is not as effective. They will taste the same either way.

If You Can't Stand the Heat

Beef Carpaccio with Lemon and Garlic Aioli

1 pound of filet mignon
Olive oil
Red onion (slivered)
Capers
Lemon and garlic aioli
Shavings of Parmigiano-Reggiano cheese

Wrap your filet in plastic wrap and get it very cold. Next get a frying pan very hot. Remove the plastic wrap and place the very cold meat into the very hot pan. Sear it on all sides and remove it from the pan. You are not trying to cook it. You are only trying to quickly brown the outside of the filet on all sides. When it cools, wrap it back up in plastic wrap and refrigerate it once again.

Aioli recipe:
1 egg
1 clove of garlic
1/2 teaspoon of kosher salt
1 tablespoon of lemon juice
1/4 teaspoon of fresh-ground pepper
1/2 teaspoon of Creole mustard
1 cup of good quality extra virgin olive oil (cold pressed)
2 tablespoons of water

Put the egg, garlic, lemon juice, salt, fresh-ground pepper, and mustard into a blender. Put it on mix, and then slowly drizzle in the olive oil. This will form an emulsion. Remove the emulsion and place it in a bowl. It should be thick for the moment. Now you want to whisk in a couple of tablespoons of water. It's kind of like making homemade mayo except that you want it to be sort of runny. This is your aioli.

Cut the cold filet into four equal slices. It's usually about one half of an inch thick each. Place a slice in between two sheets of waxed paper. Use a meat mallet and pound down until paper thin (and I do mean paper thin). Repeat for all four pieces. Place one piece of the meat on a chilled plate. Put a dollop of the aioli in the middle. Toss on a few capers, some of the slivered red onions, and then drizzle with olive oil. Add several shavings of fresh Parmigiano-Reggiano on top. Serve cold with a wedge of lemon on the side. Repeat with the other three pieces of meat.

The first time I tried to get my wife to eat this she said, "No way am I going to eat raw meat!" Then she tasted it, and after that I had to give her half. Word to the wise: make enough so that you don't have to share.

Note: To put this together faster, ahead of time, put the meat (after pounding) on a plate. Place a piece of waxed paper on top, and then put on the next pounded piece. Continue until all of the meat is done. Cover with plastic wrap and put it in the fridge. When it's time to serve, you're ready to go!

If You Can't Stand the Heat

Thai Grilled Shrimp

2 pounds of head on shrimp (big 10 count shrimp or 10 to a pound)
1/2 teaspoon of Chinese five spice
1/2 cup of Thai chili sauce

Since we always had access to fresh shrimp here in New Orleans, we cooked them a lot. Naturally the guys would get tired of the same things after a while, so we would experiment. This one was thought to be a successful experiment considering the fact that they never even made it to the table. They ate them right off the grill.

This couldn't be easier to do. Peel and wash the shrimp. Cut each one down the middle lengthways and butterfly them so they lay flat. Place them on a platter and brush on the chili sauce. Sprinkle on the Chinese five spice, and cover with plastic wrap. Make sure you do both sides. Place in the fridge for at least an hour.

In the mean time, stoke up the barbeque pit. Put the shrimp on the grill, and cook for just a few minutes. They won't take long to cook. It all depends on how large your shrimp are and how hot your grill is. It's the same thing with the chili sauce. You may not need half of a cup or you may need more. It all depends on the size of your shrimp. In any case, just judge for yourself when you think they are done. I like them with just a bit of char around the edges. Eat immediately.

Note: For a little extra kick in the taste buds, put a teaspoon of sriracha (Thai hot sauce) in with the Thai chili sauce for the marinade. Yum!

Shrimp and Oysters Pastry in Tasso Cream

1 pound of headless shrimp (peeled and cleaned)

1 pint of oysters (and their liquor)

1 small onion (finely chopped)

2 cloves of garlic (finely chopped)

1 tablespoon of flashover seasoning

1/2 cup of white wine

1/2 pound of tasso (cut into small cubes)

2 cups of whipping cream

2 puff pastry sheets (17.3-ounce box)

1 egg (beaten, for an egg wash)

2 tablespoons of butter

1/2 cup of green onion tops (chopped)

If you can find fresh big puff pastry cups already made or the frozen variety from the supermarket, all the better and easier for you. If not, use this recipe to put some together.

Roll out two sheets of puff pastry dough (get them in the bread and biscuit section of the grocery store) to one-eighth-inch thick each on a lightly floured board. You want each of the pieces of dough to be twelve inches wide. Use a ruler if you have to. That way you are sure to have at least three rounds across and get six out of each piece of dough. Cut out twelve circles with a large cup (approximately four inches). I use a mug because I don't have a cookie cutter. Place six of those circles on a silpat (non-stick baking sheet).

Take the remaining six circles and cut a hole in them with a smaller cup (approximately two and one-half inches). I use an orange juice glass because, once again, I don't have a cookie cutter. Brush the six larger circles with egg wash. Place the "donut cut" circles (along with the center that you cut out) on top of those and brush with egg wash. Be sure to put the whole piece of dough on top. You are just basically pre cutting the top inside circle.

If You Can't Stand the Heat

Slide into a 400-degree oven (or whatever the pastry box recommends) and bake for approximately fifteen to twenty minutes until golden brown. Take them out and let them cool. After they are cooled, get a knife and cut out the little caps (the two-and-one-half-inch cut "donut hole") in the center of each. Remove and you will have a little well. You may have to push the inside down with your fingers to form the well. You will be filling that well very soon. My wife likes to use the little caps as a topper when serving. Firehouse guys could care less. It's up to you whether you want a hat on your food or not.

In a large skillet, melt the butter. Next put in the tasso and fry on medium heat until slightly browned. Next add the onions and half of a tablespoon of the FOS. Cook for a few minutes until the onions are translucent. Add the garlic and cook for one minute. Now deglaze the pan with the white wine and cook down until almost all of the liquid is gone. Add the oysters, their liquor, and the shrimp. Cook until the oysters curl up around the edges and the shrimp are pink. Remove the oysters and shrimp and put aside in a bowl for the moment.

Reduce that liquid left in the pan by half. This may take a while depending upon how much oyster liquor and shrimp juice is in the pan. Now add the whipping cream and the other half-tablespoon of FOS. Reduce that by half or to thickness you desire. Then add the seafood back into the pan and mix in until they are heated thoroughly. Spoon and serve in the puff pastry cups. In fact, put in enough until they overflow. There will be plenty. Top with a sprinkle of chopped green onions.

Note: When it comes to the puff pastry, the two sheets in the box will yield only four circles per sheet as they are. That would be four total pastries once you place the "donut cuts" on top. That means you would have four larger servings than if you roll them out with a rolling pin to make then thinner. Only when you roll them out a bit will you have the ability to cut out six from a sheet or end up with just four cups. I say this only because if you are going to need only four, why not make them larger portions. Larger portions are always good.

Another note: It all sounds kind of foo foo, but sometimes foo foo can be really good.

Cheese Enchiladas

8 ounces of shredded Mexican melting cheese
6 ounces of shredded extra sharp cheddar cheese (yellow)
Enchilada sauce
3 soft corn tortillas taco size (all cut in half)
Pinch of Salt
16-ounce single serving oval baking dish (1 1/2 inches deep)

This recipe is for one individual serving of enchilada. I keep several baking dishes of the size mentioned above so I can make a few of these at once. That way I can feed more than that one greedy person (that would be me) a great dish.

Many years ago I went to visit some relatives in San Antonio. Other relatives came up from Mexico. I was used to enchiladas that were tortillas stuffed with something and topped with enchilada sauce. When they made them like this, I was hooked!

Cut a tortilla round in half. Place one half in the bottom of the dish. Brush on a thin coating of enchilada sauce (with a BBQ brush). Put one-sixth of the shredded sharp cheddar cheese on top. Add another layer of the corn tortilla (turned the other way), and brush with enchilada sauce and another one sixth of the cheese. Repeat layers until you have exhausted your supply of tortillas and sharp cheddar cheese. Finish with eight ounces of the Mexican melting cheese on top and sprinkle with a pinch of salt.

In a 325-degree oven, bake until golden brown and bubbling on top (approximately ten minutes). Let this cool a bit before serving unless you're the kind of person who likes to stick boiling hot cheese into your mouth. You never know. Some people like going to the emergency room.

Note: For my money, serve this along with refried beans, Mexican rice, and a shrimp flauta, and you have the perfect meal. Bring on the margaritas!

If You Can't Stand the Heat

Mini Muffulettas

Chicago hard rolls
Mortadella
Capocollo
Genoa salami
Sopressata
Mozzarella
Provolone
Olive Salad (see recipe)
Olive Oil

I guess the first thing that you notice is that there are no amounts behind the ingredients. Yes, that is on purpose. I will explain!

Muffulettas are a Sicilian sandwich served in New Orleans. It is usually served on a piece of bread that is approximately ten inches across and about two to three inches thick. After you add all of the meats, cheeses, and the olive salad, it's baked in the oven just long enough for the cheese to melt and the bread to get crispy. That makes for a mighty large sandwich. That is why it is normally served in either halves or quarters.

In this particular case, we are using a Chicago hard roll. Since muffuletta bread is hard to find outside on New Orleans, I tried to do individual servings on similar bread. You want something soft on the inside, capable of absorbing the olive oil in the salad, and something that will be a little crunchy on the outside after it is toasted.

The reason for excluding individual amounts for the fixings is simple. If I go to the bakery and order eight rolls, I go to the deli and order eight slices of each of the meats and cheeses. Order exactly what you need, and use it all. If you want more of one thing than the other, do it. Improvise!

Now slice a roll in half, and then put the mozzarella on the bottom, meats in the middle, and provolone on the top of that. Smother the inside top piece of bread with the Olive Salad (see recipe), and cap off your sandwich. Once you have completed the assembly of all you are going to make, brush a little of the olive oil on top of each sandwich. Bake them in the oven at 325 degrees for just about ten minutes. Depending on your individual oven, it may not take that long so keep an eye on them. You want the cheese to melt slightly and the bread to crisp up.

Serve them to the masses. They will love you! If they already love you, they will love you even more … only dripping with olive oil.

If you get to the French Quarter, stop off at the Central Grocery and get a muffuletta. Theirs is the best in the world. They invented the sandwich!

Snappy Spicy Boiled Shrimp

2 pounds of head on shrimp
1 onion (quartered)
1 whole head of garlic (cut in half down the middle)
1 small lemon (cut in half)
1 tablespoon of Zatarain's liquid crab boil
2 tablespoons of sea salt
1 tablespoon of fresh-ground pepper
1 tablespoon of cayenne pepper
Dash of Tabasco
2 quarts of water

We would normally have a huge shrimp boil and spread them out on a table with boiled potatoes and corn. That is another recipe. This recipe is just to throw together as an appetizer for a handful of folks…or a couple of firemen.

Put the water in a pot and add all of the ingredients, except the shrimp. Bring to a boil and let it continue to boil uncovered for about fifteen minutes. This will be time enough for all of the flavors to mix and come together and also time for the onions and garlic to get soft.

Add the shrimp. Bring back to a boil for one minute; then turn off the fire. Let it sit for a few minutes so the shrimp continue to cook and absorb the flavors. This timetable is variable. Occasionally take one of the shrimp out and eat it to test them. The rate that they cook depends on the size of the shrimp. If you overcook them the shells will stick, and the shrimp will become difficult to peel. I have seen people put a little olive oil in the water at the beginning of the boil. I've been told that it gets under the shells and makes them easier to peel. I have never fully tested this idea because I've always kept an eye on them, so they didn't overcook. If you want to use olive oil, it can't hurt.

Once they are done, strain, peel, and eat. Don't throw away the garlic and onions. They make great munchies on the side. Hey…lagniappe!

Note: If you are having someone over to the house that is a first date, don't serve this. You both will have garlic breath for the rest of the evening. I have found that this is not conducive to making it to a second date. If you are serving this at a firehouse, go right ahead. No one will care.

If You Can't Stand the Heat

Shrimp and Cheese Flauta

1 pound of one hundred to one hundred fifty count cooked frozen shrimp
1/2-pound block of Monterey jack/Colby mix cheese (grated)
1/2-pound block of sharp cheddar cheese (grated)
10 burrito size flour tortillas (thin)
Frying oil (preferably peanut but vegetable will do)
10 toothpicks

This is another in the long line of dishes that I picked up from my family in San Antonio and Mexico. They made them with chicken, but I thought since I am in the premiere shrimping place in the world, I would substitute shrimp for the chicken. Little did I know that there was already a shrimp flauta. So much for my ingenuity. Maybe next time I will try a pulled pork flauta. Why not?

This recipe depends a lot on how tight you roll and how pliable your tortillas are. It's fairly easy, though. Once you get the hang of it you will be whipping them out in a flash.

The first thing you need to do is to thaw out the shrimp and place them in a non-stick frying pan on low heat. The shrimp are already cooked, so all you are trying to do is to get them to release their water. This will take about five minutes. Remove the shrimp to a bowl to cool and discard the water.

Grate both blocks of cheese and separate them into two piles. Place the bowl of cooled shrimp on the side of the cheeses. Basically you are trying to make a sort of assembly line to build your flautas.

Try to find the thinnest tortillas that you can. You don't want a thick one. I have found that Azteca makes a great thin tortilla suited for this recipe. Take one of these tortillas and microwave it on high for twenty seconds. This will make the tortilla pliable and will prevent it from cracking while you are trying to roll it. Put the warmed tortilla on the counter and lay a line of shrimp down the middle. They will be small, so be generous. Don't go to the ends of the tortilla. Just about three-quarters of the way across will do nicely. Next take some of the cheese from each pile, and spread them out on the shrimp in the tortilla one at a time (two or three tablespoons of each). That comprises you filling.

Now for the so-called tricky part. First fold the left and right sides inward, and then take the edge of the tortilla nearest you and roll tightly away from you. The thing you want to be sure of is that you roll it tight. Try to get as much air out of it as you can without mashing it. Use a toothpick to hold it closed. Your finished product will look like a fat tortilla cigar. Just think. If you get to be good at this, you could always have a fallback career as a cigar roller.

Placed the finished product on a platter under a damp cloth or damp paper towels. This will keep them from cracking. You should end up with about ten flautas.

Heat your oil to 375 degrees. Place only a couple at a time in the oil and cook till golden brown. Overloading the fryer will cool down the oil and make them greasy. Remove them from the oil to paper towels for draining and cover to keep warm until they are all finished frying. Now is a good time to remove the toothpicks from the finished flautas. No sense having people poke themselves while eating.

Warning: Immediately after they come out of the fryer is not the time to serve them. The cheese inside will run out as soon as you break them open. Wait a few minutes for the cheese to cool a bit before you serve them. They will still be plenty warm inside, but your guests won't be sitting there with an empty shell in their hands and a mound of cheese and shrimp in their laps.

Top these with Mexican crema or sour cream and fresh guacamole, and they will want to know when you're going to make more.

Guacamole

2 large avocados (pitted and the insides scooped out)
2 tablespoons of red onion (finely chopped)
1 tablespoon of cilantro (chopped)
1 tablespoon of shallot (chopped)
5 cloves of garlic (finely chopped)
1 jalapeno pepper (small, chopped, and seeded)
3 tablespoons of sour cream
1 tomato (chopped and seeded)
1/2 teaspoon of flashover seasoning
Juice of one lime
Pinch of salt
1/2 teaspoon of cumin
Dash of fresh-ground pepper
Homemade tortilla chips

We cooked a lot of Mexican food at the firehouse. This is one of those dishes that you could snack on all day.

Put all ingredients into a bowl, except for the tomato and, of course, the chips. Use a fork to mash it all together and combine everything into a thick paste. Don't use a food processor unless you want a puree. I like it chunky, so I use a fork. Once it is all mixed together the way you want it, fold in the chopped tomato. Cover to keep the bright color, but try to serve right away with some homemade chips.

Chips: Just cut some taco-sized corn tortillas into triangles of four and fry in 350-degree hot vegetable oil until golden brown. Drain on some paper towels, sprinkle some salt on them, and allow them to cool just for a minute. You ideally want them to still be warm when eaten. Then you just start dippin.'

Note: If you're pressed for time, I understand tortilla chips are also sold in bags. Go figure.

Smoked Salmon Deviled Eggs

1 dozen eggs (hardboiled and peeled)
6 ounces of Nova smoked salmon (chopped small)
1 heaping tablespoon of capers (finely chopped)
1 heaping tablespoon of red onions (finely chopped)
1 large clove of garlic (finely chopped)
1/2 cup of Hellmann's mayonnaise
Pinch of kosher salt
3 or 4 turns of fresh-ground pepper

This is another variation on a theme type of appetizer. I used to make deviled eggs the way Mom made them, and everybody seemed to enjoy them. Most people make deviled eggs with a sweet flavor, but my mom had a different slant on them that made them stand out. She always served them around the holidays at home. But firefighters work every day of the week all year round. With that said, I always made them around the holidays too, even if I was at work.

One day I saw my wife eating salmon and onion on toast points at a jazz brunch. She topped them with sliced boiled eggs. That's where the inspiration came from.

I went home to experiment with the salmon deviled egg idea and finally tested out my new eggs on the guys at work. When they disappeared in just a few minutes, I knew I had something that needed to be included in this book.

Chop the salmon into very small pieces and place them in a bowl. Don't use a food processor. It just doesn't work. Get out the trusty old knife and do them by hand. It only takes a second.

Add all of your other ingredients, except the eggs, into the bowl with the chopped salmon. Fold them all together and cover. Place the bowl in a refrigerator for the time being.

Hard-boil one dozen eggs. When they are cool, peel them and cut them in half lengthwise. Place the whites on a platter and put the yolks into a bowl. Use a fork to break up the yolks. They will crumble into very small pieces. Next add your salmon mixture to the crumbled egg yolks. Blend it all

If You Can't Stand the Heat

together with a fork. It should be almost pasty and thick. If it seems a little too thick and dry, add a bit more mayo.

Next, spoon the mixture into the hardboiled egg whites. Don't worry about having enough to fill them all. There should be more than you need to not only fill the holes but to spread some across the top of the entire egg…with a bit to spare. Give them all a final twist of fresh-ground pepper from the peppermill and serve.

Note: At first, I had a tendency to keep them in the refrigerator and serve them cold. But after I made and served them a few times, I changed that. People were telling me that they tasted better when they got closer to room temperature. So I have found that if you prepare them ahead of time and need to put them in the fridge until guests arrive, be sure to take them out early enough to serve slightly chilled but not cold. On second thought, forget feeding them to your guests. Wait until they go home and eat them all yourself.

Shirley's Deviled Eggs

This is the recipe that my mom taught me for her deviled eggs. They are especially good with turkey sandwiches the day after thanksgiving!

1 dozen eggs (hardboiled and peeled)
2 tablespoons of chow chow (recipe below)
1/2 cup of Hellmann's mayonnaise
Kosher salt to taste
1/2 teaspoon of fresh-ground pepper
Paprika

Hard-boil one dozen eggs. When they are cool, peel them and cut them in half lengthways. Place the whites on a platter and the yolks in a separate bowl. Break up the yolks with a fork until they crumble into small pieces. Add all of the other ingredients, except the paprika, and mix to a soft paste. You might want to hold back on a little bit of the mayo when putting everything together. Depending on the size of the yolks, you may not need the entire half-cup. If you add it all in and the yolks are small, you will end up with a runny mixture. If it's too thick when you've mixed it all together, add the rest of the mayo. The reverse is also true. You may not have enough mayo to do the trick. If it's still too thick when all of the mayo is in, just add a little more.

With a spoon, stuff them back into the egg whites. You should have just enough to fill the holes with little to spare. Sprinkle with a light dusting of paprika and serve.

Chow chow in New Orleans is unlike any I've seen anywhere else. Just over in Mississippi, chow chow is a relish made up of mostly cabbage. It has a pink color to it. Growing up in New Orleans using Zatarain's products, I was used to their chow chow. It is basically a yellow mustard base with cauliflower and pickles. Totally and completely different. I guess the point is that if you make these using a cabbage-based chow chow, it will not taste like these. Maybe it will taste really great, but that's another recipe.

If You Can't Stand the Heat

Zatarain's chow chow is what she originally used to make this appetizer. They no longer make this product, so it was left up to us to try to make some for ourselves. Here is a quick recipe to make your own. Since you only need a little it will be easy to throw together. It's not exactly like theirs, but it's close enough for me.

2 tablespoons of yellow mustard
2 teaspoons of dill relish
1 teaspoon of pickled cauliflower (chopped fine)
A pinch of kosher salt

Mix well and let it sit in the fridge for a couple of hours. You can also make more and use it as a condiment instead of mustard on sandwiches and hot dogs.

Egg Rolls

1/2 pound of ground pork
2 cups of chicken stock
1/2 pound of cooked salad shrimp (100 to 150 shrimp)
2 cups of fresh cabbage (chopped)
1/4 cup of celery (finely chopped)
2 cloves of garlic (finely chopped)
1/3 cup of yellow onions (chopped)
1/4 cup of green onion tops (chopped)
1 cup of bean sprouts
2 tablespoons of soy sauce
1 teaspoon of dark brown sugar
2 tablespoons of peanut oil
1 quart of vegetable oil (for frying)
1 teaspoon of salt
Fresh-ground pepper (to taste)
Egg roll wrappers (can vary by how much filling you use per egg roll)
1 egg (beaten)
1 tablespoon of sesame oil (needed if you are going to pre make the egg rolls and fry them at another time)

I love egg rolls! With a little hot mustard and some sweet and sour sauce…yum! The only question I have to ask is why call them egg rolls when there are no eggs in it? They will roll, so at least half of the name is correct.

The first thing you want to do is to put the chicken stock in a pot and heat it up to a simmer. Add one tablespoon of the soy sauce and the teaspoon of dark brown sugar and incorporate. Next add the

If You Can't Stand the Heat

cabbage. Cook for just three minutes. Turn off the fire, and let the cabbage sit in the liquid for five minutes. You want it to be cooked but still crisp. Strain and put the cabbage aside in a bowl.

Get the wok hot on medium high heat, and then put in the peanut oil. Add the pork, salt, and fresh-ground pepper to the oil, and cook until the pork is no longer pink. It should take about five minutes. With a slotted spoon, remove the pork and let the oil drain back into the wok. Put the cooked pork into the bowl with the cabbage.

Turn the fire down to medium, and put the onions and green onion into the wok. Cook until onions are translucent. Add the garlic, shrimp, celery, the other tablespoon of soy sauce, and the bean sprouts to the wok. Cook for about five minutes. Fluid will form in the bottom of the wok, but don't worry about it. Most will be absorbed during the cooling process.

Now pour the pork/cabbage mixture into the wok with the rest of the ingredients already in there. Remove from the fire and mix well. Put it all back into the bowl, and taste to adjust your seasonings (salt and fresh-ground pepper). Let this cool.

Take your egg and beat it in a small bowl. Place it close by, as you will be using this as a sealer to close your egg rolls. Place one egg roll wrapper on the counter with one of the pointed ends toward you. Spoon in about three heaping tablespoons of the filling in a straight line, from left point to right point. Take the bottom point, and fold it away from you about halfway. Now fold the sides inward, left and right points. You should now have a shape that resembles an open envelope. Dip your finger into the beaten egg and run it along the edge still showing. Now roll away from you, making a tight little package. Continue until you use up the entire filling mixture.

Heat your vegetable oil to about 360 degrees. Place a couple at a time into the oil and fry until golden brown. This won't take long, so keep a close eye on them. Remove from the oil and place on paper towels for draining. Serve with plum sauce and hot mustard.

Note: If you pre-make and refrigerate these (as in not deep-frying them yet), they will stick together and be very difficult to handle. What you will want to do is to get a frying pan and heat one tablespoon of sesame oil. Put the egg rolls in and lightly brown on all sides. Remove from the pan, and from there you can store them in the fridge without worrying about them sticking together until you are ready to deep-fry them.

Pot Stickers

1 pound of ground pork
2 teaspoons of fresh grated ginger
1/4 cup of green onions (tops and bottoms of the onion, chopped)
1 tablespoon of sesame oil
1 tablespoon of soy sauce
1/4 teaspoon of white pepper
1/4 teaspoon of salt
12-ounce pack of round wrap won ton wrappers
1 tablespoon of vegetable oil
Chicken stock (enough to fill half of whatever size pan you are using)

And now for the continuous adventures of Chinese cooking in Cajun country. This is the basic recipe, but sometimes I'd add a little spicy shrimp or crawfish to the pork filling. Your choice on how creative you want to be. This is a starting block. Maybe not a block … more like a starting bowl.

In a large bowl you want to place the pork, ginger, onions, sesame oil, soy sauce, salt, and white pepper. Mix these ingredients together, and that will comprise your filling. Get your hands in there and smash it around. You can wash up later.

Next, place the wonton wrappers on the counter. Take one teaspoon of the filling and place it in the middle of one of the wrappers. Moisten the edges of the wrapper with water. Fold it over and seal the edge by pressing together. They will look like little Chinese calzones. If you can't find round wrappers and have to use square wonton wrappers, fold over from corner to corner (forming a little triangle), and seal the edge by pressing together. Some of the filling may want to come out at this time. What I do is just basically seal it on the counter, then pick it up with my hands, and press the edges together again to make sure I have a good seal. Placed the finished pot sticker on a plate covered by a damp cloth. Continue making them until you have used up all of your filling or run out of wrappers.

If You Can't Stand the Heat

Coat the bottom of a large frying pan with the vegetable oil. Over medium heat, slightly brown the pot stickers on both sides. When that is done you add the chicken stock to the pan. You only want to add enough to come almost half way up the pot stickers. Cover, and let them cook for five minutes. Take off the lid, increase the heat, and let it cook until all of the liquid evaporates. Serve with Pot Sticker Sauce (see recipe).

Note: You really don't have to use up the entire filling. Sometimes I just make enough for everybody to each get a few, and I'd freeze the rest of the filling to use at another time. I mean, if you're going to be that greedy with the food, the next thing you know you'll be joining the fire department. You already have the first qualification.

Mamoo Mac and Cheese

1-pound box of large penne pasta
1 stick (four ounces) of unsalted butter
2 8-ounce boxes of Philadelphia cream cheese
1 15-ounce jar of cheese whiz
1 12-ounce can of evaporated milk
1 16-ounce block of sharp cheddar cheese (grated)
1 cup of whole milk
1 teaspoon of fresh-ground pepper
1/2 teaspoon of kosher salt

Everybody has his or her own version of mac and cheese. This is my version. As you can see from the ingredients, this stuff will fill your arteries with everything they crave. Hey, you only live once. What a way to go out!

First thing to do is to boil the pasta until it is al dente. Drain it and set aside. Next take the butter, cream cheese, cheese whiz, whole milk, fresh-ground pepper, and salt, and put them all in a pot over medium heat. Whisk together until all of the ingredients are blended into an almost smooth mixture. I say *almost* because the cream cheese won't smooth out entirely. It's all right, though; that's the way it's supposed to be. Next you add the pasta to the pot and mix together, making sure to cover the pasta with the cream sauce as much as possible. You can really use any pasta you want, but I like to use mostaccioli or penne because it gives the sauce lots of holes to fill and places to go. Cheese needs direction!

Take a nine-by-thirteen-inch glass casserole dish and dump all of the pasta and sauce mixture into the pan. Hopefully your casserole dish is nonstick. If not, you may want to grease it up with a light layer of butter so your pasta doesn't stick. Gee, more butter; imagine that.

Next take the grated cheddar and spread it all over the top of the pasta. It will seem like a lot, but it's not. Besides, I like more than enough. Preheat your oven to 350 degrees and place the casserole dish in the center. Bake for about forty minutes or until the cheddar cheese browns lightly on top. Take it out

If You Can't Stand the Heat

of the oven to a cooling rack. As soon as it's out of the oven, take a small knife and start to make little slits in the mac and cheese. As you do, pour in some of the evaporated milk a little at a time into each slit. Do this all around. The middle, the edges, pretty much everywhere until the whole can of milk is gone. Let it sit for twenty minutes covered by some aluminum foil. This will give the evaporated milk time to be absorbed into the mac but still keep it warm. Now cut in, and serve. Gooey good!

Note: Don't let the aluminum foil cover touch the cheese. When you get ready to eat, it will have stuck to the foil and will come off. Just use the foil like a tent. Also, if you are ever in New Orleans, stop by Jack Dempsey's Seafood Restaurant. They have the best mac and cheese I've ever tasted.

Fried Rice

4 cups cooked cold jasmine rice

2 eggs (slightly beaten)

8 ounces of chopped Chinese Pork Ribs (see recipe)

8 ounces of chicken breast (diced and cooked one large breast)

1/2 cup of bean sprouts

3/4 cup of frozen peas and carrot mixture

1 cup of cooked salad shrimp (100 to 150 count cooked)

1/4 cup of green onion tops (chopped)

1 cup of yellow onion (chopped)

2 teaspoons of Chinese brown gravy

1/3 cup of soy sauce

2 tablespoons of garlic (finely chopped)

1 1/2 tablespoons of fresh ginger (finely grated)

2 teaspoons of sesame oil (for the egg)

3 tablespoons of sesame oil

1/2 teaspoon of salt

1/2 teaspoon of fresh-ground pepper

1/2 teaspoon of MSG

We ate a lot of Chinese food at the firehouse. Most of the time we ordered out, but occasionally I would prepare this at home ahead of time and bring it in to reheat.

Cook the rice according to the directions on the package. Make sure that you cook enough to yield four cups. Cover this and refrigerate for at least twenty-four hours.

You can cook this dish in a frying pan, but doing it in a wok is so much better. A wok conducts the heat better and cooks so much faster.

If You Can't Stand the Heat

Mix the salt, fresh-ground pepper, and MSG in a small bowl. Put a pinch of that mixture into the eggs and slightly beat. Put two teaspoons of the sesame oil into the wok. Heat it up and add the eggs. Scramble the egg, and break it up into little pieces. Remove the eggs from the wok and put on the side on paper towels to drain.

Pour the other three tablespoons of sesame oil into the wok and heat it up. Put in the garlic and ginger and cook for just a minute. You want to smell that great aroma breaking out before you add anything else. Don't let it get brown. Now put in the yellow onions and cook until they are translucent. Add the pork, and cook for one minute. Add the chicken, and cook for a couple of minutes until the chicken is warmed through. Add the peas, carrots, shrimp, green onion tops, and the rest of your salt, fresh-ground pepper, and MSG mixture. Cook until it is all warmed through. Toss in the bean sprouts, the cooked eggs, and the Chinese brown gravy. Stir and mix until warmed. Add the rice and the soy sauce. Mix it all thoroughly, and cook until everything is combined and heated through. That's about it. Now...eat!

Note: I used to put this on the table along with some egg rolls and some pot stickers. Throw in a couple of sauces, and you would swear you were in Hong Kong.

And just for the record, I know it's okay to serve Chinese food in New Orleans, because the last time I was in Hong Kong they were serving boiled crawfish, and there was a bottle of Tabasco on the table. I figure it's good for the world. A little cultural exchange with hot sauce on the side.

Chili Squash

10-ounce can of diced tomato and chilies
1 medium yellow squash
10-ounce can of chicken stock

This is a spicy little side dish that can be thrown together in a flash. It's a nice side item that makes the squash a little less boring to eat. I know, not everybody thinks that squash is boring, but trust me, the squash will appreciate a spicy night out.

Just cut up the squash any way you like that will make it into small bites. I usually slice it into one-quarter-inch-thick round sections. Now put them into a frying pan, and add the diced tomato and chilies and the stock. Cook on a low fire until the squash is tender but still crunchy. You don't want them to turn to mush, so watch them closely. They will cook fast. Remove and eat!

Note: Some people (my wife) like to put this together and eat it over spaghetti. Maybe you will too!

If You Can't Stand the Heat

Sautéed Spinach with Pecans

18 ounces of fresh spinach
1/2 cup of shallots (finely chopped)
1 clove of garlic (finely chopped)
1/3 cup of grape seed oil
1/2 cup of pecans (broken into very small pieces)
1 tablespoon of balsamic vinegar
Salt
Fresh-ground pepper

This is another one of my world-famous spinach side dishes. Well, maybe not world famous, but more like locally famous. Okay just ask anybody who lives in my house, and they will tell you they have heard of it. In any case, give it a try alongside of some grilled fish. Maybe it will become a hit in your world.

Clean the spinach well and drain. I like to use a salad spinner to get as much water out as possible.

Put the grape seed oil in a large pan, one that has a cover. Heat up the oil and then add the shallots. Cook until they are translucent; then add the garlic and the pecans. Cook for one minute; then add the spinach and the vinegar. On low heat, cover and cook for six to eight minutes. Remove the cover and use salt and fresh-ground pepper to taste. Serve immediately.

Elisa's Coleslaw

16-ounce bag of coleslaw mix
1 cup of onions (1/2 red and 1/2 Vidalia) (chopped fine)
1 medium granny Smith apple (diced small and not peeled)
1 teaspoon of raspberry balsamic vinegar
1/2 cup of good coleslaw dressing
1 teaspoon of Mrs. Dash seasoning blend garlic and herb
2 teaspoons of bleu cheese dressing
Fresh-ground pepper to taste

Elisa brings this over when we are having a potluck thing or sometimes if we are having a fish fry. This slaw is really good! It is even better when it has had a chance to sit in the fridge and allow the flavors to mingle. Everybody has mingled at one time or another. I'm sure you have. Interacting, finding common tastes. Well, that's what the slaw is doing, only it's doing it in a bowl in the fridge.

If you are looking for quick and easy coleslaw to make, this is it. Mix all of the ingredients together, and chill in the fridge for an hour. Serve!

Creamed Spinach

12 ounces of fresh baby spinach (washed, dried, and finely chopped)
1 1/4 cups of Béchamel Sauce (see recipe)
1 cup Parmigiano-Reggiano cheese (grated)
32 ounces of chicken stock

I love fresh spinach, but I personally do not like cooked spinach, especially creamed spinach. My wife loves it! So we make this dish a lot. I really don't have anything against spinach, but if you have ever been to Catholic school and were forced to eat everything on your plate … I need to say no more.

Heat the chicken stock in a large frying pan and add the spinach. Cook for ten minutes. Remove the spinach and place in cheesecloth. Squeeze out all excess liquid, and put the spinach in a covered bowl to keep warm. It's going to be very hot, so unless you have Teflon hands, let it cool off a bit before you squeeze it.

Have your Béchamel Sauce (see recipe) ready to go. Add the spinach to the sauce and mix in. Now add the cheese and mix in. Serve this immediately if not sooner.

Note: It may have a tendency to form a little thin layer of milk skin across the top if you wait to serve it. If this happens because you had to serve it later than you thought, just add a touch more cream to it and heat it up again.

Formally Known as Broiled Stuffed Tomato

2 large Creole tomatoes
1/2 pound of mild Italian sausage
1 cup of Italian breadcrumbs
1 cup of Parmigiano-Reggiano cheese (grated)
2 tablespoons of olive oil
4 tablespoons of butter
2 teaspoons of flashover seasoning

Once again a cook in New Orleans finds something to stuff. It's almost ridiculous. But then again, that's probably what they told the guy who wanted to stuff olives!

Cut the tomatoes in half from top to bottom. Scoop out the meat of the tomato and the seeds, and discard them. In a bowl, mix together the cheese, breadcrumbs, olive oil, and the two teaspoons of FOS.

In a frying pan, brown the Italian sausage. Make sure you brown the meat all the way through, and scrape the bottom of the pan for any brown tasty bits that might be lingering there. There is no loitering in this recipe. (This would be a good time to preheat your oven to 350 degrees.)

When the meat is cooled, put it in the bowl with the other ingredients. Now mix with your hands to combine. Don't squash it all together. Just fold it in.

Equally stuff the hollowed out tomatoes. Place one tablespoon of butter on each. Put them in an oven dish and slide it into the oven. Bake for thirty minutes. Switch over to your broiler and put them under it for as long as it takes to slightly brown the top. It won't take long, so keep an eye on it. Serve when they cool down a bit. Those babies will be really hot when they are right out of the oven.

Note: One of our friends named Bob said that he thought it tasted like a high-end pizza but without the crust. He called it a "naked pizza." So this dish is no longer a broiled stuffed tomato. It is now called a Naked Pizza.

If You Can't Stand the Heat

Smothered Potatoes

1 pound of new potatoes (creamers washed and cut into one-quarter-inch-thin slices)
2 tablespoons of olive oil
1 medium yellow onion (rough chopped)
4 tablespoons of butter
1 teaspoon of salt
1 teaspoon of garlic powder
1/2 teaspoon of fresh-ground pepper
2 tablespoons of dried parsley

My mom used to make this as a side dish to just about every kind of meat. If you are the meat and potatoes type, this dish is for you.

Heat the olive oil over medium heat in a non-stick frying pan. Make sure you have a tight fitting lid for the pan because you will be covering it later. Add the onions and sauté for five minutes. Add the potatoes and all of the spices, except the parsley, and the butter. Turn the fire down to low and toss to cover the potatoes with the seasonings. Cut the butter into eight pieces. Spread out the eight pats of butter on top of the potatoes, cover the pan, and lower the fire.

About every ten minutes you want to uncover and toss the mixture. That way the potatoes on top will have a chance to cook as well as the ones on the bottom.

Cook for thirty minutes, and remove from the fire. At this point they should break apart easily with a fork. If they don't, cook them a little longer. When they are cooked, add the parsley and mix in. Cover again and let sit for twenty minutes. Serve.

Note: You can also make this dish with a little less olive oil and using spray butter. You will cut back on the fat, but you will also lose the flavor to some degree. If you choose to cook it that way, don't let my mother find out. She has ways to make you do things properly.

Salsa

6 Roma tomatoes (chopped)
2 jalapeno peppers (seeded and chopped)
1/2 cup of fresh cilantro (chopped)
3 cloves of garlic (chopped)
Juice of two limes
1 medium red onion (chopped)
Salt and fresh-ground pepper to taste

There is nothing better than fresh salsa. Well, maybe fresh salsa and fresh guacamole. Maybe even fresh salsa with fresh guacamole and homemade tortilla chips. The only thing better than that combo is if you didn't have to share. This recipe is enough to share and then some.

Mix all of the ingredients in a bowl. Refrigerate at least two hours but hopefully overnight. Take the salsa out, and taste it. Adjust salt and fresh-ground pepper. Enjoy!

Note: This salsa will keep in the fridge for about five days and gets better tasting every day. It'll last five days of course, if you don't share.

If You Can't Stand the Heat

Cheese Grits

2 cups of quick grits
4 cups of chicken stock
2 cups of whipping cream
8-ounce block of sharp white cheddar cheese (grated)
2 tablespoons of butter
1/4 teaspoon of salt
Pinch of fresh-ground pepper
Pinch of white pepper

Not everybody likes grits. Some say they are too, well, gritty. There have been many times in the engine house that I have had grits with breakfast and grits with dinner. This is one of those recipes that you will use for breakfast or dinner. If you are one of those that don't like grits, just try these. You may change your mind.

Put the whipping cream, chicken stock, salt, and peppers in a sauté pot, and bring it up to a simmer. That takes about five minutes. When you get to that point, slowly add in the grits. While you stir—just about constantly—they will thicken up. This will take five or six minutes depending on what kind of grits you buy. I know that seems like a lot of stirring, but try to think of it as working up an appetite. Next, add the butter and stir in until blended. Slowly whisk in the cheese, and voila! You're done.

Note: I'm not sure, but I think *voila* is some French word that means it's time to eat!

Caramelized Carrot Bitters

1 stick of butter
1 cup of orange juice
16 ounces of carrots (sliced)
1 teaspoon of Angostura bitters
1/2 cup of maple syrup

This is something that my mother-in-law used to make for my wife. I think it must be something she brought down from Canada with her because it has maple syrup in it. I don't know that for sure, but it doesn't make a difference. It tastes good no matter where it came from.

I like to slice the carrots up into little circles about one-eighth of an inch thick. I just cut them up into circles and put them in a measuring cup until I have two cups.

Melt the butter in a saucepot. Add the bitters, maple syrup, carrots, and the orange juice. When it comes back up to a simmer, put your pot on a low fire and cook uncovered for forty to forty-five minutes. You want the carrots to be tender, but still have a little bite to them. In other words, you want them to be semi-crunchy and not mushy.

Remove the carrots, and reserve them on the side. Cook the sauce until you have a slightly thick syrup. You can accomplish this by reducing it down by at least two-thirds of its volume. It takes about another thirty minutes. Now put the carrots back in and cover them with the sauce. Let them soak in their for a while, and then serve. You want to use a slotted spoon and sift out the carrots, and then drizzle a little sauce on top.

Note: This makes a great side dish to barbecued pork. Try drizzling some of the carrot sauce onto the pork. It really works with the pork. Don't ask me why, it just does. Would I steer you wrong?

Cajun Dirty Rice

1/4 pound of chicken gizzards
1/4 pound of beef liver (chopped)
1 1/2 pounds of ground pork (or fresh pork sausage removed from the casing)
32 ounces of chicken stock
4 tablespoons of butter
1 cup of onion (finely chopped)
1/4 cup of bell pepper (finely chopped)
1/4 cup of celery (finely chopped)
1/8 cup of fresh parsley (finely chopped)
2 cloves of garlic (finely chopped)
1 teaspoon of salt
1 tablespoon of flashover seasoning
2 cups of rice
Salt and fresh-ground pepper to taste

Dirty rice gets its name from the fact that once you brown the meats involved in the dish, it makes the rice look "dirty" when it's added. So the fact that some people might think it involves some measure of actual dirt is wrong. Although, if you served this to a bunch of firemen and told them that there was actual dirt in it, I doubt they would mind as long as it tasted good.

Put the chicken stock in a pot and add the gizzards. Boil them uncovered for thirty minutes. If some foam should come to the surface, skim it off. Once it is done, remove it from the fire and take out the gizzards. Save the stock. When cool, put the gizzards into a food processor, pulse to chop them fine, but do not turn this into a paste. Now add the liver, and pulse the same way.

Take the leftover stock and measure out four cups. In order to get four cups, you will have to add a little more stock because some has evaporated. Put it in a pot with a tight cover along with the two cups of rice, and bring it up to a rolling boil. Turn off the fire, give it a stir, and then cover. Let this sit for forty minutes and then uncover. Whatever steam or fluid that is in the pot will be absorbed during this time, and it will cook the rice. Don't peek! Letting out the steam will only prevent the rice from cooking all the way through. It will come out like little rice rocks. Nobody likes rocky rice.

In a large frying pan, add the butter and melt it down. Put in the ground pork, gizzards, and the liver, and fry until browned. This will take a while because of all of the water that will be excreted by the meat. Now add all of the veggies, including the garlic, the teaspoon of salt, and the tablespoon of FOS. Cook on a low fire until the onions are translucent. Now add the cooked rice and mix in well. Taste for salt and fresh-ground pepper. You can cover it and let it sit for a while for the flavors to marry. This will make enough to feed an army. If you don't personally know an army, invite one for dinner. Get to know the troops.

Serve with fried chicken, fried fish—fried anything. If you want it to be extra zippy, add more FOS while you are browning the meat. It's okay. I do it all the time!

Note: If you are in a hurry, you can use two cups of Minute Rice and two cups of chicken stock. It's faster, and if you have a rice-cooking problem (some of us do), it will always be perfect. Just follow the directions on the box, but use the stock instead of water.

Green Beans with Fried Sage

1 1/2 pounds of fresh green beans
3 strips of applewood smoked bacon
3 tablespoons of butter
1 tablespoon of shallots (finely chopped)
1 tablespoon of garlic (finely chopped)
1 cup of chicken stock
Salt and fresh-ground pepper (to taste)
2 cups of vegetable oil
Fresh whole sage leaves (as many as you like, I use about 5 or 6)

In our house growing up, we always called these string beans. Somewhere along the way everybody started to refer to them as green beans. I guess I understand the logic in it. They are after all green, and they don't even remotely look like string. I suppose it's the same logic that we use when we refer to alligator pears as mirliton.

You need to start with more than one pound of beans for this (thus, one and a half pounds). You will lose quite a bit of the beans when you cut off the tips. That way you will end up with at least one pound in the end.

First cut off the tips of all of the beans and rinse them in cold water. The beans not the tips. Pat the beans dry so they won't splatter when they hit the hot butter.

Fry the bacon until crispy and set aside on a paper towel to drain. When they are cool, break them up into bacon bits and keep handy.

Drain off the bacon drippings, but leave the little tasty bits in the bottom of the pan. Heat up the butter in that pan. Scrape the bottom and then add and cook the shallots until translucent. Now add the garlic and cook for a few seconds. Don't let it brown, or it will be bitter.

Put in the beans and sauté them for two minutes to cover with the butter. Add salt, fresh-ground pepper, and the bacon bits. Over a low fire, add the chicken stock and cover the pan. This will help steam them as they cook, keeping them moist. Cook the beans for about forty-five minutes while stirring occasionally. Steam will escape every time you uncover it, but that's all right. In the end, the less liquid, the better. Once the forty-five minutes are up, uncover, and let it cook until almost all of the liquid is gone.

Heat up the two cups of vegetable oil. Put in the sage leaves and fry until crispy. This will not take long. Remove to paper towel and drain. Let them cool.

Serve the beans in individual portions. Crumble up the fried sage leaves and sprinkle on top of each portion. They will not have a strong sage taste because frying them takes away about 90 percent of that flavor. The good thing about this dish is that you also have sage infused oil left over that you could use in something else. Maybe a salad dressing or anything else you can think of. That's the beauty of cooking; there are no rules!

If You Can't Stand the Heat

McIntyre's Baked Beans

1/2 pound of ground beef
1/2 pound of bacon
1 medium onion (chopped)
16-ounce can of kidney beans (drained)
16-ounce can of pork and beans
16-ounce can of butter beans (drained)
1/2 cup of brown sugar
1/3 cup of white sugar
1/4 cup of Wendy's Smoky Honey Barbeque Sauce (see recipe)
1/4 cup of ketchup
1/2 teaspoon of chili powder
1 tablespoon of mustard
2 tablespoons of molasses

This recipe comes from one of my friends named Bob McIntyre. It is an old family recipe that we all enjoyed very much. It's easy to put together and really easy to see why it disappears from the table.

Brown the bacon in a large pot. Take out the bacon and put it on a paper towel to cool. Now add the onions to the pan, and cook until they start to wilt and become translucent. Now add the ground beef and brown it.

Next you add the three cans of beans. Break up the bacon into little bits and put it in. Mix all of the other ingredients together, and add to the pot. Once it is all mixed together, put it all in a baking dish, cover, and cook in the oven for one hour at 350 degrees.

It's ready to go!

Note: This goes great with anything from the grill. Burgers, dogs, chicken, and even gator. If you decide to grill the last one, get a really big pit.

Also, you can substitute your favorite barbeque sauce for Wendy's, but I like to make her sauce and keep some on hand at all times. You never know when a barbeque will just break out.

Mexican Rice

1 1/2 cups of medium grain Goya rice
3 1/2 cups of chicken broth
1/3 cup of vegetable oil
1 teaspoon of kosher salt
2/3 cup of onion (finely chopped)
3 cloves of garlic (finely chopped)
1/3 cup of tomato sauce
1/2 cup of green onion tops (finely chopped)
2 tablespoons of butter

This recipe comes from the Mexican side of my family. We visited with them in San Antonio when the Medina's all got together. They live in a place they just called Old Mexico. They cooked some fabulous food, and this was the way that they cooked the rice.

The first thing they did was to rinse the rice over and over until the water ran clear. They then soaked the rice in water for about fifteen minutes. They then rinsed it again and put it into a colander to drain for at least one half hour.

Next they put the vegetable oil in a pot and got it hot. They put in a few pieces of test rice to make sure it was hot enough. You will know that the oil is hot enough because the rice will "dance." What you are now trying to do is cook the rice until it turns a light golden color. Put all of the rice in and stir it a lot to prevent sticking. Remove the rice from the pot and strain out the oil in the colander.

Put the two tablespoons of butter in the pot and sauté the onions until soft. Now add the garlic and cook for another minute. Next add the tomato sauce and the salt to the pot. Mix well and then add the chicken broth. Blend that well and bring it up to heat.

Now put the rice into the pot and cook it over a medium to low heat uncovered. In ten to twelve minutes, almost all of the liquid is gone, and there are little holes forming in the rice. It will look like a lot of little volcanoes erupting. Don't forget to stir it a lot!

If You Can't Stand the Heat

Now comes the part that I thought was fascinating. They took the rice off of the fire and added the onion tops. They then put a kitchen towel over the pot. On top of that, they put the lid on over the towel and let it sit for thirty minutes. This is so that the steam will be trapped and help puff up the rice. The towel absorbs the moisture from the steam so the rice doesn't get too mushy.

Then they served it up, and wow ... it was perfect! Hope yours is too.

Jalapeno Hushpuppies

1 cup of all-purpose flour
1 1/2 cups of cornmeal
1/2 cup of green onion tops (finely chopped)
1/2 cup of jalapeno peppers (seeded and finely chopped)
1 large egg (beaten)
1 2/3 cups of buttermilk
1/2 teaspoon of baking powder
1/2 teaspoon of baking soda
1/2 teaspoon of salt
1/2 teaspoon of sugar
Peanut oil

Hushpuppies always seemed to me to be a southern tradition. Louisiana is pretty much as southern as you can get. I figured why not go even more southern than that and add a Mexican flavor. That's really Deep South!

Mix all dry ingredients in a bowl. That would be everything but the egg, buttermilk, and the peanut oil. Stir it up. Now mix in the egg and enough buttermilk to make a really thick pancake-like batter. You may not use all of the buttermilk, and you also may use a little more. It all depends on how it thickens up. You will know that you have it right when can look at it and say, "I think I could make pancakes with that," even though you can't. Put it in the fridge for at least an hour. This gives the cornmeal a chance to absorb the buttermilk and thicken really well.

Heat enough peanut oil in a Dutch oven so that your hushpuppies will float when frying. Bring the oil up to 325 degrees. Using two spoons, form balls with the mixture and drop into the oil. Don't crowd the pot. Do a few at a time. Cook until golden brown. Remove to a paper towel to drain. Continue until all of your batter is gone.

If You Can't Stand the Heat

Note: Keep a glass of warm water nearby. Dip one spoon into the water between hushpuppies. Use the other to scoop the batter, and place it on the wet spoon. It will slide off right into the oil. Be careful of oil splatter, or the next day you'll find yourself telling everybody your "How hushpuppies scarred me for life" stories! Nobody wants to hear that.

Hazel's Cracker Snacks

8 ounces of oyster crackers (soup crackers)
1 package of Hidden Valley Ranch original salad dressing
1/2 cup of corn oil
1/4 teaspoon of cayenne pepper
1/2 teaspoon of dill weed (dried)
1/2 teaspoon of garlic powder

This was a snack that one of our very good friends used to make for us. Even though she is no longer with us, her recipe carries on.

Preheat the oven to 250 degrees. Now get a large bowl. Combine all of the ingredients in the bowl, except the crackers. Whisk together then add the crackers. Mix with a wooden spoon (or with your hands) until all crackers are covered on all sides. Pour them out into a flat cookie pan and spread them around. You don't want them lying on top of each other. Now pop them into the oven. Stir them every few minutes while baking so they are evenly cooked.

Bake for twenty minutes and then remove from the oven. Allow them to cool and transfer to a Ziploc bag for storage. Either that or eat them all at once like we do!

Note: Once you get started eating them, it's hard to stop. They are addicting. I see a counselor once a week for my cracker habit. Just a word of warning.

If You Can't Stand the Heat

Pop's Sausage Appetizer

1 pound of smoked sausage
1 cup of pancake syrup

This is another example of something so simple but so good! My dad used to make this, and the first time I saw him do it I thought it was a little nutty. But after I tasted it, it made sense to me to eat it whenever I could.

Hold the sausage link in your fingers, and starting at one end, cut it up into one-half-inch-thick circles. Repeat until all of the links are cut. Heat up a frying pan. Toss the sausage in and cook until they all slightly brown. That's it! Serve them on toothpicks, and dip into the syrup. That combination of warm smoky flavor and the sweetness of the syrup can't be beat.

That's how Pops did it. I personally like to leave the links whole and throw them on the grill. I cook them until they are slightly browned and then let them rest for about five minutes. Then I cut them up as before, only this way they have that grilled flavor added to the smokiness.

Note: Sometimes I skip the toothpicks, grab a fork, and tell everyone that I'm sorry but the sausage burned. That's what they get for coming so late.

Chili Cheese Frito Bag

The following is all per serving:
1 cup of hot chili
1 small bag of Fritos (plain individual serving size)
1/2 cup of grated cheddar cheese

When I was a kid, there was this little place we would stop by on cold mornings while we walked to school. It was a long walk, so we'd get this little combo to warm our tummies on the way. I can't believe I actually used the word tummies. But hey, I was a kid, so cut me some slack.

Open up an individual serving of bagged Fritos. Scoop a cup of hot chili into the bag and top with the cheese. Now mix it all together until the cheese is melted and begins to mingle with the other ingredients. Once they get to know one another well enough, grab a spoon, and dig in. It will warm the cockles of your heart...and any other places cockles would hang out!

Note: The chili will be hot, so use some napkins to insulate the bag from your fingers. Plus if it's cold out, it will keep the food warmer longer.

If You Can't Stand the Heat

Entrées

Chicken and Andouille Jambalaya

2 pounds of chicken thigh meat (with the skin on)
1 pound of andouille sausage (sliced into 1/4-inch square pieces)
1 large Vidalia onion (chopped)
1/2 cup of bell pepper (chopped)
1/4 cup of celery (chopped)
4 cloves of garlic (finely chopped)
1 cup of green onions tops (chopped)
2 1/2 cups of chicken stock
2 cups of medium grain rice
4 teaspoons of flashover seasoning
1 teaspoon of salt
1 teaspoon of dried thyme
2 bay leaves

Once again, there are more varieties of jambalaya than one can count. I like to break it down into two categories—red and brown. You can use any combination of ingredients in either color of jambalaya. You can use duck, shrimp, sausage, chicken, or even rabbit. You can use pretty much anything. Normally the brown is pork and chicken, and the red is pork and seafood, but it really doesn't matter. All you need to know is that if you brown the meats in the pot and add the rice and stock, you have a brown jambalaya. But if you add any tomato product, it becomes a red jambalaya. This recipe is for a brown jambalaya. I prefer brown to red. Nothing wrong with red, but this is the one we make most often. We'll save the red for another time.

First thing to do is to get out a big Dutch oven. Preferably, what we call the big black iron pot. If you don't have one, you can use another kind of pot, but it has to be something that distributes the heat evenly and that has a tight cover.

If You Can't Stand the Heat

The next thing you need to do is to rub down the chicken pieces with two teaspoons of FOS. Now remove the skins, and save them on the side. Remove the chicken meat from the bones, and cut into bite-sized pieces. Put them aside for now.

Put the pot on the stove, and heat it up on medium heat. Place the chicken skins in the pot, and brown the skins on all sides. Remove the skins and discard. That should give you a little chicken fat in the pot. Now add the andouille sausage and one teaspoon of FOS, and brown this meat also. Be careful. Take your time. If you burn it the least little bit, you will have to start over. Scrape the bottom and sides constantly to get the tasty browned bits incorporated into the meat. When they are slightly browned (three to four minutes), remove the meat to a bowl, and keep it handy. Now add the chicken, and slowly brown the meat. Cook it until the meat is no longer pink. Once you have done this, remove it, and put it in the same bowl as the andouille.

Put the onions, celery, bell pepper, and the last teaspoon of FOS into the pot. Slowly cook these down until the onions have browned slightly. You will be trying to slowly caramelize the onions. That's where more browning (brown jambalaya) comes in. Scrape the bottom of the pan a lot to release and mix in any little brown bits. Now add the garlic and cook for one minute.

Rinse the rice in cold water to help remove some of the starch. Add the rice, stock, thyme, bay leaves, salt, and then stir. Bring it all up to a low simmer, and then cover. Put it on a low fire for twenty minutes (or as long as is called for on the package of rice you are using).

Now add the meats and the green onion tops. Mix in well, cover, and again cook on a low fire for ten more minutes. Remove it from the fire, and then let it sit covered until all of the fluid is absorbed. I usually like to just leave it alone for half an hour.

Do not open it! There is steam that will help cook the rice that may not have completely cooked, and if you open it prematurely you will release all of that cooking power. Your rice will taste like it has little rocks in it, and people will leave the kitchen looking for their nearest fast food outlet. Patience first…then pop the top and eat.

Note: *Jambon* comes from the French word meaning "ham." *Ya* is an African word that means rice. I guess it should have been called "Jamboya." In any case, all jambalayas have pork in them. Those clever Cajuns. Gotta love 'em!

Mom's Stewed Chicken

1 hen (cut into pieces)
1 1/4 quarts of chicken stock
1 10-ounce can of chicken gravy
1 10-ounce can of cream of chicken with herbs
1 whole head of garlic (finely chopped)
2 large yellow onions (chopped)
6 whole green onions (chopped)
1 teaspoon of Kitchen Bouquet
1/3 cup of vegetable oil
3 teaspoons of Paul Prudhomme's poultry magic
1/3 cup of flour
Salt and fresh-ground pepper
1 teaspoon of Zatarain's liquid crab boil

Normally when I come across a recipe that I like, I might be tempted to change it to suit my taste and that of the guys at the firehouse. But there are some things that you just can't improve upon. This recipe is one of them. My mom has made this since I was a kid, and I like it just the way it is.

First, you salt and fresh-ground pepper the chicken. Put the vegetable oil in a large pot, and bring it up to a high temperature. Add the chicken pieces skin side down and start to brown it. Once you have done that on all sides, remove the chicken to a bowl.

Add the flour into the oil, turn down the fire, and make a brown roux. Be sure to scrape the bottom of the pot because there will be little brown chicken pieces stuck to it. Don't burn them, or it is all for naught. Cook and scrape until the roux is just past golden brown, kind of like the color of Franco American turkey gravy in the can. Add the veggies (except the garlic), two teaspoons of Poultry Magic, and mix in. Continue to scrape the bottom of the pan and cook the veggies until the onions are translucent. Add the garlic and cook for two minutes.

If You Can't Stand the Heat

Next, add the stock and the Kitchen Bouquet. Mix well; then cover and simmer on a low fire. Cook for sixty minutes, and then uncover. Add two cans of gravy (chicken and cream of chicken), the other teaspoon of Poultry Magic, and the liquid crab boil. Stir in well and cook for another half hour. Add the chicken and cook covered for an additional half hour to forty-five minutes depending upon how big the chicken pieces are. Remove from the fire, and let it sit covered for at least a half an hour. Serve over cooked white rice.

Note: Share some with your mom.

Chicken and Shrimp Pasta with Pancetta Cream Sauce

2 quarts of lightly salted water
1/4 pound of pancetta slices (sliced into thin strips)
24 ounces of whipping cream
1/2 pound of chicken (cut into small bite-sized pieces)
1 1/2 pounds of shrimp (40 to 60 count peeled, rinsed, and deveined)
10 ounces of Capanelle pasta
1/2 stick of unsalted butter (cut into tablespoons)
2 tablespoons of olive oil
6 cloves of garlic (finely chopped)
1 1/2 cups of Parmigiano-Reggiano cheese (grated)
1 cup of white wine
2 teaspoons of flashover seasoning
4 tablespoons of fresh basil (chopped)
Fresh-ground pepper (to taste)

We like to use cream sauces with seafood, meats, or just pasta. This is just another example of what happens when you leave me alone in a kitchen with a cream sauce on the brain.

Peel the shrimp and dust with one teaspoon of FOS. Do the same with the chicken, and put them in the fridge for at least one hour.

Boil your pasta in the lightly salted water and cook until al dente. Drain, but do not rinse the pasta.

First put the olive oil into a large frying pan. Render down the pancetta on medium heat until it is slightly crispy. Remove it from the oil and place it on a paper towel to drain and cool. Add the garlic to the oil and cook for two to three minutes. Now add the white wine and reduce for five minutes. Be careful when you pour it in, as it will splatter.

If You Can't Stand the Heat

Add the butter a piece at a time, and melt it in. Now put in the chicken pieces. Cook for five minutes.

Crush up the pancetta into little bacon-like bits. Add the cream, the pancetta, and a pinch of fresh-ground pepper, and blend in. Cook that for about five minutes to reduce by one-third. Add the shrimp. Cook them for a few minutes or until they are pink and cooked through. Add the cooked pasta to the sauce and toss well. Sprinkle a cup of the cheese on top and mix in. So serve it already!

Sprinkle the rest of the cheese on top of the individual plates as they are served. Also top each with a little of the fresh basil. You should not need any salt. The pancetta will probably have plenty enough salt for the dish. Taste it at the end just in case your pancetta isn't as salty as it could be. Serve with some crusty bread.

Note: Between the FOS and the pancetta, there is probably enough salt in the dish. I have made this using one-third pound of pancetta, and the dish was too salty. I only say this because if you decide, like I did once, to add more meat, don't. You may end up with a dish that will test the limits of your blood pressure.

Cajun Cordon Bleu

4 chicken breasts (with skin on)

4 ounces of tasso (cut into strips)

4 slices of baby Swiss cheese (cut into strips)

4 tablespoons of olive oil

4 teaspoons of all-purpose flour

8 leaves of fresh basil (cut chiffonade style)

1/2 cup of shallots (finely chopped)

4 cloves of garlic (finely chopped)

1 cup of white wine

4 Roma tomatoes (chopped)

1 cup of chicken stock

4 teaspoons of flashover seasoning

1/2 teaspoon of kosher salt

8 ounces of angel hair pasta (cooked al dente)

I always liked chicken cordon bleu. Most of the time they are chicken breasts that have been stuffed, rolled, breaded, and baked or even fried. And as much as I love to stuff and fry things, I decided this time to go a different route. This is a zippy baked tomato basil version. We'll save the old version for another time. The good thing is … it's still stuffed. I suppose that when it comes to changing things, I'll only go so far!

The first thing you need to do is get the chicken really cold. Once it is very chilled, take a breast and flip it over on the kitchen counter with the skin side down. Take hold of the ribcage bones, and pull them away while using your thumb on your other hand to push the meat off in the opposite direction. It's really easy to do. You don't need a knife to de-bone the breast. There may be a small pin bone up at the top of the breast that has to be removed, but it's also easy to just pull out. You should now have a de-boned breast with the skin intact. Repeat for all four.

Take the chicken breasts and rinse them well. Pat them dry with paper towels. Make a slit in the side of the meat, down the middle, to almost butterfly it. Don't cut it in half. You will be forming a pocket that you can open up like you would a squeezable coin purse. Equally divide into four, the strips of cheese and tasso. Place one-fourth of the strips of cheese in and put one ounce of the tasso strips on top of the cheese. Do this for each breast. Fold the meat back over and press the edges together. Sprinkle one-half teaspoon of FOS onto the skin side of each breast. Pat it into the skin with your fingers so that it will stay on. Refrigerate them covered for at least one hour so the seasoning has time to adhere to the skin.

Use a frying pan that you are able to cover, and be sure it can also be put into the oven. Dust one-half teaspoon of the flour on each side of each breast. I use a flour sifter to do this, but you can just sprinkle it on by hand. Put the olive oil in the pan and get it really hot. Now place the chicken into the pan skin side down. You want to brown the chicken on that side. This will take approximately two minutes. Turn the chicken over, and cook on other side for two minutes. Remove the chicken to a plate.

Now add the shallots to the pan and cook for about two to three minutes. Next, toss in the garlic and cook for one minute. Now pour in the wine to deglaze the pan. As always, scrape the pan to get up the good tasty brown bits off of the bottom and incorporated into the sauce. Once you've done that, add the chicken stock, the other two teaspoons of FOS, the salt, and cook to reduce by one-third. Now put in the tomatoes, the basil, and return the chicken to the pan along with any juices that may have settled in the plate. Cover and put in a 325-degree oven for twenty minutes. When it is done, place equal portions of the cooked pasta on four plates. Put a cooked chicken breast on each bed of pasta. Pour sauce equally over each breast. Serve immediately.

Stuffed Artichokes

8 fresh artichokes
24 ounces of Italian breadcrumbs
8 ounces of grated Parmesan and Romano cheeses
4 ounces of grated Parmigiano-Reggiano cheese
4 ounces of olive oil
2 heads of garlic (finely chopped)
1 large onion (finely chopped)
1 big lemon

Yes, boys and girls, what we have here is another stuffing project. When you are finished with this project people will want to hug and kiss you. It's a natural reaction to introducing them to something so delicious. But watch out for them … garlic breath.

The first thing that I like to do with this dish is to make it safe. I know that sounds weird, but I will explain.

Artichokes have these little thorn like ends on all of the leaves. The very first thing I do is to cut these off with a pair of kitchen scissors (just the tips). As you will eventually be putting these leaves into your mouth, the points have to be removed. No sense in having an artichoke accident.

After that is done, I pull back the leaves a bit to open up the artichoke. Rinse them and drain upside down on paper towels. When they drain thoroughly, cut off the bottom stem so that they will sit flat on the countertop.

Next get a large bowl. Pour in the breadcrumbs, garlic, onion, and the Parmesan and Romano cheese. Mix all of the ingredients well, and then add the olive oil a little at a time. Mix it in bit by bit. You eventually want to end with a mixture that is slightly moist but still crumbly. If you need more olive oil, use it. If you need less, use less. The thing is to get the texture right.

Now take the artichokes one at a time and place them in the bowl. Pull back the leaves and start to fill them from the bottom leaves up with the breadcrumb mixture. Just stuff it in there. It will end up being a lot larger than the little choke you started with. Once one artichoke is filled all the way up, put it in a pot with one-half inch of water at the bottom. Repeat this until you have done them all and you have filled the pot so that there is no chance that any of them will fall over. Squeeze the lemon over the tops of all of the artichokes. Next you sprinkle the Parmigiano-Reggiano over the tops of each of the artichokes. If you like, some folks like to place a lemon slice over the tops, but that is a personal preference that I usually do not do.

Turn on the heat and cover. Put them on a low fire as you are trying to basically steam them for about thirty-five to forty-five minutes. Once they are done, remove to a tray and serve. Each leaf should be filled with the breadcrumb garlic cheese mixture that is "oh yeah!" yummy. Just start pulling the leaves off one at a time, and eat it as you would an artichoke that you steamed and dipped in lemon and butter sauce. You'll get the artichoke taste along with the great taste of the stuffing.

Note: Make sure your pot is big enough to accommodate all of the stuffed chokes. They can get pretty big once they are stuffed. If not, use two pots, four in each. Just make sure they can't fall over or the water will destroy the stuffing.

There is one other little thing that you might want to try. Chop up three or four large shrimp per artichoke, and add to the stuffing mixture. Be sure to season the shrimp with a little FOS before you add them. Then, stuff as before. It is mucho good!

Another little "by the way" is that if you have made too many stuffed artichokes, wrap them in plastic wrap and then in foil. Freeze them until another time. Just thaw them out and steam in a steamer for ten to fifteen minutes. They are going to be just as good as the first time.

Mexican Spaghetti

2 pounds of ground chuck
2 tablespoons of flashover seasoning
2 tablespoons of chili powder
2 tablespoons of cumin
1/2 teaspoon of salt
1/2 teaspoon of fresh-ground pepper
4 cloves of garlic (finely chopped)
29-ounce can of tomato sauce
16-ounce bag of Mexican cheese
16 ounces of cooked spaghetti (al dente)

Sometimes we would be busy at multiple fires and didn't have time to prepare anything that was time consuming. This is one of those dishes that you can throw together in little or no time, and it still tastes great.

Brown the ground meat in a pot. Add the garlic and cook for two to three minutes. Add the dry seasonings and cook for two to three minutes. Add the tomato sauce; turn to low heat and cover. Cook for one hour.

Plate up the pasta and pour the Mexican spaghetti sauce over the pasta. Sprinkle cheese (as much or as little as you like) on top while still hot. That was quick, wasn't it?

Now grab a fork, and get your share before it all disappears.

Note: This stuff is also great to serve on top of tortilla chips as a snack. Oh, if you do it this way, keep the cheese and lose the pasta.

If You Can't Stand the Heat

Deep Fried Turkey

1 10- to 13-pound turkey (thawed, rinsed, and patted dry)
16-ounce bottle of Cajun butter flavor injector
1 can of turkey gravy
1 stick of melted butter
1 tablespoon of Tony Chachere's Cajun seasoning
Peanut oil
Turkey fryer
Propane gas burner and bottle
Submersible thermometer (usually comes with the fryer and the fryer stand)

People are always talking about the difficulties you can encounter when frying a turkey. They also talk about the fact that if you eat a fried one, you'll never go back to baked. Another firemen friend of mine named Tony Palisi, who has sadly left us, lived across the street from me. He was one of my converts from baked turkeys. The first time I fried one for him and his family, I got to ask him the next day how they liked it. He said when he last saw his kids they were sucking on the bones. Enough said!

There is no danger in turkey frying as long as you remember to do it outside away from your house, and don't overfill the oil. People have a tendency to fill it up, heat the oil, and then put in a turkey. The oil spills over, and they burn down the neighborhood. There is a simple way to avoid this. Whatever the size of your turkey fryer, put in the largest turkey you are going to fry (we usually fry multiple turkeys in the same oil). Fill the fryer with water until it just about covers the turkey (just leave the tip of the leg bones sticking out). Mark that spot on the inside of your fryer. That is the oil level you will fill up to the next day when you fry. Pour out the water and dry out your fryer. Now you know how much peanut oil to put in without overflowing the pot.

It also should be noted that you should only use peanut oil. We have tried this with less expensive oils, and it doesn't work out or taste the same as it does with peanut oil. If the expense is too much, fry a couple for the neighbors and split the cost. They will love you for it. The only drawback to this is that you will be frying for them every year after that, so be prepared. Also, before you throw the turkey wrapper away, make sure you know how much it weighs. You will need that bit of info when it comes to the timing of the cooking of your bird.

Put the Cajun butter flavor sauce, the butter, the Tony Chachere's, and the turkey gravy into a saucepan. Heat them up and whisk them into a sauce mixture. Let it cool down, and then use the injector to inject your sauce into as many of the turkey muscles as you can. Inject the wings, legs, thighs, and breasts in as many spots as you can until you run out of sauce. Now place your turkey into a couple of plastic garbage bags and seal it up. That way nothing will spill out into your fridge while the turkey marinates overnight.

When it is time to fry, fill the fryer with peanut oil up to the line you found the day before. Put the pot on the burner, and start up your fire. Place the thermometer inside and make sure that you can read it at all times. The thermometer should have a clip that will allow you to attach it to the side of the fryer pot. Get your oil up to 300 degrees, and its ready.

While the oil is getting hot, you want to take your turkey out of the fridge and mount it. There will be a flat stand with a long rod attached. Slide your turkey, with the legs facing up, over the rod through the turkey cavity. The loop at the top of the rod is used to lower the turkey into the oil. When the temperature is right, slowly lower the turkey with the hook into the hot oil. Be very careful because it will splatter a bit. Once it is in the oil, crank up the heat until it comes back up to 300 degrees. Now turn the fire down low and check your watch.

I have heard of a thousand different ways to do this, but trust me this is the best way. Making sure you always keep the temperature at 300 degrees, you cook the turkey for three and one-half minutes per pound. Period! No three minutes per pound at 350 degrees. No two minutes per pound at 375 degrees. Just do it this way, and your turkey will be cooked perfectly inside as well as have a golden brown color on the outside. For some reason I have seen people cook them until they are black on the outside, and there is no sense in that. I have cooked hundreds of turkeys in this way, and in my humble opinion, this is the best way to do it.

When the time is up, pull the turkey up to drain, and then remove the turkey to a pan that is lined with paper towels. This will absorb the excess oil after frying. That's about it. You will now be a convert. I guarantee it!

If You Can't Stand the Heat

Note: Peanut oil can be strained and put back into its container for use at another time. It will probably look like used motor oil, but once you thoroughly strain it, it can be used again to fry more birds at later dates. I like to start over with fresh oil every time, but I have seen firemen use the same oil for quite a few frying sessions before opening their wallets to buy more. Hey, we're underpaid—what can I say?

Another note: Try to use only turkeys that weigh between ten and thirteen pounds. Anything larger than that are usually tough, and besides that, they probably won't fit into the average-sized fryer.

Smothered Chicken and Onions

1 whole cut up chicken
1/3 cup of oil
1/3 cup of flour
1/2 pound of bacon
4 large onions (cut into thin slivers)
1/2 cup of bell pepper
1/4 cup of celery
3 cloves of garlic (finely chopped)
48 ounces chicken stock
2 tablespoons of flashover seasoning

Get a large Dutch oven. I use a big black iron pot, but that's just me. I like the old-fashioned way of smothering down food. But I digress. Let's get to it.

Fry the bacon in the pot until it is crispy. Remove it and place on paper towels to cool.

In another pan, make a dark brown roux with the flour and oil. Set aside and let it cool.

Rinse the chicken pieces and pat them dry. Now rub the FOS all over the chicken. Going back to your original bacon pot, heat up the bacon drippings and brown the chicken pieces on all sides. It may take a couple of batches to do it all, but that's all right. Place the browned chicken on some paper towels for now.

Put the onions, bell pepper, and celery in the pot with the chicken fat and bacon drippings, and sauté them down until they are wilted. I use a heat resistant spatula to mix things around and, in the process, scrape the bottom of the pan. That way all of the tasty brown bits will mix with the veggies. Now add the garlic and cook for a minute more.

Next put the chicken stock into the pot and heat it all up to a simmer. Scrape the bottom of the pot to release any of the browned bits that might still be there. Once the stock is hot, slowly add the room

If You Can't Stand the Heat

temperature roux a little at a time, and blend it in. Now add the chicken; then crumble up the bacon and put it in the pot. Cover and place into a 350-degree oven for one hour.

Remove from the oven, and let the pot sit for a half hour covered. No peeking!

After that, taste and adjust the seasonings as you like. Serve this over cooked white rice.

Note: If I have the time and I'm at home making this, I will remove the chicken from the bones and put it back in the gravy. That way no one has to pick the meat from the bones while they are eating. It can get a little messy. When I was at the firehouse I never did that. Those guys liked being messy.

Chicken with Tomato Basil Arrabbiata

4 boneless skinless chicken breasts (coated with a thin coating of olive oil)

1/3 cup of olive oil (plus a tablespoon to rub on the chicken)

5 large cloves of garlic (finely chopped)

4 ounces of hot capocollo (cut into small pieces)

28-ounce can of whole tomatoes (you will crush them by hand)

1 teaspoon of flashover seasoning

1 tablespoon of dried Italian seasoning

1 cup of chicken stock

2 tablespoons of fresh basil (chopped)

6 small dried red jalapeno peppers

8 ounces of angel hair pasta

1 cup of grated Parmigiano-Reggiano cheese

This is a little old Roman pasta dish with a kick. Who knew that the Romans liked a little zip in their pasta? Hail Caesar!

Get your grill hot and ready to cook the chicken. Rub a tablespoon of olive oil on the chicken. Sprinkle the FOS over the chicken breasts. Now that they are ready to grill, you should start on the sauce.

Drain the tomatoes and put them into a bowl. Crush them with your hands to break them up. There were no food processors in Rome. Get into it. Set them aside for now.

Put the olive oil into a pot and heat it up. Add the capocolla and cook for two minutes. Now add the garlic and cook for another two minutes over low heat. You want to extract the garlic flavor without burning any of the garlic. Next, add the red jalapeno peppers. Cook for another two minutes.

Pour in the crushed tomatoes and mix in. Add the Italian seasonings, the cup of chicken stock, and cook uncovered for thirty minutes while stirring often.

If You Can't Stand the Heat

Remove the peppers from the sauce and discard. Now stick an immersion blender in there to mix everything well and make a smoother sauce. Because there will be some olive oil floating on top, you will need the immersion blender to help incorporate it into the sauce as well as make the tomato chunks smaller. Make it as smooth or as chunky as you like. Your sauce is now done. Keep it warm and start your chicken.

Put the breasts on the grill and cook until done. Set them aside covered to rest for about fifteen or twenty minutes.

Using four plates, put one-quarter of the pasta on each. Slice the chicken into one half-inch strips and place one cut up breast on top of the pasta on each plate. Cover each with equal amounts of sauce and top with equal amounts of cheese. Sprinkle each with the same amount of chopped fresh basil.

Note: Put it on the table and move back quickly. You don't want to be in the way with all that cutlery flying around!

Mandarin Chicken

The batter:
1/2 cup of cornstarch
1 teaspoon of sugar
1 teaspoon of baking soda
1 teaspoon of baking powder
1/2 teaspoon of salt
1 large egg
2/3 cup of cold water

The chicken and roux:
2 chicken breasts (boneless and skinless)
2 cups of vegetable oil
1/2 cup of flour

The sauce:
2 cups of chicken stock (room temperature)
1 teaspoon of fresh-ground anise seeds
1/2 teaspoon of curry powder
1/2 teaspoon of onion powder
1/2 teaspoon of garlic powder
Pinch of salt
Pinch of fresh-ground pepper
1 tablespoon of crushed peanuts

The serving:
4 teaspoons of crushed peanuts
4 tablespoons of chopped green onion tops
2 cups of cooked white rice
2 cups of lettuce (shredded)

If You Can't Stand the Heat

No one knows why you can't find this dish outside of Louisiana. Trust me, we have tried. A Chinese dish found strictly in Cajun country. After eating it five thousand times we finally figured out what went into it. So this is my version of a New Orleans favorite. Don't let the amount of ingredients intimidate you. It's really pretty easy.

First thing you do is to mix up all of the dry ingredients in the batter mix. Now beat the egg into the water, and mix it like you were going to make scrambled eggs. Put that into the bowl that contains the dry stuff. Mix it all until it looks like smooth and thin pancake batter.

Cut your chicken breasts in half as if you were filleting them. You want the breast in two pieces but thinner than they are, like butterflying them but cut all the way through. Put the chicken pieces into the batter and just let it sit for a moment until they are all thoroughly coated.

Get your vegetable oil up to about 375 degrees. Carefully place the chicken into the oil and fry on a medium heat until they are golden brown. This should take about ten to twelve minutes or so depending on the thickness of the meat. You want the chicken to cook all the way through but still end up with that golden brown look. Remove to a paper towel to drain. Keep warm.

Strain away all but one-half cup of the cooking oil. Now add the half-cup of flour and make a roux. This should be a light brown roux, something a little bit darker than the peanut butter roux in color. As a reference, it is kind of the same color as Franco American Turkey Gravy. Next add room temperature chicken stock a little at a time. Mix in well to incorporate into the roux. Now add the spices for the sauce and the tablespoon of peanuts. Once again, mix well. Slowly cook this down until it thickens up enough to cover the back of a spoon without dripping off. That may be too thick for you, but that's how I like it. If you want it thinner, just make it thinner. Your call!

Slice your fried chicken pieces into one-inch-thick strips. Place a bed of lettuce on your plate. Put the chicken on top and spoon on the gravy. Sprinkle a few crushed peanuts on top followed by a few of the green onions. Serve with a scoop of cooked white rice on the side of the same plate so they can mix it in with the mandarin chicken and the sauce. Everybody gets a half of a cut up breast. This will naturally serve four.

Note: Most places just serve this with white rice. I like to serve it with Fried Rice (see recipe) to just give it a bigger flavor, not that it needs it. If you want to go with the white rice, just go for it. It's your choice. Whatever floats your sampan.

Paneed Back Strap of Venison

(Known around the Firehouse as Deer Candy)

1 pound of venison back strap
1 cup of flour
1 cup of milk
1 egg
1 cup of Italian breadcrumbs
Olive oil
Salt and fresh-ground pepper

The back strap is the filet mignon of venison. You could cut it into steaks and grill them, but this is what we usually did with them. Everybody would eat them as they came out of the fryer, and they were subsequently named "candy." They're addicting.

Cut the venison into one-quarter-inch-wide pieces. They will look sort of like thick meat potato chips. Salt and fresh-ground pepper the meat and set aside for the moment.

Put the flour into a bowl. Combine the egg and milk in another bowl to make an egg wash. Into the last bowl goes the breadcrumbs. One at a time put the venison candy into the flour. Shake off the excess and then into the egg wash. Drip off the excess and then into the breadcrumbs. Shake off the excess.

Heat some olive oil in a frying pan. Make it just deep enough to cover the breaded meat. Get it up to 375 degrees. Now put in the venison and cook until they are a nice golden brown on both sides. Don't overload the pan. Do a few at a time. Once they are cooked, set them on a paper towel to drain.

This is the clever part. Since you are cooking you get to test one for salt and fresh-ground pepper after cooking. Add any if you need it. Serve!

Note: Because you were the cook and had to sample the goods before serving them, you get to have one more piece than anybody else. Clever!

If You Can't Stand the Heat

Regular Good Old Fashioned Osso Buco

4 veal shanks (cut about 3 inches thick)
1/2 cup of olive oil
1 cup of flour
4 cups of onion (chopped)
1 cup of celery (chopped)
1 1/2 cups of carrots (chopped)
4 cloves of garlic (chopped)
2 6-inch sprigs of fresh lemon thyme
1 6-inch sprig of fresh rosemary
2 bay leaves
2 tablespoons of tomato paste
1/2 pound of Roma tomatoes (peeled, seeded, and chopped)
1 cup of red wine
28 ounces of beef stock
1 tablespoon of flashover seasoning
Salt and fresh-ground pepper

I call this a regular good old-fashioned Osso Buco for a reason. Lately I have seen it made with lamb shanks, turkey legs, and all sorts of things. I figured I'd leave that to the "let's try this and see how it comes out" crowd. For me it has to be the old way. That's the best way. If it weren't, there would be no old way, just whatever happens to be the fad today.

Use a big Dutch oven, something that will conduct heat really well in the oven (one with a tight lid). Pour in your olive oil and start bringing it up to a high heat. In the mean time, salt and fresh-ground pepper your shanks. Now dredge them in the flour and shake off all of the excess. Once your oil is hot, put in the shanks. You are trying to brown them on all sides. Once you have browned them, remove them from the pot and put them aside for now.

Add the onions, celery, and carrots (mirepoix) to the pot, and lower the fire. Cook them until the onions are translucent; then add the garlic. Cook for one minute; then add the tomato paste. Cook until the tomato paste starts to turn slightly brown. Now deglaze with the red wine. Put in the tomatoes. Get a piece of cheesecloth and wrap up your bay leaves, lemon thyme, and the rosemary. That is your bouquet garni. Put it in the pot. Add the one-tablespoon of FOS. Mix it all in well then add the beef stock.

Once it is all incorporated, put the shanks back into the pot. Cover and put it in a preheated oven at 350 degrees. Cook for two hours. I like to check it occasionally to baste the shanks and to check the level of the stock. You don't want it to cook away and dry out. Always try to keep the level of the gravy about one third to half of the way up the shanks.

Once it is done it should be falling off of the bone. Check it now for salt and fresh-ground pepper, and adjust it to your taste. Take it out of the oven and set it on the stove. I like to let it sit there covered for another half hour at least to let all of those flavors hang out together and get to know one another really well. That's about it. Grab some French bread and butter and go for it! Don't forget to get rid of the garni. It may wind up on someone's plate, and they will think they found the door prize.

While the Osso Buco is cooking, I also like to cook up some multi-colored orzo to serve on the side. You can use the regular-colored orzo, but the other one adds more color to the plate (as if it needs it). If you don't want to use that, try some risotto or even some polenta. That's the beauty of cooking—there are no rules. Serve it with whatever side dish you like. Try it with mashed potatoes. It's not exactly Italian, but who cares? You will love the Osso Buco either way.

Note: Some people like to use a little butcher's twine to tie around the shanks before you start to cook them. They are supposed to help hold the shanks together until you serve them because they have a tendency to fall apart when they are done. I usually don't do this, but if it makes you more comfortable, by all means, do it. Just don't forget to cut the strings off before you serve them. Nobody wants to eat and floss at the same time.

If You Can't Stand the Heat

Lasagna a la Lori

1 1/4 pounds of ground beef

9 lasagna noodles (pre boiled al dente in lightly salted water)

26-ounce jar of tomato, onion, garlic Prego (reserve just enough to put a thin coating on the bottom of your baking dish)

15 slices of mozzarella cheese

12 ounces of ricotta cheese

1 cup of onions (finely chopped)

1/2 medium sized green bell pepper (finely chopped)

3 cloves of garlic (finely chopped)

2 tablespoons of olive oil (for sautéing the vegetables)

1 tablespoon of olive oil (for the pan)

1 1/2 tablespoons of dried Italian seasoning

1 1/2 tablespoons of Pickapeppa sauce

2 teaspoons of Tabasco

1/2 tablespoon of flashover seasoning

1/4 teaspoon of fresh-ground pepper

1/2 teaspoon of kosher salt

This recipe is for a lasagna that my wife makes. Although she is a great cook, she rarely gets into the kitchen because there's already someone in there—me. When she does manage to squeeze in there this is one of her specialties!

Make sure that you have your noodles ready to go. They may come twenty to a box, but since you will be using a nine-by-nine-inch casserole pan for this, you will only need nine noodles for three layers. Preheat your oven to 350 degrees.

Heat up the two tablespoons of olive oil for sautéing the onions and the bell pepper. Put them both into the pan with the oil, and then add the salt, fresh-ground pepper, and dried Italian seasoning. Cook until the onions are translucent. Next add the garlic and cook for two minutes. Now add the ground beef. Cook the beef until it is browned.

Add the pickapeppa sauce, the FOS, and the two teaspoons of Tabasco. Mix well. Continue to cook over medium heat until cooked through and thoroughly mixed. Add the Prego (except the reserved portion), and let it simmer ten minutes over low heat to cook out some of the fluid and thicken up the sauce.

In your nine-by-nine-inch pan, put in the olive oil (for the pan), and coat the bottom and sides. Next, you will put in the reserved Prego to coat the bottom of the pan on top of the olive oil. After that, you put in your first three lasagna noodles to cover the bottom. Cut the noodles to fit the bottom of the pan. You should have to cut about three inches off of the length of each one. She usually does the first one by measuring, and then she just stacks them on top of each other and cuts the rest of them all at once.

Now divide your sauce into thirds. Divide the ricotta and the mozzarella slices into thirds also. One-third of the sauce goes on top of those noodles. Spread it out evenly to cover the lasagna noodles. Next comes the ricotta cheese and then the mozzarella slices. Use four ounces of ricotta per layer and five slices of mozzarella per layer. When you are putting in the ricotta, it is impossible to spread. Just put in little dollops at a time all over the sauce until you use all four ounces. You will also have to cut the last slice of mozzarella for each layer. The first four will fit but will leave an edge on two sides. Cut the last slice into four pieces and fill in the gaps.

Follow that with another layer of noodles and then another third of the sauce. The same amount of ricotta and mozzarella as you used on the previous layer is next. After that, the last layer of noodles followed by the last of the sauce. The last of the ricotta is next, and then cover the whole thing with the last layer of mozzarella.

Put the pan in the oven and cook at 350 degrees for forty minutes. The cheese on top should be a nice slightly browned color. Once it is done, take it out and let it cool for a bit before you cut and serve.

A little garlic bread and some wine, and you are in for a great dinner!

New Orleans Style Bracciole

3 pounds of round steak (or beef sirloin tip thin cut)
2 cups of Parmigiano-Reggiano cheese (finely grated)
2 cups of olive oil (one half cup is for browning the steak)
15 ounces of Italian breadcrumbs
4 cloves of garlic (finely chopped)
1/2 teaspoon of kosher salt
1/2 teaspoon of fresh-ground pepper
4 hardboiled eggs (chopped)
6 large basil leaves (finely chopped)
3 quarts of Basic Tomato Gravy (see recipe)
1 cup of red wine

This is really old line New Orleans cooking. I like to think that some wonderful Italian, way back when, was into stuffing. They stuffed eggs, they stuffed artichokes, why not figure out a way to stuff meat? That's my own personal conjecture. Either way, it's really good stuff!

The first thing you do is to get a meat mallet and pound the steak until it is one quarter of an inch thick. Try to do this so that you end up with eight pieces, eight inches by eight inches or something close to that. Keep in mind that you are pounding down the meat in order to stuff and roll them up. Set the meat aside when you are done. You could make smaller ones if you like, but I like them big. Use your own judgment for whomever you are feeding.

In a bowl, mix together the breadcrumbs, salt, fresh-ground pepper, cheese, garlic, hardboiled eggs, and basil leaves. Begin adding the olive oil, and put in a little at a time until the mixture is moist and starts to clump together. Don't just pour it all in there, because you will not need it all; plus, you will need one-half cup to brown the steak.

Once you have it to the texture that you like, evenly spread it out onto each piece of steak. Be generous, there will be plenty. Leave a little space around the edges. Now roll them up one at a time and secure them with toothpicks to hold them together. You could use butcher's twine if you like, but tooth-picks will do. Use colored toothpicks; they are easier to find when you are through cooking.

Now get out a big pot that you can cover and put the rest of your olive oil into it. Heat it up, and then put the rolled up steaks into it. Brown them on all sides and remove to a plate. Deglaze the pan with the red wine and scrape all of the brown tasty bits off of the bottom. Put your Basic Tomato Gravy (see recipe) into the pot and mix in. Heat it up, and then put the steaks into the pot and cover. Put it on a low fire and cook for one hour or until the meat is tender enough to cut easily. Taste-test it while you are cooking. Who will know?

Serve over fettuccini noodles. You might even want to sprinkle a little more Parmigiano-Reggiano on top. One more thing: don't forget to take the toothpicks out after the steaks are cooked. You wouldn't want your guests to encounter the toothpicks while they are in the process of eating instead of after they eat. Not a good thing!

Venison Tenderloin Marsala

1 pound of venison tenderloin (back strap)
1 1/2 cups of Marsala wine
8 ounces of beef stock
1 cup of flour
6 tablespoons of olive oil
5 tablespoons of butter (unsalted)
2 tablespoons of shallots (finely chopped)
1 clove of garlic (finely chopped)
Salt
Fresh-ground pepper

You can make this dish with veal instead. Actually, it is normally made with veal, but I like to use venison when I can get it. If I make it at home, I use veal. When I was at the firehouse, a lot of guys would deer hunt. Sometimes they would bring in a nice back strap of venison, and I would use it in place of veal. Sometimes we did a combo of both.

First, take the venison and cut it into about one-quarter-inch-wide pieces. Once that is done, place each piece, one at a time, between sheets of waxed paper and pound them down with a meat mallet. You are just trying to flatten them out a bit without making them paper-thin. You want some substance, and you don't want your substance too thin. Just pound them until their width is increased by half. After that is done, salt and fresh-ground pepper each piece on each side and set aside.

In a large frying pan, put three tablespoons of the olive oil and two tablespoons of the butter. Heat it up, and when the butter is melted, dredge each piece of venison through the flour. Shake off the excess. Now fry the venison in the pan for a minute or two on both sides. Cook until the flour coating is nicely browned. Put the finished pieces on paper towels to drain. When you are halfway done, you will probably be out of oil and butter. Add two more tablespoons of olive oil and two more tablespoons of butter. Finish frying your venison, and keep it on a plate covered with paper towels nearby.

In the pan, add the last tablespoon of olive oil and heat it up. Now add the shallots. Cook for a minute, and then add the garlic. Cook another minute, and then deglaze with the wine. Cook to reduce by half then add the beef stock. Reduce this to your desired thickness, and add the last tablespoon of butter. It should not be thick but more of a runny constancy. Mix it all together, and then put the meat back into the sauce. It is already cooked so you are just trying to heat the meat up.

Serve this with some simple buttered noodles on the side. It's a "can't miss" hit!

If You Can't Stand the Heat

Fried Meatballs and Gravy with Orzo

1 pound of ground beef
1 pound of ground pork
1 pound of ground veal
3 cups of day old bread (crust removed and cut into small pieces)
2 cups of olive oil (plus three tablespoons)
2 cups of whole milk
5 eggs
2 cups of plain breadcrumbs
3/4 cup of onion (finely chopped)
3 cloves of garlic (finely chopped)
1/4 cup of parsley (finely chopped)
Fresh buffalo mozzarella slices (one per meatball)
Orzo (cooked as per instructions on the box)
Salt and fresh-ground pepper (to taste)
3 quarts of Your Basic Tomato Gravy (see recipe)

Over the years, I met so many firefighters of Italian descent it isn't even funny. Every one of them had an old family recipe handed down from their grandmother's grandmother. There was this one old guy from years ago who made the best meatballs I ever had. This is his recipe. He wasn't one for giving out secrets, especially old family ones. He would give you the recipe but always leave something out. He was so clever. Luckily he always left out a different ingredient every time he gave out the recipe. His cleverness eventually led me to this. His grandmother would not be amused.

The very first thing that needs to be done is to take the three tablespoons of olive oil and sauté the onions until translucent. Next, you add the garlic and cook for one minute. Remove from the fire, and then drain this mixture in a strainer. Put the strained onions and garlic in a bowl with all of the meats. Have your tomato gravy hot and ready to go in a big enough pot to hold it plus the meatballs.

Soak the bread in the milk for about fifteen minutes. While it's soaking, mix the meats together with the sautéed onions and garlic, the parsley, and a pinch of salt and fresh-ground pepper. Now squeeze the milk out of the bread and add the bread to the meat bowl. Make sure that you break the bread into little pieces before you put it into the meat mixture, otherwise you'll have big chunks in the middle of your meatball.

Next put in the eggs. Mix by hand, and try not to mash too much. If you mix it and squeeze the mixture too much it will make for very dense meatballs. Try to just fold all of it together while mixing thoroughly.

Now take the mixture and form it into whatever size meatballs you like. I personally like to make them large. Two to a serving is perfect for me. This recipe makes about a dozen big boys. That's over a quarter of a pound apiece. I know it sounds like a lot, but if you can handle a quarter pounder with cheese, you can handle one of these.

Once you have them all rolled out, begin to heat up the two cups of olive oil in a pan. Roll the meatballs in the breadcrumbs to cover each one, and then fry them in the oil. You are just trying to brown the outside, but you are trying to brown the entire outside. You are not trying to cook them completely—that comes later. Roll them in the oil so all sides are browned and then remove them to paper towels to drain. Once they are drained, put them in the hot tomato gravy pot and cook covered on a low fire for thirty minutes. Now the meatballs are cooked. You can do this ahead of time and keep it warm until you are ready to serve.

What you do next is to get out a big casserole dish, maybe even two depending on the size of your casserole dish. Line up as many meatballs in the dish as possible. Next, pour enough gravy into the dish so that the meatballs are covered a little more than halfway up the meatball. Now place a good slice of mozzarella cheese on top of each meatball. Slide your casserole dish under a broiler until the cheese slightly browns. Remove and put a portion of the cooked orzo on a plate. Put the meatballs and gravy on for each serving. Sometimes I throw on a little shredded fresh basil if I have some left over. If there is any gravy left over, it freezes well!

Note: To make it a little bit more authentic Italian, when you are making the meatballs, put a piece of fresh mozzarella inside of each. Nothing major, just a marble sized piece so that when someone goes to eat the meatball he or she will find a nice surprise inside. Not only is it more authentic Italian, it's also kind of like eating a meatball Cracker Jack. Those of you who are old enough will know what I mean!

If You Can't Stand the Heat

Veal Parmesan with Mac and Cheese

Veal cutlets:
6 veal cutlets
2 cups of Italian breadcrumbs
2 eggs
1 cup of milk
2 cups of flour
1 teaspoon of flashover seasoning
1 cup of olive oil for frying
Salt and fresh-ground pepper to taste

Sauce:
4 cloves of garlic (finely chopped)
2 medium onions (finely chopped)
48 ounces of San Marzano tomatoes (broken up)
1 tablespoon of tomato paste
1 tablespoon of dried Italian seasonings
1/2 cup of olive oil
Pinch of sugar
2 cups of beef stock
Salt and fresh-ground pepper to taste

Before baking:
2 cups of Parmigiano-Reggiano cheese (freshly grated)

After baking:
Mamoo Mac and Cheese (see recipe)

One of our favorite places to eat lunch is a place in St. Bernard called Rocky and Carlos. They serve huge portions of veal Parmesan on top of their macaroni and cheese. This is basically our homage to a wonderful neighborhood eatery.

In a good-sized pan (that has a cover), heat up the olive oil for the sauce. Now add the onions and cook until they are translucent. Now add the garlic and cook for a minute or two. Next add the tomato paste and cook until it slightly browns. After that you put in the San Marzano tomatoes and cook for five minutes.

Now pour in the beef stock, Italian seasonings, sugar, salt, and fresh-ground pepper. Cook covered for sixty minutes, uncovered for ninety minutes, and then set it aside but kept warm. This uncovered time is approximate. You basically want to cook it to the thickness that you desire. The ninety-minute time is what I use. That will generally give me a thick and rich sauce to complement the veal. You can do this ahead of time and keep it warm.

Put the olive oil (for frying) in the veal cutlet portion of the recipe into a frying pan, and bring it up to heat. You guessed it; this is to cook your veal cutlets. Aren't you the clever one?

Go to cutlet ingredients. Now get three bowls lined up side by side. In the first, put the flour. In the second, the eggs and milk beaten together. In the third, the breadcrumbs. Season the flour with a teaspoon of FOS. One at a time, put the veal into the flour, shake off the excess. Now into the egg wash, followed by the Italian breadcrumbs. Shake off the excess, and then place into the hot olive oil. Fry until golden brown on both sides, and then remove to paper towels to drain. Salt and fresh-ground pepper to taste. Continue the process until all are finished.

Get a large baking dish. Place the cooked breaded cutlets into the dish and cover with your tomato gravy. Now sprinkle the two cups of Parmigiano-Reggiano cheese on top. Bake in the oven at 325 degrees for thirty minutes.

To serve, put a healthy portion of Mamoo Mac and Cheese (see recipe) on the plate. Now spoon on a generous portion of gravy followed by a piece of veal. That's it!

If You Can't Stand the Heat

Veal Stuffed Bell Peppers

6 medium-sized bell peppers
2 cups of bread
3 cups of milk
1 medium onion (finely chopped)
2 cloves of garlic (finely chopped)
1/4 cup of celery (finely chopped)
1/4 pound of pancetta (cut into small pieces)
2 teaspoons of flashover seasoning
2 cups of Parmigiano-Reggiano cheese (freshly grated)
1 pound of ground veal
Salt and fresh-ground pepper to taste

This recipe is for a half dozen peppers, provided they are smaller peppers. If you buy huge peppers, you may only get four. If you want this for an appetizer, use small ones. If this is for a meal, use larger peppers. It's your choice.

Cut the tops off of the peppers. Clean out the insides of seeds, membranes, and make it hollow. Place them in boiling water for four minutes, and then remove. Drain them and dry them and set aside.

Break up the bread and soak it in the milk for about thirty minutes. While it is soaking, fry the pancetta as you would bacon. Once it is crispy, remove it and place on a paper towel to drain. Now put your onions and celery into the drippings and one teaspoon of the FOS. Cook until the onions are translucent. Now add the garlic and cook for another minute or two. Add the ground veal, and cook until the meat is browned and almost all of the liquid is gone. Now would be a good time to turn your oven on to 375 degrees. That way it has time to preheat while you are finishing the peppers.

Once the meat is browned, squeeze the milk out of the bread, break it up as much as you can, and put it into the pan with the meat. Add the other teaspoon of FOS along with the pancetta. Mix well and cook until it is all warmed up. Taste for salt and fresh-ground pepper, and add what you need. Now mix in one cup of the Parmigiano-Reggiano.

Stuff the mixture into the peppers. Don't fill them all the way to the top. Leave a little room to put the other cup of Reggiano cheese on so that it will not overflow. Top the peppers with the rest of the cheese that you have, evenly distributed on each pepper. Place them into a baking dish, and then add enough water to make it about one half inch in the bottom of the pan. Put this into the oven and cook for twenty to twenty-five minutes.

Your peppers are done and will eagerly be consumed by whomever you have decided to bestow this blessing upon. I hope I'm invited!

Note: Your peppers should have golden brown cheese on top. It varies with different ovens. You can also add a little tomato sauce on top of your stuffing before you put the cheese on. That will give it a little bit of a difference in taste but also delicious.

Simple Sizzling Steak

4 steaks (1 pound each, preferably thick rib eyes)
Salt (kosher)
Fresh-ground pepper
Garlic powder
12 tablespoons of unsalted butter (that is 3 tablespoons for each steak)
2 teaspoons of dried parsley flakes (1/2 teaspoon for each steak)

Who doesn't love a good steak? The thicker the better. If I could fit a cow on my grill, I would!

Sprinkle a little salt, fresh-ground pepper, and garlic powder on each steak. Make sure you do it on both sides. After that, put the butter in a pan along with the parsley flakes and bring it up to heat. Melt the butter and mix with the flakes. Put it aside for now.

Preheat your grill, and then put the meat on. Cook one side (depending on the thickness of your steak) for just a few minutes. If you have a hot enough fire and can put a little char on that side, do it. Flip the steaks over and cook them until you have reached the desired temperature that you or your guests like to eat your steak. Only turn the steak over once, and don't press down on it with a spatula. You want to keep those juices in there.

I personally like to take my steak off when it is about 145 degrees internal temperature. That is rare. Use a meat thermometer to tell unless you are one of those people who are able to ascertain the temperature by feel. I never could. Besides, nobody likes his or her steaks being manhandled.

While you are grilling, turn on the broiler in your oven. Get it hot!

From this point on, I like to use ovenproof platters for the steaks. I take the steak from the grill and put it on an individual platter. After that, I take one-quarter of the butter/parsley mixture and pour it over the steak. Now slide it under the broiler until the butter slightly browns.

That's all there is to it. Great steaks bubbling in butter... yummy!

Note: Make sure when you serve these that you tell whoever will be eating it that the platter is hot... really hot. I also like to use these silicone mats on the table to put the platters on. They can stand up to 500 degrees, and they keep the hot platters from messing up your table. There is nothing worse than having to replace a table after eating just one meal. I suppose there are worse things, but that ranks right up there to me.

Daube and Spaghetti

4-pound bottom round roast
12 ounces of bacon (reserve 4 strips for roast)
3 cups of onions (coarsely chopped)
1 cup of celery (coarsely chopped)
2 cups of carrots (coarsely chopped)
1 cup of bell pepper (coarsely chopped)
8 small cloves of garlic (peeled and whole)
8 small pieces of parsley leaves (cleaned and whole)
2 tablespoons of flashover seasoning
2 cups of red wine (Cabernet)
4 cups of low sodium beef broth
1 28-ounce can of San Marzano tomatoes (drained and chopped)
1 teaspoon of fresh thyme (finely chopped)
1 teaspoon of fresh oregano (finely chopped)
1 4-inch long sprig of fresh rosemary
4 hardboiled eggs (peeled and left whole)

Daube is a French word meaning "to braise in wine and or stock." Some say it was derived from a Spanish word meaning the same thing. I say it's just a word that means good!

The first thing you do is preheat your oven to 375 degrees. You're off to a great start.

Now you must prepare the meat. Take the two tablespoons of FOS and rub it all over the roast. Next, cut up the four bacon strips into eight individual pieces. Just cut them in half. Now place a clove of garlic and a piece of parsley on the bacon strip and roll it up. Repeat with all eight. One at a time, make slits into the roast, and stuff each one with the bacon, garlic, and parsley balls. Try to get a little of the FOS in the holes along with it. Place the roast on the side for now.

Take what is left of your twelve ounces of bacon and fry it in a big Dutch oven (one you can cover). When it is done, remove the bacon, but leave the bacon drippings in the pot. Use the bacon to make a BLT sandwich for lunch because you won't need it here, just the drippings.

While the drippings are still hot, put the roast in the pan and brown it on all sides. Once you have it nice and browned, take it out of the pot and set it on a plate for now.

Into the pot, put the onions, bell pepper, celery, and carrots. When you do this, it will cook in the oil and loosen all of the tasty brown bits from the bottom of the pan. Stir your veggies around and heat until the onions are translucent and wilted. That's when you add the aromatics. That would be your thyme, rosemary, and oregano. Stir them around and cook for another two minutes. Now add the tomatoes and cook for two minutes.

Deglaze what's left with the wine, and bring the whole thing back up to heat. Pour in the beef broth, and then carefully slide the roast back into the pot. Cover and cook in the oven for three and a half to four hours. Baste it every so often with the braising liquid. If you like, you can turn it over on occasion since the roast will probably be sticking out of the liquid.

After the time is up, take the pot out of the oven and remove the roast to a cutting board. Carve your roast into whatever thickness you desire. I like them at about one-half-inch thick each. Check your gravy for salt and fresh-ground pepper. Add it if you need it. Remove the sprig of rosemary and discard.

Now place the roast slices back into the gravy and cover. Put it back in the oven for another thirty to forty-five minutes. Remove the pot from the oven and put the hardboiled eggs into the pot to soak. Let the pot sit for one hour before you serve it.

Ladle the sauce out over spaghetti and with a big chunk of some crusty bread and butter on the side. Slice up the eggs and serve a little on top of the meat. We also like to top it off with a little grated Parmigiano-Reggiano cheese. Or even a lot of cheese. Your call!

If You Can't Stand the Heat

Paneed Veal Pasta Rosa

When I first heard the name of this dish, I thought he was saying Ponderosa instead of pasta rosa. I thought it might be a Bonanza thing. You know … like hitting the Bonanza. Either way, cook this and make Hop Sing proud.

Veal:
1 pound of veal (shoulder chops will do)
1 cup of all-purpose flour
1 cup of olive oil
1 cup of milk
2 eggs
2 cups of Italian breadcrumbs
1 teaspoon of flashover seasoning

Mix the eggs and milk together in a bowl.

Butterfly the chops; only go all the way through until each chop yields two pieces. Pound down each piece of the veal with a meat mallet until they are about one-fourth inch thick. Continue until all of the meat is done.

Mix the FOS in the flour. Dredge the meat through the flour. Shake off the excess. Now dredge the meat through the egg and milk wash and then through the breadcrumbs. Shake off the excess.

Get the olive oil hot and fry the meat until brown on both sides. You have paneed veal! Put finished meat on the side on paper towels. When all of the meat is done, put aside and keep warm.

Sauce:

6 ounces of tasso (cut into very small cubes)

2 tablespoons of olive oil

1/2 cup of onions (finely chopped)

4 cloves of garlic (finely chopped)

1 1/2 cups of grated Parmigiano-Reggiano cheese

1 cup of Roma tomatoes (diced into small cubes)

1/2 teaspoon of fresh thyme (chopped fine)

1/2 teaspoon of fresh oregano (chopped fine)

1 teaspoon of fresh basil (chopped fine)

3 cups of whipping cream

4 tablespoons of unsalted butter (for sautéing)

2 additional tablespoons of unsalted butter (for later)

1 heaping tablespoon of tomato paste

1 cup of white wine

1/2 teaspoon of salt

1/2 teaspoon of fresh-ground pepper

12 ounces of fettuccini noodles (cooked al dente)

In a large frying pan, heat up the olive oil and then add the tasso. Cook this for about five minutes or until the tasso is slightly browned. Now melt the four tablespoons of butter in the pan one at a time. When that is incorporated, put in the onions, thyme, basil, and oregano. Cook on a medium heat until the onions are soft and wilted. This should be about four to five minutes. Put in the garlic and cook for one minute more. Sprinkle in the salt and fresh-ground pepper. Next, add the tomatoes, tomato paste, and blend together. Cook for an additional three minutes.

Deglaze the pan with the white wine, and reduce by half. This could be anywhere from five to eight minutes. Add the additional two tablespoons of butter and blend it in with the dish. Pour in the whipping cream and bring it up to a simmer. Cook this for approximately eight to ten minutes, or until it reaches your desired thickness. You are looking for a reduction that will be not too thick and at the same

If You Can't Stand the Heat

time not too runny. If it gets too thick to cover all of your pasta, just add a little more whipping cream and blend it in.

When that point is reached, add the cooked (al dente) fettuccini noodles. Mix well until all of the noodles are covered with sauce. Sprinkle the cheese on top and mix again. Now get ready to feast!

Put a couple of pieces of the paneed veal on a plate. Put some of the pasta and sauce on top and serve in individual portions. Make sure there is plenty of crusty Italian bread or slices of French bread on hand!

Note: If you like, you can substitute four ounces of pancetta instead of the tasso. You just do everything the same way except that you fry the pancetta until slightly crispy (it is after all a kind of bacon), and you have to watch out for the salt. The pancetta is pretty salty by itself. If you choose to go this route, you will lose the depth of flavor and smokiness that comes from the tasso, but it will still be a great dish nonetheless.

Rosemary Rack of Lamb in Demi glace

2 racks of lamb (one pound each)

4 basil leaves (chopped)

2 6-inch long stems of fresh rosemary (leaves removed from stem & chopped)

1 6-inch long stem of fresh oregano (leaves removed from stem & chopped)

3 cloves of garlic (finely chopped)

4 tablespoons of olive oil

1 cup of red wine

Salt

Fresh-ground pepper

2 tablespoons of butter

2 heaping tablespoons of roasted veal demi glace

1 cup of warm water (to mix with the demi glace)

The first thing you need to know is that you can buy the demi glace on the Internet. You can also buy it at some specialty markets. Your third option is to make it yourself, but that takes many hours of work. It's just easier to buy it already made. I prefer to use Aromont, but there are many others to choose from.

The two racks of lamb should have eight bones in each rack. Cut them in half so that you have four racks with four bones each (each enough for a serving). Take the basil, rosemary, oregano, and garlic, and mix together. Take all four racks of the lamb and place them in a bowl. Rub down the meat with two tablespoons of olive oil; then take the mixed herbs and spread them over the lamb racks to cover as much as possible with the fresh seasonings. Salt and fresh-ground pepper and place all in a Ziploc bag. Now pour in a half-cup of red wine, mix, and marinate overnight.

When it's time to cook, take a skillet and add the last two tablespoons of olive oil. Heat the olive oil on high heat on the stove. Sear the meat on all sides. Try to brown it nicely without burning it. The idea is to sear it until the meat is sealed. Remove the skillet from the heat, take the meat, and put it on a

If You Can't Stand the Heat

preheated grill. Insert a meat thermometer into one rack. Cook until the center is 145 degrees. Remove all of the meat from the grill and let it rest.

While the meat is cooking on the grill, go back to your skillet and heat it again. Deglaze with the other half-cup of red wine then reduce by half and incorporate two tablespoons of butter. Mix the demi glace in the warm water until it is dissolved. You can do this ahead of time. Add it to the pan. Reduce by half or to the thickness you desire. When the meat is done on the grill and has rested for five minutes, plate them up and serve with a generous portion of the sauce.

Note: I always served this with roasted garlic mashed potatoes. There is usually plenty enough gravy that spills off of the lamb. Somehow it always seems to quietly work its way over to the potatoes. I think it has to do with the magnetic attraction of potatoes and meat but that is not based on any scientific fact. It is purely speculation on my part.

Chuck Pot Roast/Debris and Gravy

3-pound chuck roast
4 medium onions (chopped)
1 cup of bell pepper (chopped)
1/2 cup of celery (chopped fine)
8 cloves of garlic (4 cut in half to stuff and 4 cloves chopped fine)
1/4 cup of vegetable oil
1 cup of dark brown roux
32 ounces of beef stock (room temperature)
1/2 teaspoon of salt
1 teaspoon of fresh-ground pepper
1 tablespoon of flashover seasoning

Make slits in the roast all over and stuff with eight pieces of garlic (four cloves cut in half). Mix salt, fresh-ground pepper, and FOS, and sprinkle on meat. Rub it in well. Get the oil hot in a Dutch oven. Put in the meat and sear on all sides. It will make little good brown tasty bits on the bottom of the pot. Remove the meat from pot and put it aside for the moment.

There should be a little oil left on the bottom of the pot that didn't stick to the roast. Now add the roux and scrape all of the little brown goody bits off of the bottom of the pot. Heat it all up until the roux is melted and warm; then add the onions, celery, and bell pepper. Cook until the onions are translucent. Add the garlic and cook for another two minutes. Start pouring in the beef stock a little at a time and blend it all together.

Put the meat back into the pot. Cover and cook on low fire for two hours. Uncover and cook for another ninety minutes. The actual time will depend on different factors. Either way, after the allowed time is up, stick a fork into the meat and twist it. If the meat breaks away easily, it is done. If not, cook it a little longer until it is tender. Check for salt and fresh-ground pepper, and if it needs any, add it now.

If You Can't Stand the Heat

Once your time is up or the meat is cooked to your liking, take the meat out, slice it, and put it back into the gravy and cover. Let it sit for thirty minutes and allow the meat to absorb some of the gravy. That's it. Serve with a side of mashed potatoes or cooked white rice. These are only suggestions of course. Serve it with whatever you like. This gravy will make an old shoe taste good.

Debris:

Making debris is basically the next step in breaking the meat down into very small pieces. After you have finished cooking the roast as indicated above, remove the roast and gravy and put it all into a Crock-Pot on low for twelve to fifteen hours. It may not take that long, and then again it might take a bit longer; it all depends upon the meat itself. Just check on it. Stir it often so it doesn't stick to the bottom of the Crock-Pot. The idea is to cook it until it completely falls apart in the gravy. That is what we here in New Orleans call Debris.

I like to serve this on hot biscuits with butter for breakfast. We also like it over mashed potatoes. You can try that or you could try the old shoe. Use your own discretion.

Roasted Garlic Butter Steak

4 filet mignon (at least 2 1/2 inches thick)
Garlic Butter (see recipe, but leave out parsley)
2 tablespoons of butter (for the sauce)
2 tablespoons of olive oil
Pinch of salt (for the garlic butter)
Pinch of fresh-ground pepper (for the garlic butter)
Fresh-ground pepper (for the steaks)
2 ounces of red wine
1 heaping tablespoon of roasted veal demi glace
1 cup of water

These are big steaks for guys who love big steaks. That would be me! We ate a lot of steak at the firehouse. One guy I worked with used to eat them almost raw. We don't talk about him; we just stayed out of his way.

The very first thing that you need to do is to prepare your Garlic Butter (see recipe, but leave out the parsley because it clogs the injector). Add pinch of salt and pepper.

Take your Cajun injector and fill it with the garlic butter. The meat should be chilled from the fridge. The processed butter should be about as thick as a cake batter but not runny like melted butter. If it's melted it will just squirt out of the other side of the meat. Inject the garlic butter in equal parts into the center of each steak. Move the needle from side to side while you are injecting so you will get the maximum amount of butter into the steak. If some runs out, don't worry about it. Put fresh-ground pepper on each and place in a Ziploc bag. Refrigerate the steaks for the rest of the day or overnight if possible.

It's time to grill! Start by getting your grill hot and ready to use. Back to the kitchen, use a large frying pan and heat up olive oil on high heat. Place the steaks in and sear the meat on all sides. Remove the meat when seared, take the pan off the fire, and save the contents in the pan for later.

If You Can't Stand the Heat

Put the steaks onto the grill and put the meat thermometer into one. Some people can feel with their fingers when a steak is done. I don't happen to be one of those people. That's why I use a thermometer. Unless you are one of those magical people, I suggest you use one too. Cook the steaks to the desired temperature, and remove from grill. Let them sit and rest while you prepare the sauce.

While your steaks are resting, add the tablespoon of demi glace to the water in a small pot and heat to dissolve and mix. You could also do this ahead of time (while the steaks are cooking) and help speed up the process.

Go back to that frying pan you had earlier and put it on medium heat. Add the two tablespoons of butter. Heat to barely brown the butter, and then pour in the wine. Deglaze with this and scrape the bottom of the pan. Add the demi glace mix and reduce to desired thickness. Pour over the meat and serve.

Note: You can actually make the whole finished sauce while the steaks are grilling. I find that if I do this instead of doing it while the steaks are resting, guys will come into the kitchen and snatch a steak before they have had time for a proper rest. It's just a courtesy to the steak. It's been through a lot and deserves to be treated properly and with respect!

Smoked Brisket with Horseradish Cream

5-pound brisket (after trimming fat)
6 cloves of garlic (whole)
2 tablespoons of garlic (finely chopped)
32 ounces of beef stock
2 tablespoons of flashover seasoning
3 tablespoons of bacon fat
1 twelve-ounce bottle of dark beer
1 tablespoon of tomato paste
1 large onion (roughly chopped)
2 bay leaves

If at all possible, this brisket should be stuffed with garlic, covered with bacon fat and spices, and refrigerated overnight. I tell you this now so that you are not half way through the recipe and have to say, "Wow, I should have started this yesterday." If you can't marinate it overnight, at least try to do it for a few hours.

Rinse off the brisket and pat dry. Trim off the excess fat to about one half-inch thick left on the brisket. Make small incisions all over with a paring knife and insert the whole cloves of garlic into the openings. If they are too big, cut them in half and make more incisions. The garlic won't mind. Rub the outside with two tablespoons of the bacon fat, and then sprinkle on the FOS. The fat will help it stick to the brisket. Rub it in really well, and place it in a big Ziploc bag then slide it into the refrigerator. Keep it this way overnight if possible.

When you are ready to cook, set up your smoker to use indirect heat. That would be placing your coals on one side and the meat on the other so that the coals are not directly beneath the brisket. Ideally you would use a smoker with a separate smoke chamber from the coals. With that said, rev up the smoker and get it going.

If You Can't Stand the Heat

Heat up a large Dutch oven until it's really hot. Put in the last tablespoon of bacon fat and melt it. Take the brisket and sear it on all sides until it browns on all of those sides. Take the Dutch oven off of the fire. Remove the brisket and place it in a shallow pan that has been lined with aluminum foil. Place this pan with the brisket on the smoker (fat side up), add your wood, and close the lid of the smoker. Let it smoke for about four hours. I like to use hickory chips that have been soaked for an hour for the smoking wood.

While that is happening, take that same Dutch oven that has all of that good stuff in it from the browning of the meat and bring it up to a medium heat. Toss in the onions and sauté for a couple of minutes, scraping the bottom as you go to release any little brown bits from the bottom. Next add the tablespoon of tomato paste. Cook for another couple of minutes or until the tomato paste browns slightly. Add the two tablespoons of chopped garlic and cook for one minute. Don't burn the goody bits that are stuck to the bottom of the pan. If they won't come off while you are cooking and start to get too dark, just use a splash of beef stock to loosen them up. Now pour in the beef stock and the beer. Mix it all in well. Simmer this until it reduces by half. You'll have plenty of time to do this, so don't rush. The brisket will be on the smoker for four hours. When your stock is done, remove from the fire; add the bay leaves and set aside covered.

Preheat your oven to 325 degrees. After the four hours are up, take the brisket from the smoker and put it in the Dutch oven down in the gravy. If there are any drippings from the meat left in the foil in the smoking pan, pour them in too. Place in the oven covered for another three hours. Baste about every hour with the juices. I also like to flip the meat over in the pot at these times.

If you can stick a fork in the brisket and twist it without any resistance, it is done. If it isn't done after the three hours, just put it back in and cook it a little more. After it reaches that point (finished cooking), you need to take it out of the juices and set it on a cutting board. It should be pretty much falling apart at this point. Let it rest on the cutting board for about twenty minutes, and then slice it up thin. Remove the bay leaves. Take your brisket slices and put them back into the juices that are left and cover the pot again. Let it sit for about a half hour covered while the meat absorbs the juices. Heat and eat!

Serve it with Horseradish Cream (see recipe).

Note: If you happen to be feeding some folks from neighboring states that happen to think that their brisket is better, just stick this in their mouths and watch as they become very quiet … unless they happen to chew loud.

Uptown Pesto Pasta

4 large cloves of garlic (finely chopped)
1 pound of shrimp (peeled and deveined)
1/2 cup of olive oil
1/2 cup of white wine
4 tablespoons of butter
1 pint of whipping cream
8 ounces of Fresh Basil Pesto (see recipe)
2 cups of Parmigiano-Reggiano cheese (grated)
1/4 cup of fresh basil (cut chiffonade style)
8 ounces of bow tie pasta (cooked al dente)
Fresh-ground pepper (to taste)
1 cup of either Your Basic Tomato Gravy (see recipe) or a good bottled spaghetti sauce

I have been making a pesto and pasta sauce for years. I used elbow macaroni so all of the sauce would have a place to hide out until my mouth found it. Then I went to a great place in New Orleans called Semolina's. They used to make something really similar but with bow tie pasta and used a tomato sauce for a base. That's when I decided to change those two things in the recipe. You can do it any way you want, but I like this way much better.

Use a big non-stick frying pan and heat up the olive oil on medium heat. When that is done, lower the heat and add the garlic. Cook for two minutes; then add the white wine. Cook for an additional five minutes or until almost all of the wine liquid is gone.

Turn the heat back up for a moment then whisk in the whipping cream. Cook for ten to twelve minutes to reduce the mixture until it thickens up. Just remember to stir it a lot for those few minutes to prevent burning it. About five to six minutes after adding the cream, slowly add the butter a tablespoon at a time. Blend it in thoroughly. Now whisk in the pesto and the fresh-ground pepper and then blend. Cook this for another three to five minutes.

If You Can't Stand the Heat

Toss in the shrimp, and cook for another three to five minutes or until the shrimp is barely cooked through. Put the pasta in and stir to heat it back up. Sprinkle the cheese over it all and mix it in with a wooden spoon. Turn off the fire.

On your plate you will spoon on a little of the spaghetti sauce. Use just enough to put a thin layer on the bottom of the plate. Spoon the pesto shrimp and cream sauce on top and garnish with the ribbons of basil. Mix and eat! Share this with three others, or be greedy and eat it all yourself. Once you taste it you might be tempted. You remind me so much of … well, me.

Note: If you are ever in New Orleans, stop by Semolina's. It's a great place for pasta. Like I said, I made this dish, which is similar to theirs, for years, but I never thought of putting tomato sauce in it. I borrowed that idea from them. I hope they don't mind.

Low Fat Lo Mein

Wok Fry:
1 pound of headless fresh shrimp (peeled and rinsed clean)
1/4 pound of fresh green beans
1/2 cup of bean sprouts
10 ounces of baby corns
1 teaspoon of sesame oil
1 1/2 cups of chicken stock
1/2 pound of wide pasta ribbons (cooked al dente, save 1/2 cup of pasta cooking water)
1/2 cup of pasta water
1/2 teaspoon of Chinese five-spice powder
1 small onion (chopped fine)
1/2 cup of green onion tops (chopped fine)
2 cloves of garlic (chopped fine)
1 teaspoon of fresh ginger (chopped fine)
1 tablespoon of soy sauce
Salt and fresh-ground pepper to taste

Sauce:
Leftover chicken stock (from the blanching)
1 teaspoon of cornstarch
1/2 cup of warm water

I was looking for something a little light to cook for dinner one day, and I sort of stumbled upon this. The shrimp was a sure thing. I walked around the store and just grabbed the rest because it was there. Impulse buying at its best!

If You Can't Stand the Heat

First, put the chicken stock, five-spice, and the green beans into a pot. You want to heat it up to a simmer and then just blanch the beans. You don't want them too soft. I like them with a bit of a crunch still in them. Remove the beans to a bowl and set aside for now. Save the stock.

Mix the cornstarch and warm water together until the cornstarch dissolves. Slowly add this to the leftover chicken stock and simmer until it thickens slightly. I like it to be able to coat the back of a spoon. This might take a while, so do it before you start the stir-fry. Set it aside for the moment.

Now heat up the sesame oil in a wok. Next toss in the shrimp and cook them until they are cooked through. Remove them from the wok and set aside for now. They will leave behind a lot of water. That's all right. It is full of low-fat flavor.

Add the onions, green onions, garlic, and ginger to the wok. Put them into any remaining shrimp juice and start to stir-fry them. Cook them until the water has evaporated, and then they will begin to stick to the bottom of the pan. That is when you want to add the pasta cooking water. Cook on a low fire until the onions are translucent. By that time, all of the water will have evaporated.

Put the shrimp back in along with the bean sprouts, the green beans, baby corn, soy sauce, and the pasta. Now pour in your chicken stock sauce. Mix thoroughly and make sure everything is covered and heated through. Salt and fresh-ground pepper to taste. Serve it up.

Note: This will make four relatively decent-sized servings or two fireman-sized servings.

I have also done this using other ingredients. Try leaving out the corn and use water chestnuts. Throw in some broccoli. Mix and match. Despite what you have been told your entire life ... play with your food!

Stuffed Pork Loin Roulade with Calvados Sauce

Loin and stuffing:

3-pound pork tenderloin

2 slices of applewood smoked bacon

2 teaspoons of fresh thyme (chopped fine, 1 teaspoon for the rice and 1 for the end)

2 tablespoons of fresh sage (chopped fine, 1 tablespoon for the rice and 1 for the end)

1/2 teaspoon of garlic powder

1/4 cup of shallots (chopped fine)

6 ounces of long grain and wild rice

3 cups of chicken stock (2 for the rice and 2 1/2-cup portions for deglazing)

2 ounces of chopped pecans

1 large granny smith apple (peeled, cored, and diced small)

Salt and fresh-ground pepper

2 tablespoons of olive oil (for browning after it is stuffed)

Sauce:

2 tablespoons of chicken demi glace

1/3 cup of Calvados apple Cognac

1/2 cup of white wine

1 cup of chicken stock

The hardest thing about making this dish is cutting the meat, and that really isn't all too difficult. Rinse and pat dry your loin and set it on a cutting board. Start by making an incision right down the middle lengthways that is about an inch deep. Turn the knife to the right, and make a lengthwise incision again about one inch deep. This will lay it open just a little. Now turn the knife to the left side of the incision you just made and cut along that edge. Keep making these incisions on the left until the loin is about

If You Can't Stand the Heat

one inch thick and flat. That is your goal…from round loin to an inch-thick, flat piece of meat. Salt and fresh-ground pepper on each side, and set aside in a Ziploc bag in the fridge.

Loin and stuffing:

For the rice, I use a boxed wild rice, but I use chicken stock instead of water, and I don't use the seasoning packet. Put the rice in a pot and add two cups of the chicken stock. Add one tablespoon of sage, one teaspoon of thyme, the garlic powder, and a pinch of salt and fresh-ground pepper. Bring to a boil and cover. Lower the fire and cook for twenty-five minutes. Let it sit covered for ten minutes after that so the rice will absorb all of the stock.

In a large frying pan, fry down the bacon until it is crispy. Remove them from the pan and set on paper towels to drain. Once they are cooled, break them up into bacon bits. Add the pecans into the pan and toast for a minute. Now add the shallots and cook them for a minute. Next add the apples and the bacon bits. Deglaze the pan with one half cup of chicken stock. Cook until the liquid is gone. Now add the cooked rice, the last tablespoon of sage, the last teaspoon of thyme, and mix well. Check for salt and fresh-ground pepper. Let your stuffing cool.

Take out your pork loin and lay it flat on a board. Spread the stuffing evenly across the pork loin. Leave about a one-inch space around the edge. Now roll it back up, and you will have a loin stuffed like a pinwheel. Tie it every inch or two with butcher's twine. Make sure you tie off the ends well. You don't want any of your hard-earned stuffing slipping out. Preheat the oven to 350 degrees, and you are ready to go.

I like to use a Dutch oven large enough to hold the loin. Pour the olive oil into the pan and bring it up to a good hot heat. Put your loin inside and brown it all the way around. Pour in the last half-cup of the chicken stock. Cover and put in a meat thermometer that you can read from the outside of the oven. I use a Polder Digital Thermometer with a long wire. If you don't have one, just check it after about forty to forty-five minutes to see if it has hit an internal temperature of 160 degrees.

Once it is at that point, remove it from the oven and from the pan to a cutting board. Let it rest for fifteen minutes before you cut it. Also make sure you cut off the twine that you tied it up with once it cools a bit. Save the drippings in the pot.

Sauce:

I like to make the sauce ahead of time. It will take awhile to reduce this until it thickens up. You can even make it a day ahead and save yourself the trouble of having to do everything at once.

Add all of the sauce ingredients into a pot and slowly simmer until it reduces by one third or until it thickens to your liking. Make sure you completely dissolve the demi glace in the sauce. You don't want any lumps in the sauce, as they are really strong.

When you take the loin out of the roasting pan to rest, pour this sauce mixture into the loin drippings and mix in. Get all of the drippings from the bottom of the pan and the sauce, blend them together, and heat them up.

Cut the loin into one-inch-thick serving slices and drizzle a little sauce on top.

Note: If by chance you should happen to grab a pork loin in a pack that turns out to be two small loins in a pack, don't sweat it. Butterfly them both flat. Put the stuffing on each, and stack them on top of each other. Now roll and tie, and treat it like a large three-pound loin.

If You Can't Stand the Heat

Particularly Potent Pork Powder Boneless Ribs

2 1/2 pounds of boneless pork ribs
1 gallon of water
2 tablespoons of Zatarain's liquid crab boil
2 tablespoons of pork powder
Pork powder:
3 tablespoons of kosher salt
2 tablespoons of fresh-ground pepper
1 tablespoon of garlic powder
2 teaspoons of MSG

Mix all of the spices together to make the pork powder, and use it as a rub for the ribs. You will only use two tablespoons for now. Save the rest for another time. Try it on some chicken. It's good there too.

My "brother from another mother" Miles and I used to make this during football season. Every Sunday we would crank up the pit down at his restaurant in the French Quarter and throw some ribs on it. They were gargantuan good!

Get a large pot and put in the gallon of water. Add the crab boil and bring the water up to a simmer. Place the racks of ribs in the water and bring it back up to a simmer. Cook for twenty minutes and remove the meat to a plate. Let it cool, and then put the pork powder on the meat. Rub it in well, and then place the meat in a plastic Ziploc bag. Refrigerate for at least six hours.

Have your grill ready and hot. Take the ribs out ahead of time to get them to almost room temperature. Put the ribs on the grill and cook for a few minutes on both sides or until they are as done as you personally like them. Some people like them a little more done than others. Just don't leave them on so long as to dry them out. The meat is actually pretty much cooked from the simmering in the water. If your ribs are about one and a half inches thick, they will be slightly pink inside. If they are thinner, they will naturally need less time to cook. All you really want to do is brown the outside of the ribs on the pit. If you are not sure, check them with a meat thermometer. Now let the meat rest for about fifteen minutes before you cut up and serve.

Note: These are not ribs that you eat with a sauce. Their flavor comes from the combo of the zippiness of the crab boil and a savory taste of the rub. So before you start brushing barbeque sauce on them, try them au natural!

Pasta "Bolonaise"

12 ounces of fettuccini noodles
6 tablespoons of butter
4 cloves of garlic (finely chopped)
2 cups of Pecorino Romano cheese (grated)
1 cup of Parmigiano-Reggiano cheese (grated)
1/2 cup of olive oil
4 teaspoons of fresh basil (chopped)
4 teaspoons of fresh oregano (chopped)
1 teaspoon of salt
1 teaspoon of fresh-ground pepper

This isn't the typical Bolonaise sauce that you are probably used to. That particular sauce has meat and tomatoes in it. It isn't even spelled like the part of the country in Italy where Bolognese originated (Bologna). This is a bastardization that was put together by my wife and me. Thus the "bolo" part (our names are Bob and Lori). We usually use this as a side dish instead of a main dish. Well, sometimes we used this as a main dish served with lots of Italian bread and butter. What can I say…gluttons for good stuff!

Boil your pasta until it is al dente, drain. In a large pan, heat up the olive oil and the butter. When it is melted, add the garlic and cook for one minute. Now add the drained pasta and top with salt and fresh-ground pepper. Mix well. Now add the basil and oregano and mix. Add the cheeses and mix well. Serve.

Note: It's so simple…even I can't screw it up!

Stuffed Mirliton

6 mirliton
1 pound of mild Italian sausage
1 pound of ground beef
1 pound of fresh shrimp (peeled, rinsed, and chopped)
1 large onion (chopped)
1/2 cup of bell pepper (chopped)
1/4 cup of celery (chopped)
4 cloves of garlic (chopped)
1 cup of Italian breadcrumbs (for the stuffing)
1/2 cup of Italian breadcrumbs (for dusting the top of the mirliton)
4 tablespoons of butter (2 for the sautéing and 2 for the brushing)
5 teaspoons of flashover seasoning

These little things are called chayote or alligator pears elsewhere. In New Orleans they are called mirliton. No matter what you call them, when they are stuffed, you just call them delicious!

First, you want to slowly boil the mirliton in water until they are fork tender. Once that is done, you need to let them sit in a colander and drain until they are cooled. They will drain for a long time, as they will absorb a huge amount of water while they are boiling. Once they are cooled and drained, you want to cut them in half lengthwise. Remove the seeds and throw them away. That is the seeds, not the mirliton. I only say this because someone was reading my recipe and said, "Why do you throw them away? I thought we were going to eat them."

Using a spoon, scoop the "pulp" of the mirliton out and reserve it in a colander to drain some more (a lot of water in there). The pulp refers to the green insides of the mirliton. It's like scooping out a baked potato down to the skins.

In a very large non-stick frying pan, brown the ground meat, sausage, and one teaspoon of FOS. When that is done, set up a metal colander over a bowl. Pour the meat out of the pan and into the colander. Let it drain into the bowl. Put the meat on the side for now.

There should be lots of juice and fat in the bowl. Pour it back into the frying pan. Add two tablespoons of butter and melt it down. Mix them together and bring it up to heat. Now add the onions, celery, bell pepper, and another teaspoon of FOS, and sauté until the onions are translucent. Now add the garlic and cook for one minute.

Add the drained pulp from the mirliton to the pan and cook for five minutes. Now add the shrimp and another teaspoon of FOS. Cook until the shrimp are pink.

Now add the meat back into the pan. Heat it all up then remove the pot from the fire. Put in the Italian breadcrumbs and another two teaspoons of FOS. Mix thoroughly and let it get cool enough to handle.

Take the mirlitons that you have scooped out and begin to stuff them with the mixture. There will be a lot, so don't be afraid to stuff them full and pile up more into a mound on top. Melt the remaining butter and brush on top of each mirliton. Sprinkle a little of the remaining one half cup of Italian breadcrumbs on top of each. The butter will help make it stick to the stuffing. Put them on an oven tray. Bake them in the oven at 375 degrees for fifteen minutes or until they are browned on top.

Note: If you have any stuffing left over (and you will), cook it the same way but in a casserole dish for anyone who might not want to eat the mirliton shell. Just don't remind them that they are eating the inside pulp. Then again, go ahead and tell them. That will leave more for you!

Rabbit Tchoupitoulas

2 whole rabbits (cut up)
12 ounces of applewood smoked bacon
2 large onions (chopped)
1/2 cup of bell pepper (finely chopped)
1/2 cup of celery (finely chopped)
3 cloves of garlic (finely chopped)
12 ounces of tasso (cut into small pieces)
2 tablespoons of flashover seasoning
64 ounces of chicken stock
1/2 cup of vegetable oil
1/2 cup of flour
1 cup of red wine
Salt and fresh-ground pepper

There are a lot of firemen that hunt. I'm not one of them. I'm just the cook. I once had a vegetarian friend ask me how I could cook and eat a rabbit. I just told him to think of all the lives of all the carrots I just saved. I don't judge; I'm just the cook.

Use the half-cup of oil and the half-cup of flour to make a dark chocolate roux. Remove from the pot and allow it to cool.

Season the rabbit pieces with salt and fresh-ground pepper. Put them aside for now.

In a large pot that you can cover, fry the bacon until crisp and remove. You won't need the bacon, just the bacon fat, so plan on making some BLT's for lunch that day.

Put the rabbit pieces in and fry them in the bacon fat until you slightly brown the pieces. Remove and keep handy. Now add the onions, bell pepper, celery, and one tablespoon of FOS to the pot. Cook the veggies until the onions are translucent. Now add the garlic and cook for two minutes. Next add the tasso and cook for one minute. Now add the wine and mix in. Cook this until almost all of the liquid is gone.

If You Can't Stand the Heat

Now add the other tablespoon of FOS. Mix in and then slowly pour in the stock. Bring it up to a simmer, and then slowly, a little at a time, add the room temperature roux. Once that is mixed in, cover and place over a low fire for one and one half hours.

Put the rabbit pieces in and cover again. Cook the dish for one hour. Uncover and cook for an hour more or until the rabbit is very tender. Serve over cooked white rice.

Note: If you are feeling especially generous, make this a day ahead of time and allow it to completely cool. Take out the rabbit and remove the meat from the bones. Put the meat back into the pot and discard the bones. It's not necessary, but it does make it easier for everyone to eat. I don't do this at the firehouse. They will quite literally suck the meat from the bones. Savages!

Smoky Barbeque Pork Ribs

8 pounds of pork ribs
Dry rub
1 cup of Wendy's Smoky Honey Barbeque Sauce (see recipe)

Dry rub:
1 cup of brown sugar
4 tablespoons of garlic powder
4 tablespoons of onion powder
2 tablespoons of cumin
2 tablespoons of chipotle chile pepper
1/4 cup of paprika
1/4 cup of kosher salt
1/4 cup of packaged (not fresh-ground) black pepper

This recipe is for a lot of ribs done at the same time. Eight pounds of pork ribs is about three racks. Of that, you can cut the racks in half. That means that you can feed about six normal people or three firemen.

Mix all of the ingredients for the dry rub together. I find it easier to put them all in a Ziploc bag. Even a new box of brown sugar will clump together. In a Ziploc bag, you can use your fingers to mash up the little sugar clumps without spilling the rub everywhere.

Rub the rub (not redundant) all over the meat, and put the rubbed ribs into another really large Ziploc bag. Try saying that three times fast. Refrigerate it overnight to let the rub get into the meat. The recipe for the rub is a lot more than you will need for three racks. It's actually enough for maybe six to eight racks. Use as much as you like to cover the ribs on both sides. What is leftover can be saved in a Ziploc bag for future use. You can cook more ribs (or chicken) without having to mix up the rub again. If you want to only make enough for now, just cut the recipe in half. You still may have a little leftover and maybe not. It depends on the size of your racks and how liberal you want to be.

I use a smoker with indirect heat. If you have a big barbeque pit, just put coals on one side of the pit. That way you have indirect heat. I also use hickory chips that have been soaked in water for thirty minutes. Drop them over the coals and cover the pit to keep most of the smoke in. I take the meat out of the fridge at least half an hour before I put them on the pit. The meat should stay on that low indirect heat for four hours. Low and slow! After that, move the ribs to a big tray.

Next, lay out some aluminum foil. Put the ribs on individual pieces of foil and heavily brush on Wendy's Smoky Honey Barbeque Sauce (see recipe). Now wrap them up in the foil so no air can get in or out. Try to make it like a bunch of tents. Place these in your oven at 225 degrees for two hours.

That's all there is to it. Cut open your tents (watch out for the steam; it can burn), and slip out some really zippy tender ribs. Serve this with a little Smashed Potato Salad (see recipe) on the side. Maybe some ears of corn swimming in butter would also go well. You've heard of Memphis ribs and Kansas City ribs, well… these are New Orleans ribs, so keep the cold beer handy!

Snap Beans and Potatoes

1 pound of fresh snap beans (trimmed and rinsed)

1 pound of either pickle meat, ham chunks, or pork stew meat (cut into small cubes)

1 pound of potatoes (peeled and cut into 1-inch cubes)

4 cups of chicken stock

14.5-ounce can of beef gravy

1/4 cup of shallots (chopped fine)

1 clove of garlic (chopped fine)

Salt

Fresh-ground pepper

My mom brought this recipe from Kansas when she moved to New Orleans. We ate it quite often growing up. I ended up bringing it into the firehouse kitchen as a side dish. Eventually, when prepared in large quantities, it ended up being a full meal. After all, it has veggies, meat, and potatoes. If there was a way to incorporate a dessert into it, I would have found it by now, so don't even try.

Put the pork into a pot with a little salt and fresh-ground pepper on it. Not too much salt as the pork will be pretty salty. On a medium to high heat, cook the pork until slightly brown. Next add the shallots and garlic and cook for one to two minutes. Now add the chicken stock and basically deglaze the pan. Scrape the bottom to release any tasty brown bits there. Pour the beef gravy into the pot and mix in. Bring it up to a simmer and add the beans. Bring them up to a simmer again; then cover and put on a low fire. Cook them for one hour, and then uncover. Turn the fire up a bit to a simmer, and cook for another thirty minutes.

Once the beans are cooked, put the potatoes in the pot. Cook until fork tender. Take the pot off of the heat and check for additional salt and fresh-ground pepper.

Now eat!

Note: If you like, add in a little splash of red wine vinegar to a bowl full of the beans to brighten up the dish! That's what Mom used to say. I thought it was pretty bright all by itself.

Homemade Pizza

Dough (see Pizza/Calzone Dough recipe)
Sauce (see Pizza Sauce recipes)
Toppings (your choice)
Mozzarella cheese (your choice about how much)
Pizza stone
Pizza paddle (also called a peel)
Corn meal

When I was a kid there was no pizza to be had except for Chef Boyardee in a box, unless you count that cardboard-like substance that passed for pizza at the drive-in theatre. Today you can find it on practically every corner. Even though this is true, homemade is better and fun. Invite people over for a "roll your own" party. That's where they bring the toppings of their choice, and you supply the sauce and the dough. Everybody can have a personal pizza of his or her own with very little cost.

Get your oven as hot as you can. The hotter the better. If you can crank it up to 500 degrees, do it. Put your pizza stone in, and let it get hot.

On a flat surface that has been sprinkled with corn meal, roll out your dough into a twelve-inch circle and to the thickness you want. You'll want to make a little ridge around the edge so your ingredients don't fall out. Just think of it as a pizza levee. You remember what happened when the levee broke don't you? I thought so.

Put the dough on a pizza paddle that has been sprinkled generously with corn meal. This will help it slide off of the paddle and onto the stone. Brush on your sauce, and then add your toppings. Now put on the cheese and slide it into the oven and onto the hot stone. How long you leave it in will depend upon what temperature your oven is and how thick your pizza is. Keep an eye on it. When the edges of the dough start to slightly brown or your cheese begins to brown on top, it's done. Stick your paddle back under it, and pull it out and onto a tray for cutting.

Use whatever toppings you like. With the tomato sauce I like to use shrimp and red onion (a personal favorite). With the garlic sauce I like to use Italian sausage. There are no rules. Our friend Stan liked his with sun-dried tomatoes, anchovies, and smoked oysters. Not my cup of tea, but obviously it's his. Be creative. You know what you like.

Note: When sliding the pizza onto the stone, it doesn't always like to slide off. You may have to give it a quick little flick of the wrist. That takes a little practice to get it right without having half of the pizza hanging off the back of the stone. If you don't feel comfortable doing it that way, use some oven gloves and take the hot stone out of the oven. Set it on top of the stove and then use the back of a long knife to help push the pizza onto the stone. Now put it back in the oven without losing any toppings. Use the gloves! It will be wicked hot. You don't to be walking around with people calling you "pizza hands" now do you?

Stuffed Eggplant Pirogue

Pirogue portion:
2 medium eggplants
2 cups of flour
1 tablespoon of flashover seasoning
2 eggs
2 cups of milk
2 cups of Zatarain's fish fry
1 quart of vegetable oil (for frying)

Sauce portion:
1/2 cup of tasso (finely chopped)
1/2 cup of onion (finely chopped)
1/4 cup of bell pepper (finely chopped)
2 cloves of garlic (finely chopped)
2 tablespoons of butter
1 tablespoon of flashover seasoning
1 pound of headless shrimp (peeled and rinsed)

Stuffing portion:
1/2 pound of white lump crabmeat
2 cups of Mornay Sauce (see recipe for Béchamel Sauce)
1 cup of plain breadcrumbs
1 cup of Parmigiano-Reggiano cheese (grated)

As you can see, this little recipe is divided into three portions. We'll just go through them one at a time, and you will see how they come together as one dish.

First, take the eggplants and peel them. Cut them in half lengthways. Now use a spoon or melon-baller to scoop out all of the insides until you leave about a one-quarter to one-half-inch-thick shell. This is your pirogue. In case you don't know, a pirogue is a small boat used in Cajun country. That's what you are making—four small boats.

Get three bowls and place them side-by-side. In the first bowl place the flour and the FOS. Mix well. In the second bowl, mix together the eggs and milk. In the third bowl, add the fish fry. Heat your oil in a deep pan to 375 degrees. One at a time you want to put the eggplant boats into the flour, remove and shake off the excess. Next it goes into the egg and milk wash. Remove it and let it drip, and then it goes into the fish fry. Shake off the excess. From there you place it in the hot oil and cook until golden brown. Don't overcrowd the pot. Do a couple at a time. Place on paper towels, and they are now ready to stuff.

The second portion is the so-called sauce. I say so-called because it is really not a sauce but more of a way to sauté the veggies so you can add them into the dish.

Put the two tablespoons of butter into a frying pan and melt. Now add the tasso and cook for a minute. Now add the onion, bell pepper, and the FOS. Cook until the onions are translucent. Now add the garlic and cook for another minute. Lastly, put in the peeled shrimp and cook until pink.

Now part three. Add two cups of the Mornay sauce (see Béchamel recipe) to the wilted veggies, shrimp, and tasso sauce. Now you need to add the breadcrumbs so they will absorb the liquid. Once you've done that, all that's left to do is to very gently fold in the crabmeat and half of the cheese. You now have the stuffing.

Scoop this stuffing into your eggplant pirogues. Dust the tops with the last of the Parmigiano-Reggiano cheese. Place them all on a cookie sheet, and put under the broiler until the cheese is slightly browned.

That's it. This is a guaranteed hit, so just serve and take your bows!

Fried Soft-Shell Crab Choron

4 large soft-shell crabs (cleaned and rinsed)
1 cup of flour
2 cups of milk
3 eggs
2 teaspoons of flashover seasoning (and a few pinches)
2 cups of Zatarain's fish fry
1 cup of Choron Sauce (see recipe)
1 quart of peanut oil

Who doesn't love soft-shell crab? What's not to love? If you don't, you will after you try this.

Put three bowls side by side. In the first you want the flour. Put a teaspoon of the FOS into the flour and mix. In bowl number two, mix together the egg and milk, and whisk to combine. In the third bowl, put in the fish fry and the other teaspoon of FOS. Mix them well, and then get your oil heated to 375 degrees.

One at a time put a crab into the flour, and then shake off the excess. Now it goes into the milk and egg mixture. Let the excess drip off, and then put it in the fish fry. Shake off the excess, and then put it into the oil. Don't crowd the pot. If you try to cook too many at one time you will have greasy crabs, and that will be disgusting not to mention demeaning to the crabs. Fry in the peanut oil until golden brown, and then place on a paper towel to drain off oil. Sprinkle a pinch of FOS on right after it comes out of the oil. Repeat until all are done.

Plate them up and drizzle on one-quarter cup of Choron Sauce (see recipe) on each. If I have some, I will sometimes also sprinkle on a little bit of fresh white lump crabmeat. Serve this with your favorite side dish and watch the eyes light up around the table. If they don't light up, tell them that they need to have their eyes checked!

Fried Fish Meuniere

1 pound of fresh grouper filets (redfish, snapper, or speckled trout will do also)
1 cup of flour (seasoned with a pinch or 2 of flashover seasoning)
2 tablespoons of unsalted butter (soft)
1 stick of unsalted butter (cold and cut into tablespoon-sized pieces)
2 tablespoons of veal demi glace
1/2 tablespoon of fresh lemon juice
1 teaspoon of flashover seasoning
1 cup of white wine

The word *meuniere* actually means "miller's wife." I suppose the miller was making the flour needed for this dish while the wife was making the butter. Maybe the kids were in the kitchen making the demi glace. Either way, this family knew how to work together!

First, you should have four filets. I used grouper in this because I happened to have some today. Practically any other white flesh, salt-water fish will do. Redfish, speckled trout, red snapper, and even flounder filets will suffice for this. Lightly sprinkle the teaspoon of FOS onto the fish. Use it on both sides of the filets.

Dredge your filets in the seasoned flour and shake off the excess. Heat up the two tablespoons of soft butter in a large frying pan until it starts to slightly brown. Place your filets in the pan and sauté until golden brown on one side. Turn them over and do the same to the other side. Remove them from the pan and keep warm.

Deglaze the pan with the white wine. Scrape the bottom to get all of those brown tasty bits from the pan. Add the lemon juice and the demi glace and blend in. Cook this for about five minutes or until it starts to thicken. Once that is done, start putting in the tabs of butter one at a time and incorporate them into the sauce with a whisk. Cook until blended and thick enough to coat the back of a spoon.

Serve it right away because this sauce will break easily. Just make sure that you keep whisking. That's about it. Evenly pour the sauce over the four filets and serve.

Note: Just remember, fish is brain food. It will tell your brain to forget about all of the butter and just enjoy it!

If You Can't Stand the Heat

Cedar-Smoked Salmon

1 pound of fresh salmon (cut into 4 equal sections)
1/2 lemon
1/2 teaspoon of salt
1/2 teaspoon of fresh-ground pepper
1 teaspoon of dill
4 tablespoons of unsalted butter
Cedar plank

I know salmon isn't native to New Orleans or the area in general, but we eat a lot of it anyway. I have a friend in Seattle (named Bob Baker or B.B. for short), and we initiated the first cross-country food exchange program. I send him crawfish etouffee, and he sends me salmon. I send him gumbo, and he sends me salmon. I send him … well, you get the idea.

Put all of the ingredients in a saucepan (except the salmon … and of course the cedar plank). Melt and mix together. Brush this on the fish. Brush it on all sides. There will be some left over, but try to put on as much as you can. I sometimes will let it sit there on a platter for half an hour before I put it on the pit. That way it will absorb more of the lemon butter sauce. Not to mention the fact that the butter will congeal and have a better chance of staying on the fish and not rolling off onto the plate. Also, unless you like salmon briquettes, make sure that you soak the cedar plank in water for at least an hour before you use it to cook with.

Get your grill hot and ready to go. Put the soaked plank on the pit, and heat it up until it starts to make steam. Now put the fish on the cedar plank. Cover the grill, and let it cook for approximately ten to fifteen minutes. It really depends on how thick your fish is. It should break apart easily with a fork when it is done.

If the plank should catch fire, put it out with a little water spray. You want that smoke flavor from the grill and the charring cedar plank flavor without burning the fish.

That's about it. Put the fish on the table on the plank. It makes a great presentation; plus, it will help keep the fish warm if you don't serve it all at once. I like to pair it up with a little wild rice on the side and maybe a salad.

Note: It's a great way to bring the taste of Seattle to your own home! That is, unless you happen to live in Seattle. I guess in that case it would just be considered home cooking.

If You Can't Stand the Heat

Fried Soft-Shell Crab Nest with Crawfish Cream Sauce

6 large soft-shell crabs
2 cups of flour (with a pinch of flashover seasoning added)
1 egg
1 cup of milk
2 cups of Zatarain's fish fry
1 quart of vegetable oil
3 tablespoons of butter (for the roux)
1 tablespoon of butter (for the tasso and onions)
3 tablespoons of flour
6 ounces of tasso (chopped into small pieces)
1 medium onion (finely chopped)
3 cloves of garlic (finely chopped)
1 tablespoon of flashover seasoning
3/4 cup of white wine
24 ounces of crawfish tails and fat
4 cups of whipping cream
1/2 cup of green onion tops (finely chopped)
12 angel hair pasta nests

The first thing that you need to do is to clean the soft-shell crab. We're not talking about taking them into the shower with you. No, this is a little different. First you have to cut off the mouth and eyes. One quick slice with a sharp knife will do the trick. Lift up the shell and remove the lungs on both sides, rinse in cool water. Put them aside until you are ready to cook.

Heat up a frying pan, melt a tablespoon of butter, then put in the tasso. Cook over a low to medium heat until the tasso browns slightly. This should take from five to seven minutes. Add the onions and one-half of the tablespoon of FOS. Lower the fire and cook until the onions are translucent; then add the garlic. Cook for one minute, and then deglaze with the white wine. Cook it until almost all of the liquid is gone. Remove it from the fire and set aside for the moment.

In another large pan, melt the three tablespoons of butter. Add the flour and whisk into a golden brown roux. Warm up the whipping cream just slightly. You don't want it boiling or even simmering, just slightly warm. Not cold! Now add the cream a little at a time to the roux. Try to whisk it in and incorporate it into the roux. Now cook it on a low fire until it starts to thicken up. When you reach that point, put the tasso and onion mixture from the other pan into the reduced roux and cream mixture. Add the last half-tablespoon of the FOS. Stir in well to incorporate it all. Cook until your desired thickness is reached. Also remember that adding the crawfish tails will dilute the cream somewhat. I like my sauce a little thicker than most. Sorry, I just don't like runny sauce. Now toss in the crawfish and cook until they are heated throughout. Keep warm.

You can prepare the crabs ahead of time. Not the frying portion but the breading portion. I like to get the breading over with and let them sit in the fridge until it's time to fry. It also gives the fish fry time to adhere to the crabs before frying. That way you have less of the coating coming off in the oil while you are frying them.

Now it's time for the crabs. Use a little pinch of the FOS to season the flour. One at a time, dredge the crabs in flour. Mix the egg and milk together and beat well. After you shake off the excess flour, put the crabs into the milk and egg wash. Remove, let the excess drip off, and then dredge in the fish fry. Shake off the excess. Place the crabs in 375-degree vegetable oil. Fry until golden brown and remove to paper towels. Keep them warm.

In a shallow pan, cook the angle hair nests until al dente. Using a wide shallow pan will keep the nests from all sticking together. You should try to time it so that they are ready when it's time to eat.

Now plate two nests and spoon the sauce and crawfish tails over them; then sprinkle a few green onion tops on each. Place a crab on top of the nests and drizzle a little sauce over it.

Repeat until all of the plates have been filled. Now sit back, and watch all of the plates empty!

Note: Sometimes it is hard to find big soft-shell crabs. On occasion I have been able to only find what my dad calls "buster crabs." These are just smaller versions of the same thing. In that case you might want to serve two little ones instead of one big crab per person.

If You Can't Stand the Heat

Baked Bass Veloute

4 1/4-pound bass filets
2 teaspoons of flashover seasoning
1/2 cup of shallots (finely chopped)
1/2 cup of white wine
1 cup of whipping cream
1/4 pound of butter (cut into tablespoon portions)
1/2 pound of white lump crabmeat (picked over for shells)
Pinch of fresh-ground pepper
Pinch of sea salt

This is a great way to serve practically any fish. I used to use redfish to make this dish, but I found that I liked it much more using bass. If you want to do this with redfish, be my guest. I'm sure the bass population will be greatly appreciative.

The first thing you need to do is to set the oven to 325 degrees. Now take the filets of bass and lay them out on a strip of aluminum foil. Season them with the FOS. Make sure that you have a long enough piece of foil to do the job. Basically you are trying to lay the filets flat on the foil and form a pouch for them. You want to seal them inside so that it forms a little enclosed tent. Cook them for twenty minutes and remove them from the oven. Let them rest for about five minutes so more liquid will be released from the fish.

Now, being careful not to burn yourself from the steam, using scissors cut the top open on your tent. Pour out the liquid from the inside directly into a frying pan. Next add the shallots, the wine, and reduce this down until you have a couple of tablespoons of liquid left among the shallots. Whisk in the whipping cream, and then incorporate the butter one tablespoon at a time. When this is done, strain into a small saucepan. Now gently fold in the crabmeat, fresh-ground pepper, and sea salt, and keep it warm. Plate up the filets and pour the crabmeat veloute sauce on top.

What are you waiting for, a handwritten invitation? Eat!

Note: I know there are a lot of dishes that contain cream and are a thick and stick-to-your-ribs kind of sauce. This one is not like that at all. This sauce is very light and delicate … almost a work of art. So if you are looking to get away from the heavy sauces but still serve something loaded with flavor, this is your dish.

Another note: I have tried this with many different kinds of fish, and they all worked pretty well with the exception of catfish. Naturally, don't try this with an oily fish like salmon. Stick to the white flesh fish. Just trust me on this one.

If You Can't Stand the Heat

Baked Stuffed Flounder

4 1-pound flounders (de-headed, cleaned, and scaled)
2 cups of Crabmeat Dressing (see recipe)
4 tablespoons of butter
1/2 cup of white wine
1 lemon (quartered)
2 teaspoons of flashover seasoning

I always thought Picasso must have eaten a lot of flounder. You know … both eyes on the same side of the head. Get it? Anyway … this is one dish even Picasso would be proud of.

After the flounder is cleaned and scaled, you want to have the dark side of the fish facing up. With a sharp knife, cut a slit right down the middle of the fish lengthways. Just cut it until you hit the spine, and not all the way through. Now take your knife and cut along the ribs on each side to form a pocket on both sides. Pull back the pockets on each of the sides and stuff them with one half cup of Crabmeat Dressing (see recipe). Sprinkle a half-teaspoon of FOS on each fish. Place the fish in a shallow baking dish. It may take two dishes to fit all of the fish.

Melt the butter, and mix in the white wine. Pour over the fish, and then squeeze a quarter of a lemon on each fish. Place uncovered into a preheated oven at 375 degrees. Cook for twenty-five minutes, remove, and serve.

Note: If you don't want to deal with a whole flounder or can't find any, use filets instead. Put one filet on the bottom and spread out the dressing on top; then cover with another filet. It's rather like making a stuffed fish sandwich. Everything else is the same except the cooking time. Fifteen to twenty minutes should do it. It all depends upon the thickness of your fish.

Shrimp Fettuccine Diablo

1 pound of fettuccine noodles

2 pounds of shrimp (peeled, rinsed, and butterflied)

1 quart of whipping cream

2 sticks of butter

2 tablespoons of garlic (chopped)

2 tablespoons of shallots (chopped)

3 tablespoons of flashover seasoning

2 cups of grated Parmigiano-Reggiano cheese

If you use the word *Diablo* in cooking, it means to cook with some heat. I know what you're thinking, another shrimp dish. You would figure that after awhile we would run out of shrimp dishes. You would be wrong. Didn't you see *Forrest Gump*?

After the shrimp are peeled and butterflied, cover them with the three tablespoons of FOS. Mix well and cover. Place in the fridge for a couple of hours.

In a very large pan, melt the butter. Add the garlic and shallots and cook for just a couple of minutes. Add the whipping cream and put on a low fire to reduce by a third.

While it's reducing, cook the pasta until it is al dente. You'll have plenty of time. The reduction takes awhile. Make sure you stir it a lot. Try to keep it blended. It has a tendency to want to break. Place the pasta on the side for now.

After the sauce is reduced, add the shrimp. Cook until pink. This won't take very long. Now add the fettuccine and mix to cover. Toss in the cheese and mix again. Serve with some crunchy bread and butter.

It is Diablo. It should have a slight bit of a bite to it. I love food that bites me back ... don't you?

Note: Sometimes, as a bit of a change up, I will add a small can of baby peas to the dish around the time I add the shrimp. It gives it some color plus it gives it a slightly different texture.

If You Can't Stand the Heat

Panko-and-Peppercorn-Encrusted Tuna with Wasabi Ginger Sauce

Fish:
1 pound slice of fresh tuna
1 tablespoon of black peppercorns (broken into small pieces)
1/4 cup of panko
Pinch of salt
2 tablespoons of wok oil

Sauce:
1/2 teaspoon of wasabi
1/4 cup of soy sauce
1 tablespoon of fresh ginger (chopped)

We didn't get a lot of tuna in New Orleans; it's more of a Japanese thing. But when we did get some, we knew how to treat foreign visiting dignitaries! That would be whoever it was that brought in the fresh tuna!

First thing you need to do is to make the sauce. Put the wasabi, ginger, and soy sauce into a bowl and mix well. Cover and place in the fridge for at least an hour. This is the dipping sauce.

Grind the peppercorns in a mortar and pestle. I like to use a coffee grinder that I keep just for grinding up spices. Ten or twelve pulses will break them up without making them into fresh-ground pepper. Now mix the pepper with the panko. Brush some wok oil on both sides of the tuna. Rub the panko and peppercorn mix on both sides of the tuna.

Heat the remaining wok oil in a frying pan. When very hot, sear the tuna on the first side. After three minutes, flip the tuna over and sear the other side. Cooking time will vary depending upon the thickness of the tuna filet. A one-inch-thick piece of tuna will be about four minutes per side on medium-high heat. You want it to be cooked and crispy on both sides but still a little pink in the middle. Plate it up and use a pinch of salt over the tuna to taste. Use the sauce for dipping.

Note: This is one of those dishes that will depend heavily upon the size and shape of the tuna. If your slice is not thick but more flat like a thin rib eye, it will naturally cook in less time. If your tuna steak is more like a thick filet mignon, it will take more time to cook. The general idea is to sear the peppercorns and panko on both sides while cooking the tuna, but not all the way through. You can see through the tuna on the sides, and watch it cook. That will be your gauge as to how long you want to cook it on each side. Having it a little rare in the middle is perfect.

It's a pound of tuna. Share it with someone special.

If You Can't Stand the Heat

Seafood Stuffed Potato Canoes

1/2 pound of shrimp (headless, peeled, and cleaned)
1 pound of crabmeat (back fin, picked over for shells)
4 large baking potatoes
3 ounces of sharp cheddar cheese (grated)
6 ounces of Colby and Monterey Jack cheese (grated)
4 tablespoons of butter
5 teaspoons of flashover seasoning (1 teaspoon in the shrimp when they cook, 3 teaspoons in the stuffing, and 1 teaspoon reserved to sprinkle over the tops of the potatoes)

Some people call these "potato pirogues." Some call them "potato boats." I call them "potato canoes." Not because of the way they are prepared, but because of something my nephew said when he was a small child. The first time he saw me tackle one of these he said something akin to, "Canoe eat dat all by you self?"

Try to find the biggest potatoes that you can. The more the merrier. Scrub them clean, and then wrap them in aluminum foil. Boil them in a pot of water for about thirty-five to forty minutes. Heat the oven to 375 degrees. Place the potatoes in the oven and bake for one hour leaving the foil on. (You might want to put a pan under them to catch any water that would come out and stain the bottom of your oven.)

Remove and let cool. After they are cool, cut them in half lengthwise and use a spoon to scoop out the cooked potato while leaving the skin intact. Think of it as making a little dugout canoe.

Chop up the shrimp. In a small frying pan, melt the butter; then place the shrimp in. Sprinkle on one teaspoon of the FOS. Cook for only a minute or two; then pour the shrimp and butter into the bowl containing the potatoes that you scooped out of your "canoes." Mix in the crabmeat, the cheeses, and three more teaspoons of FOS. Once you have it thoroughly mixed, get a big spoon and stuff the mixture back into the potato canoes. Sprinkle the last tablespoon of FOS evenly on top of each.

Have the oven ready at 375 degrees. Place the potatoes on a flat metal pan and slide them into the oven. Bake them for fifteen minutes. Remove from the oven, and then give everybody a paddle (spoon) to eat with.

Note: This will make eight big potato halves. Unless you work—or should I say eat—with long-shoremen (or firemen), it will feed eight people.

If You Can't Stand the Heat

Fish Tacos with Cilantro Infused Coleslaw

1 1/2 pounds of tilapia filets
Batter:
1 cup of all-purpose flour
1 tablespoon of baking powder
1 cup of lager beer
1 egg
Pinch of salt
Pinch of fresh-ground pepper
Frying and assembly:
Peanut oil (enough for whatever sized fryer you use)
Flashover seasoning to taste
10 taco-sized tortillas (for stuffing with the fish and coleslaw)
Coleslaw:
1 cup of Cilantro Dressing (see recipe)
2 tablespoons of chipotles in adobo (added to coleslaw Cilantro Dressing during prep)
2 tablespoons of Mexican crema (added to the coleslaw Cilantro Dressing during prep)
5 cups of shredded purple cabbage

Fish tacos have become the rage lately. I don't know why it took off all of a sudden, but it did. We have been making these things for as long as there have been fish. Well, maybe not that long, but you get the idea.

Heat the peanut oil in a deep fryer to 375 degrees. If you don't have a deep fryer, you can use a deep frying pan. Just fill it half way with the oil. You don't want it to boil over.

Mix all of the ingredients of the batter together and set aside for the moment. Cut the tilapia filets into one-inch-wide strips. Dip the fish strips into the batter, and then put them into the hot oil. Don't overload the fryer. Do a few at a time. Fry them until they turn a nice golden brown color. Remove, and let them drain on a plate with paper towels. Sprinkle on some FOS as soon as they come out of the fryer. Continue until they are all done.

Keep the tortillas warm until you are ready to assemble and eat. The recipe for the cilantro dressing calls for adding the chipotle and crema to the food processor while making the dressing for this particular dish (see Cilantro Dressing recipe note). Once it is all mixed, put the shredded cabbage into a bowl and pour on the dressing. Mix well. You can make this ahead of time, but keep it handy and at room temperature.

Put some of the fried fish into a warm tortilla and cover with a helping of coleslaw.

There should be enough there for ten tacos. Once again, that should be enough to feed four or five normal people or a couple of firemen.

If You Can't Stand the Heat

Barbeque Shrimp

1/2 cup of olive oil

3 pounds of shrimp (very large and head on, 10 count shrimp are perfect)

3 sticks of butter

5 tablespoons of flashover seasoning

1/2 bottle of dark beer

1 teaspoon of Worcestershire sauce

3 cloves of garlic (finely chopped)

1 six-inch long fresh rosemary sprig

Whenever you meet someone from outside of New Orleans, they think this dish is something you grill on the pit. I'm not certain how it acquired the barbeque moniker, maybe it was from the boys down at Pascal Manale (a great barbeque shrimp place on Napoleon Avenue in New Orleans) but it really doesn't matter. The fact is that this dish is killer! This is one that will win you friends for life. Albeit greasy friends in the end, but they will love you once the French bread gets to flying!

In a very large frying pan, put in the olive oil and turn on the heat. Sauté the garlic in the olive oil and one tablespoon of the FOS. Cook for about two minutes. Don't burn the garlic. Add the butter and let it melt. When it slightly browns, pour in the beer, Worcestershire sauce, another tablespoon of the FOS, and toss in the rosemary sprig. Mix well and bring up to a moderate heat.

Now put in the shrimp and sprinkle them with the remaining three tablespoons of the FOS. Cook until the shrimp turn pink. You will note the change in color as they cook. Make sure to mix and toss a lot to cover the shrimp with the butter sauce while they are cooking. You want that sauce to get all over and under the shrimp shells. When they are done (the shrimp is cooked through), remove the rosemary sprig and discard.

Serve immediately in individual bowls with plenty of French bread for dipping!

Always use head-on shrimp for this; the larger the better. There is fat in the heads that will dissolve and mix with the butter and seasonings that will give it a flavor unlike that of cooking with headless shrimp. So leave the shrimp intact. Let them go out with some dignity!

Note: If you don't use individual bowls and opt for a community plate, some people (I will not name names) will do a lot more dipping than they will shrimp eating. Watch out for these people. They will suck up all of the precious juices and leave you with none.

Crawfish St. Charles

24 ounces of crawfish tails (with fat)
4 tablespoons of butter
3 cups of whipping cream
2 tablespoons of garlic (finely chopped)
3 teaspoons of flashover seasoning
10 ounces of rotini pasta (cooked al dente)
1/2 cup of green onion tops (finely chopped)
1 teaspoon of salt

This is actually a dish that you can throw together pretty fast. The reducing takes a couple of minutes, but other than that it goes quickly. We needed things like this at the engine house, things we could put together fast. Once it hit the table it went pretty fast too!

In a large frying pan, put in the butter and heat on medium until slightly browned. Toss in the garlic and a teaspoon of the FOS and cook for two minutes. Add the whipping cream, salt, and another teaspoon of FOS. Keep whisking continuously until it reduces by one-third (or until it thickens up to your liking), making sure that the mixture doesn't break.

Pour in the crawfish and fat, and stir together. Since the crawfish is already cooked, just mix in well and heat the crawfish up to temperature. This will add a lot of liquid to the dish. Keep the heat on medium, and once again, reduce by one-third or until it thickens to your liking.

Put in the green onions and the remaining teaspoon of FOS, and stir in. Now add the pasta, and once again, mix in well. Serve immediately.

Note: You can also do this with oysters and crabmeat instead of crawfish. Either way it's a quick and delicious dish. The crabmeat will already be cooked, so just heat it until the oysters cook through and begin to curl up on the edges. That would be one pound of crabmeat and one pint of oysters (drained). More if you like. It's your pasta dish!

Crab Cake Carondelet with Chipotle Remoulade

2 pounds of white lump crabmeat

3 cups of breadcrumbs (one-half cup is used to bind the cakes)

1/2 cup of Homemade Mayonnaise (see recipe)

1 large egg

2 cups of flour

2 tablespoons of flashover seasoning

3 cloves of garlic (finely chopped)

1/2 cup of green onion tops (chopped)

1/2 cup of yellow bell pepper (chopped)

1/2 cup of Vidalia onions (chopped)

2 tablespoons of butter

1/2 cup of olive oil

1 cup of whole milk

1 1/2 cups of Chipotle Remoulade (see recipe)

Shrimp cakes, fish cakes, crab cakes … why cake? Don't they look more like a burger? But who am I to question the difference? I'm just the cook. Now, go make some cakes.

Melt the butter in a frying pan. Add the veggies (except the garlic), one tablespoon of the FOS, and sauté until the onions are translucent. Add the garlic and cook for two minutes. Remove from the heat and let cool.

Pick through the crabmeat to be sure there are no pieces of shell that may have been left behind during their initial cleaning. Be careful not to break up the lumps. Put the crabmeat into a large bowl. Add the mayo and the now-cooled mixture of cooked veggies. Also add one-half cup of the breadcrumbs. Gently fold the whole mixture together until incorporated well while keeping the crabmeat lumps as whole as possible.

If You Can't Stand the Heat

Now take the mixture and divide it into twelve equal parts on a tray. Form each into a crab cake one by one. Cover the cakes and refrigerate them for a minimum of one hour.

Place the other two and one-half cups of breadcrumbs in a bowl. In a second bowl, put the flour and the other tablespoon of FOS. Mix well. In a third bowl, mix the egg and milk together.

Take one crab cake at a time and dredge it in the flour. Shake off excess. Place the cake into the milk and egg wash and then into the breadcrumbs. Shake off excess.

In small batches, fry them in the olive oil about two minutes per side. Lift them occasionally to make sure you are not burning them. They should be a nice golden brown color. Remove to paper towels to drain. Plate it up, and drizzle the Chipotle Remoulade (see recipe) over them and serve.

Once that remoulade starts hanging out with those crabs...look out...its party time New Orleans style!

Baked Italian Shrimp Au Jus

2 pounds of headless shrimp (twenty-six to thirty count, peeled and rinsed)
4 cloves of garlic (finely chopped)
1/2 cup of green onion tops and bottoms (chopped)
1 cup of shrimp stock (see Shrimp/Seafood Stock recipe)
1 tablespoon of flashover seasoning
1 tablespoon of dried Italian seasoning
2 sticks of unsalted butter
1/4 cup of olive oil
1/2 pound of whole milk mozzarella cheese (grated)
1/4 cup of white wine
1 teaspoon of lemon juice

There are a million different versions of this dish. Everybody bakes shrimp with cheese and olive oil. Throw in some garlic, and how can you go wrong? This version is similar to one that I learned to make from one of the guys who worked out of old Engine 7 many years ago. I changed things a bit but basically it is the same. I can't help it…I like to experiment.

Put your shrimp into a bowl. Pour in the olive oil and use it to coat the shrimp. Now add the FOS and mix in well to cover the shrimp. Put this in the fridge and let it marinate for at least one hour.

Melt one stick of the butter in a frying pan on medium heat. Cook until it slightly starts to brown. Next add the garlic and the green onions along with the dried Italian seasoning. Lower the fire and cook for just a minute or until it starts to bubble up in the pan. Add one-half of the stock and cook for five minutes on a low fire. Add the other stick of butter one tablespoon at a time. Incorporate; then add the other half-cup of stock, the lemon juice, and the white wine. Cook for ten minutes. Turn off the fire and let it cool.

I have these ovenproof dishes that I use all of the time. They are about one and one-half inches deep and hold approximately sixteen ounces of liquid. That should give you a gauge to go by. I line four of

If You Can't Stand the Heat

these dishes with equal amounts of shrimp until the entire two pounds are gone. Next I mix up the butter sauce and spoon it out equally into the dishes over the shrimp. After that I top each dish with equal parts of the grated mozzarella.

Preheat the oven to 350 degrees. Take the shrimp out of the fridge a half hour before you cook them. You don't want them to be cold when you put them in the oven. Barely room temperature is just fine. Bake them for about twenty minutes. Switch to the broiler and keep the dishes in until the cheese browns on top. Serve with crusty bread for dipping.

Note: As you can tell from the recipe, this dish is not for the faint of heart. I mean that literally. There is enough butter and cheese in here to sink a ship. For those of you who normally eat two percent cheese and spray butter, you might need to eat this once in awhile just to remind your arteries what the good stuff is like.

Filleted Fish Fry Feast

1 pound of fresh-filleted fish
1 cup of all-purpose flour
3 tablespoon of flashover seasoning
1 cup of Zatarain's fish fry
2 jumbo eggs
1/2 cup of evaporated milk
4 cups of vegetable oil
2 sliced lemons
Salt and fresh-ground pepper

Practically all New Orleans firefighters go fishing. Best relaxation in the world. It's also a bonus for those guys who don't fish because those that do would usually bring their catch into work and share them with everyone. Their reward ... not having to wash the dishes. At the engine house, it's better than gold.

Start with three bowls. In one place the flour and a tablespoon of the FOS. Mix together. In the second, place the eggs, milk, and another tablespoon of the FOS. Mix that one together too. In the last you will place the fish fry and the last tablespoon of FOS seasoning, and you guessed it ... mix together. Heat the vegetable oil in a pan to 375 degrees. Use a thermometer if you have one.

Dredge a fish filet in the flour and shake off excess. This will give the fish a barrier so the cooking oil doesn't get into the meat of the fish and the fish will stay moist on the inside during frying. Next put the filet into the egg and milk bath. Let the excess drip off, and then dredge through the fish fry. Shake off the excess. Now place the filet in the hot oil and fry until golden brown. Only fry a couple at a time. If you put in too many, it cools the oil off and the fish don't get crispy.

When they are done, remove and place on paper towels to drain. Squeeze lemon over them and sprinkle on a little salt and fresh-ground pepper. Repeat until all of the fish are done.

Serve them with Twenty Megaton Tartar Sauce (see recipe). You'll be happy, the fish will be happy, and the people who sell garlic for a living will be extremely happy.

Note: You can use this for catfish, bass, perch, redfish, trout, flounder, snapper, drum, grouper, amberjack, mahi mahi ... did I leave out a fish?

If You Can't Stand the Heat

Firecracker Shrimp

1 cup of Homemade Mayonnaise (see recipe)
3 cloves of garlic (finely chopped)
4 heaping tablespoons of Thai sweet chili sauce
1 tablespoon of Sriracha hot sauce
1 pound of medium headless shrimp (peeled and rinsed)
1 cup of buttermilk
1 cup of flour
1 cup of Zatarain's fish fry
1 twelve-ounce bag of fresh spring greens

A lot of firemen in New Orleans go out and trawl for shrimp. On many occasions they would bring some into work so they could get help from all of the guys to remove the heads for freezing. In exchange for all of the extra helping hands, we would receive free shrimp to cook for dinner. I tried many different concoctions attempting to come up with a spicy shrimp dish patterned after something I had once in Hawaii. After all, I had free shrimp to experiment with. They would use the Thai sauce and the Sriracha as a marinade on shrimp while they barbequed them on bamboo sticks. Of course, we are in New Orleans, so why not deep-fry them? It could only make it better. Look what it did for the Snickers bar.

Take that cup of Homemade Mayo (see recipe) and add the three cloves of finely chopped garlic. Now add the four heaping tablespoons of Thai Sweet Chili Sauce; then add the one-tablespoon of Sriracha hot sauce. I found that you don't need a specialty store to find this item. I got it at Wal-Mart. It's in a bottle that has a white rooster on it. Tuong Ot Sriracha. Mix well and put the sauce aside. The flavors will become fast friends.

If you're cooking for just a couple of people, all you'll need is to peel one pound of headless shrimp. Don't use large shrimp. I've found that medium is best. Cooking large shrimp like this makes them mushy. Dredge the shrimp in flour. Take them out of the flour, shake off the excess, and place them in the buttermilk. Put fish fry in a bowl and take the shrimp directly from the milk and dredge them in the fry meal. Coat them, shake off the excess, and then fry in 375-degree hot oil until golden brown. Remove from the oil to a paper towel to drain.

Next place the shrimp in a bowl (while they are still warm), and pour the sauce over them a little at a time. Turn with a spoon until the shrimp are coated well. The sauce will adhere to the shrimp. This does not work if the shrimp are cold. Now place the shrimp on top of a bed of torn spring greens and serve. You don't really need the greens, but I saw a dish similar to this at a restaurant, and they served them with greens. It looked good so I used it for a nice presentation for guests at home. Firemen don't care how it looks, just how it tastes.

Note: I like to make the sauce the day before and refrigerate it overnight to marry the flavors. Make sure you let it sit out to room temp before you put it on the hot shrimp. They get sort of yucky if you don't.

Also, if you like them with even more spice, just add more Sriracha sauce. After you make them a couple of times, you will figure out how to make them your own.

If You Can't Stand the Heat

Flashover Smoked Salmon

2 8-ounce fresh filets of salmon
2 tablespoons of melted butter
1 tablespoon of flashover seasoning
1 Cameron's stovetop smoker

The first thing you need to know about this recipe is that you will need a stovetop smoker. This is a handy little item that you will find many uses for besides cooking this salmon. It comes with everything you need to smoke just about anything without the trouble of cranking up a big smoker outside when you want to cook for a smaller group than let's say... a Super Bowl party. I got mine over the Internet, but I have also seen them at kitchen shops.

The recipe is fairly easy. Another plus is that, if you like, you can get everything ready the day before you actually cook. What a deal!

Brush the melted butter on the filets; then sprinkle the FOS in equal parts on both pieces of fish. Cover and refrigerate until cooking time. Take them out twenty minutes before cooking.

When you are ready to cook, set up the stovetop smoker with your favorite choice of wood chips provided in the smoker. I prefer alder smoke chips with salmon. I just like the taste of that wood with the fish, but use any one you want. Follow the instruction for the smoker, and in just about twenty minutes you will have some of the most delicious and moist smoked salmon you have ever tasted.

I like to pair this with a wild rice dish. There is also a great recipe for smoked potatoes that comes with the smoker. Throw some in while you are smoking the fish, and you can have a "kill the two birds with one stone" type deal.

Note: If you find that after you use it for a while your smoker leaks out more smoke than you want it to, just wrap some aluminum foil around the top before you put it on the stove. Leave one corner uncovered so it can release that first puff of smoke that lets you know when to start timing the cooking process. (In the instructions that come with the smoker it will tell you that once you see the first puff of smoke you should count twenty minutes from that point and the salmon will be done.)

This is perfect for just two people like my wife and me. If you need to serve more than two salmon filets, this smoker will accommodate them. Just double up on the recipe and smoke away.

Pete's Crawfish Pasta

3 12-ounce bags of rainbow rotini pasta
17 ounces of olive oil
16 ounces of mild cheddar cheese (grated)
2 pounds of California blend frozen vegetables
2 pounds of crawfish tails (and their fat)
1/3 cup of parsley (finely chopped)
1/2 cup of garlic (finely chopped) (one heaping tablespoon is for the crawfish tails)
Salt and fresh-ground pepper to taste

One of my good friends who I worked with for many years used to make this at the firehouse. Pete Frisch would throw this together in one of two styles. In this version he used crawfish. In another version he used pepperoni. In either case it was enough to feed a lot of people. He was in a double house (a pumper and a ladder truck), so he had to feed a double crew. This recipe is for two crews, so if you only want to feed your crew at home, cut the recipe in half (but still be very liberal with the garlic).

Start by boiling your pasta in a little salted water. Pete usually boiled the frozen veggies in the same pot as the pasta. They normally would be ready at the same time if boiled separately, so why not do it all at once?

While that is going on, put two ounces of the olive oil in a big pan. Heat it up on a medium fire; then put in the crawfish tails, their fat, and a heaping tablespoon of garlic. Put in a little salt and fresh-ground pepper. Cook everything for a few minutes, and then put the pan aside and keep it warm. You just want it to cook until everything is really heated up well. Be careful for splatter when the water from the crawfish hits the hot oil.

When your pasta is al dente, drain it well. Put the pasta and veggies back into the hot pot that you just dumped them out of; then add the leftover garlic (minus the heaping tablespoon you used earlier) to the pasta and veggies. Mix it in so the heat of the pot and the heat of the food in it will release the garlic's aroma and flavor. Put in salt and fresh-ground pepper.

If You Can't Stand the Heat

Now pour the leftover fifteen ounces of olive oil into the pot. Mix it around to coat everything well. Now add the cheese, the parsley, and mix it around. The cheese will melt and get nice and gooey. Next add the crawfish and garlic that you cooked earlier. Check again for salt and fresh-ground pepper to taste. Serve while hot.

Note: This is actually the second incarnation of this dish. The original recipe called for two pounds of pepperoni instead of crawfish tails. You can do it either way. I prefer the crawfish, but others prefer the pepperoni. As always, it's your choice. Try it both ways, and figure which one your crew likes the best.

Urky Lurky

2 pounds of head on shrimp (peeled and cleaned, reserve peelings for stock)

3 quarts of water

1 pound of Italian mild sausage (fried, browned, and drained)

1/2 teaspoon of Zatarain's liquid crab boil

3/4 pounds of angel hair pasta

1 cup of onions (chopped fine)

1/4 cup of celery (chopped fine)

1/4 cup of bell pepper (chopped fine)

1/3 cup of garlic (chopped fine)

1/2 cup of olive oil (to start)

1/4 cup of olive oil (for the end)

2 tablespoons of flashover seasoning

14-ounce can of marinated artichoke hearts (8 1/2 ounces after draining liquid, chopped)

6-ounce can of black olives (rough chopped)

1 cup of Parmigiano-Reggiano cheese (grated)

How can you have a firefighter's cookbook without including Urky Lurky? But what is Urky Lurky you might ask? All you really need to know about Urky Lurky is that a New Orleans fireman invented it and that he supposedly used whatever was "lurking" around in the fridge. There is another story that says it's called Urky Lurky because there is so much garlic in it that no one will lurk around you for very long after you eat it, and they would be irked at you.

Who really knows … or cares? I can tell you that every firehouse in New Orleans has somebody who can cook it (all different). This recipe is based off of one that I got from Mike Langston at Engine 33. I happen to think his is the best, and I am not alone.

You start by making a stock out of three quarts of water, the shrimp peelings, and the liquid crab boil. Cook uncovered for one-half hour then strain well. I use cheesecloth to make sure that I get out all of

If You Can't Stand the Heat

the shell fragments. Now add your pasta to the stock and cook it until al dente. While the pasta is cooking is also a good time to cook the sausage. Besides, what else are you going to do, stare at the pasta?

In a very large pan (enough to hold all of the ingredients), put in the half cup of olive oil and heat it up. Add the onions, celery, bell pepper, and a tablespoon of FOS. Cook until the onions are translucent. Now add the garlic and cook for one minute. Put in the artichoke hearts and the olives. Cook for a couple of minutes or until they are warmed through.

Add the cooked Italian sausage and the shrimp and the last tablespoon of FOS. Cook until the shrimp are pink and cooked all the way through and then put it all into the pasta. Now add the last quarter cup of olive oil. Mix it all in thoroughly. Cook until everything is warmed through. Sprinkle the cheese on top, and then mix thoroughly.

Despite the confusion over the origin of the name, there won't be any of it lurking around once it hits the table. Serve this with a loaf or two of French bread and butter.

Note: This recipe is the way it was made at work because we had a lot of guys to feed. If I were doing this at home I would make it a little differently. I would use less pasta. On the flip side, if you needed to stretch the meal for more people (common at the firehouse), you could use a pound of pasta instead of three-quarters of a pound. It will slightly take away from the taste of the ingredients overall, but it will still be really good because you cooked the pasta in shrimp stock, and that imparts a lot of flavor.

Another note: If you want to taste more of the meats and veggies, use less pasta. I sometimes use only one-half pound of pasta because I want to taste more of the shrimp, sausage, garlic, olives, and artichokes. It will still serve eight or more people, but the flavors will be more intense.

Crawfish Boil

40 pounds of fresh crawfish (cleaned and rinsed)

46 quarts of water

1 16-ounce bottle of Zatarain's liquid crab boil (approximately, you may want more)

32 ounces of sea salt (approximately, you may want more salt or less)

1 sixteen-ounce bottle of cayenne pepper

3 pounds of onions (cut in half)

15 whole heads of garlic (cut in half)

1 large bag of lemons (cut in half)

1 five-ounce bottle of Tabasco

2 sticks of butter (one half pound)

5 pounds of red creamer potatoes

20 ears of frozen corn on the cob

4 pounds of smoked sausage or andouille (cut into 3-inch lengths)

Crawfish boils are a way of life in Louisiana. Having a "boil" has now moved into other states. It wouldn't surprise me to find folks as far away as Texas cooking crawfish.

As far as the ingredients are concerned, they will vary. This recipe is just a guideline. Some people may want to have their crawfish a little saltier than others. Some would add more pepper spice. Some more or even less lemons. It all depends on your individual taste. The basics are usually the same. Potatoes, onions, garlic, sausage, corn, and of course the crawfish are the norm.

If adding all of the spice ingredients seems a bit overwhelming, Zatarain's does sell something called "Pro-Boil." It comes in a fifty-three-ounce plastic bottle. It contains enough of everything to cook forty pounds of crawfish all by itself (the usual amount of crawfish in a sack). No measuring. I like to use it as a base and then add more lemons and spices at my own discretion.

The first thing we need to do is to dispel an old myth about crawfish boiling. When I was growing up we would "purge" them with salt water to clean them. That was supposed to make them expel any

If You Can't Stand the Heat

contents inside of them. Well, it's not true. All it really does is kill any small ones, and it doesn't make them excrete anything. All you need to do to purge them is to rinse them in cool water until the water runs clear. That's it. They are freshwater creatures, and saltwater is not good for them.

Now get out your boiling pot, set it on the burner, and fill it up a little past halfway. If you fill it up too much, you will have a boil over. Not good. I use a eighty-quart pot, so I would put forty-six quarts of water into it. If you have a smaller pot, you would naturally use less water. A bigger pot, more water. Put in your basket/strainer at this point.

Once the water is in you add the salt, cayenne, lemons (squeeze them into the water, and then toss them in), crab boil, and the Tabasco. Mix it all in well, and then taste the water. You want it to have a nice salty and lemony taste to it with a little zip on the side. Turn on your propane tank and light your burner. Crank it up to high and cover the pot. That will make it come to a boil faster than if it was uncovered. When you see steam coming out from around the lid, that means the water is boiling, and it's ready.

I have these two mesh nylon laundry bags. I usually will fill one with the sausage and potatoes. In the other I usually put the onions and garlic. That way, when the boil is done I can find all of the items I put in and separate them into piles for whoever wants each item. You can throw them all in (the traditional way) without separating them. I just find it easier with the bags.

Once the water is boiling, put in the onions, garlic, sausage, butter, and potatoes. Boil these and check the potatoes after a while. They are your gauges. Once they are right at fork tender, it is time to add the crawfish. Adding them will make the water stop boiling. When the water comes back up to a boil, cook for three minutes uncovered. Now turn off the fire.

Put the still-frozen corn into the pot and stir it around. This will help to stop the boiling process, and the water will still be hot enough to cook the corn. Now comes the soaking time. The longer you let them soak, the spicier they will get. I usually let them soak for about twenty to twenty-five minutes. If you let them soak too long, they will be hard to peel, so watch it.

If you happen to be the one who is cooking the crawfish, that job comes with an added bonus. You are the one who gets to check them and pronounce them "ready to eat." So that means that you have to check them by eating several during the soaking time. Poor you. You should continue to sample them until they are spicy enough to eat without being overcooked to the point that the peelings are sticking. Be sure to stir them up so you get to taste some of the ones that are on the bottom.

Once you have taste-tested to your satisfaction, strain; then pour them out on a table and tell everybody to "suck some heads and pinch some tails!" You probably won't have to say anything. I think they'll know.

One may think that forty pounds of crawfish is a lot but your average person will consume between five to seven pounds at a sitting. Make sure you invite plenty of friends!

Note: Adding the two sticks of butter is something that not everyone does. I was told many, many years ago that adding butter to the pot helps them peel easier. Something about the butter getting under the shells. I'm not really sure if that actually works, but I always do it anyway. When grandma says put in the butter, you had better put in the butter.

Seafood and Tasso Crepes

1 cup of tasso (chopped into small pieces)
2/3 cup of green onion bottoms (the white part, chopped small)
2/3 cup of red bell pepper (chopped small)
1 stick of unsalted butter
1 quart of whipping cream

3 tablespoons of flashover seasoning
1/4 cup of flour
3 pounds of shrimp (3 pounds of 26 to 30 count shrimp with heads on before peeling)
1/4 cup of green onion tops (the green part, chopped small)
1 pound of fresh white lump crabmeat (picked over for shells)
16 Crepes (see recipe)

You can fill crepes with just about anything. This is a savory dish that has some good old Cajun pork and fresh Louisiana seafood. What could be better? Eating it of course! This recipe is for feeding eight people, so hunker down and invite the masses.

This dish happens pretty fast, so be ready with all of your ingredients.

Get a big pan and put it on the stove. It needs to be deep enough to hold all of the ingredients. Put in the tasso and heat it up to release some of the oil. Slightly brown the meat, and then add the green onion bottoms, one tablespoon of the FOS, and the bell pepper. Cook for just a couple of minutes, and then add the butter. When it melts, it will begin to bubble. That is when you add the flour and another tablespoon of the FOS. Cook and scrape the bottom of the pan for just about one minute, and then add the cream. Stir in to blend nicely and bring up to a simmer.

Reduce the cream by one-quarter, and then add the shrimp and the last tablespoon of FOS. In case you think it might be too thick, remember the shrimp will release a lot of water, so it will thin out your cream mixture.

Once the shrimp are cooked through, lightly fold in the crabmeat and the green onion tops. Try not to break up the crab. The bigger the lumps, the better they are. If not, they would call it scattered crabmeat instead of lump crabmeat, now wouldn't they?

Once it is all incorporated, take a crepe and place it on a plate. Spoon some of the crabmeat, shrimp, and tasso in the middle, and roll it up like a cigar. Use two crepes per person. Once you have made the two stuffed crepes, spoon a little of the sauce on top. Serve while hot.

Note: This recipe will make a lot of crepes. Enough for eight people. If you want to feed less people, just cut all of the ingredients in half. Either that or eat more of them yourself. I won't tell.

Spinach and Crabmeat Ravioli

I've made all kinds of ravioli. You can pretty much stuff anything into pasta in a cream sauce, and it will taste good. I have made crabmeat dishes with asparagus. I have made them with artichoke. I have made them with broccoli. So one day I thought, why not make ravioli with spinach? Nobody complained… everybody loved it, so I wrote it down.

Dough:
2 large eggs and one egg yolk
2 tablespoons of water
2/3 cup of all-purpose flour
1 cup of semolina double 00 flour

Stuffing:
6 ounces of fresh baby spinach
16 ounces of chicken stock
1/2 cup of milk
1/2 cup of whipping cream
1 tablespoon of unsalted butter
1 tablespoon of flour
Pinch of fresh-ground pepper
1/2 pound of fresh white lump crabmeat (picked over for shells)
2 tablespoons of shallots (finely chopped)
1 tablespoon of unsalted butter
Pinch of kosher salt
3/4 cup Italian breadcrumbs

Sauce:

2 cups of whipping cream

2 tablespoons of butter

2 cups of Parmigiano-Reggiano cheese (1 cup grated for the sauce and 1 cup grated for the broiler)

Salt and fresh-ground pepper (to taste)

Make the dough:

Mix all ingredients in a bowl, and knead for five minutes. Oil the inside of a bowl and add the dough to it. Cover with plastic wrap and set aside in a cool, dry place for two hours.

Make the stuffing:

Put your spinach in a food processor and pulse it until it is chopped fine. Heat up the chicken stock in a pot and add the chopped spinach. Cook for five minutes, and then strain through a cloth. Squeeze out all of the water. Put it aside for now.

Mix the milk and whipping cream and put it into a pot. Bring it up to heat and let it simmer but not boil. In a separate pot, melt a tablespoon of butter and add the flour. Heat it up and stir it to make a golden brown roux. Now slowly add the warm milk mixture a little at a time until it is all incorporated. Heat and stir until the sauce reduces and begins to thicken. Remove from the fire and put in the spinach. Once you mix them together, add the fresh-ground pepper and the crabmeat and gently fold it in.

Take the other tablespoon of butter and melt it in a pot. Put in the shallots, the pinch of salt, and cook until the shallots are translucent and soft. Mix it in the crab and spinach. Now gently fold in the breadcrumbs. That is your stuffing for the ravioli.

Assembly:

Break off a piece of dough and put it on a floured surface. Roll out the dough until it is very thin. Most people will roll out a big sheet of dough and then put down dollops of stuffing then cover it with another thin sheet of rolled out dough. That way they can save time and make many at once. I don't do

If You Can't Stand the Heat

that. I'm only going to make sixteen or twenty, so what I do is make them individually. Some are bigger than others, but it lets people know that you took the time to make it all by hand.

Roll out enough dough to make a single, large ravioli. Cut out a square to the size of ravioli you want. Cut that square dough in half and put water on the edges of one piece. Put the stuffing in the middle of that piece, and cover with the other layer of dough. Use a fork to seal the edges, and then start on another one.

The amount of filling will vary with the size of your ravioli. Just make sure that whatever size ravioli you make you put in enough stuffing without overstuffing it. They are going in boiling water, and you don't want them to pop open. Full and well sealed. Continue until you have all of the ravioli you need or have run out of ingredients.

Heat up some water in a pot and keep it hot. In a pan, melt the butter for the sauce. Add the whipping cream, salt, and fresh-ground pepper. Heat until it begins to thicken, and then add half of the cheese. Remove from the fire, but keep warm.

Turn on your broiler and have it ready. Put the ravioli in the pot with the simmering water and cook the pasta for three to four minutes. Remove them and place four in an ovenproof bowl. I use sixteen-ounce and one-inch-deep bowls for mine. They are elongated, so the ravioli fit in there nicely. Spoon some of your sauce over the ravioli and make sure it's coated on all sides; then sprinkle some Parmigiano-Reggiano cheese on top. Place the plate under a broiler and slightly brown the cheese on top. Repeat until you have four servings with four ravioli apiece. Serve with some crusty bread.

Note: This recipe will make many small ravioli or a few large ones. I make about sixteen large ones. I always opt for the large ones because I think it's better to serve more filling than more dough. The only time I want more dough is when I'm in Vegas, but that's another story.

Grillades and Grits

1 pound of veal
12 ounces of applewood smoked bacon
1 tablespoon of flashover seasoning
1/2 cup of flour
2 large onions (chopped)
1 cup of bell pepper (chopped)
1/4 cup of celery (chopped)
2 cloves of garlic (chopped fine)
4 large Roma tomatoes (chopped)
3 cups of beef stock
1 cup of red wine
2 bay leaves
1 tablespoon of dried Italian seasonings
Cheese Grits (see recipe)
Salt and fresh-ground pepper (to taste)

Where the word *grillades* comes from is anybody's guess. Some say it was a poor man's meal that eventually became a rich man's meal. It used to be made with inexpensive cuts of beef like round steak. Now it's made with veal. Rich man, poor man—who cares? Throw this on the table, and everyone will feel like a million.

In a Dutch oven, cook the bacon, and then drain it on paper towels. You won't need the bacon in this dish, so keep it until tomorrow and make some BLT's. When it's all cooked, measure the drippings in the pot. You need one-half cup of bacon fat. If the drippings do not equal that amount, supplement it with olive oil to reach a half-cup.

If You Can't Stand the Heat

Divide the meat into four pieces. Pound the meat down with a meat mallet until it's thin. One-half inch thick would be nice. Salt and fresh-ground pepper the veal. Heat up the fat, and then, in small batches, brown the veal in the bacon drippings. Remove the meat, and put it on paper towels to drain.

Now add the flour, and over a really low fire, make a brown roux, somewhere between peanut butter and chocolate. It will almost be a dark rusty red color. Once you have your roux, put in the onions, bell pepper, celery, and the tablespoon of FOS. Cook until the onions are translucent then add the garlic. Cook for two minutes more then deglaze the whole thing with the red wine.

Add the tomatoes and mix well. Now add the beef stock, Italian seasonings, and the bay leaves. Put on a low fire, and cook covered for one hour. Stir it occasionally.

Now uncover the pot and add the meat. Cook uncovered for another hour.

Check for salt and fresh-ground pepper. Turn off the fire and let it all sit covered for at least one hour. Serve each over a plate of Cheese Grits (see recipe). It's enough for four people to enjoy.

Note: It is so much better when you cook this the day before and let it sit all night in the fridge. This makes one hell of a dinner, but it also is a really great breakfast. You can find this item on many menus in New Orleans for either mealtime. If I were you, I'd make enough to eat it for both meals!

Bananas Foster Stuffed Pain Perdu (Lost Bread)

Toast:
1 cup of milk
2 eggs
4 tablespoons of unsalted butter (one tablespoon per serving)
8 slices of Texas toast
Powdered sugar (to your liking)

Stuffing:
1 stick of unsalted butter (divided in half)
1 cup of light brown sugar
1 teaspoon of cinnamon
2 bananas (cut up into 1/2-inch slices)
1 teaspoon of banana extract

Everybody and their sister-in-law makes a version of Bananas Foster. Usually it's a dessert. This one is a non-alcohol breakfast version. Who wants alcohol for breakfast? I mean ... really! That's why I usually serve this right before a Saint's game and right alongside a good Bloody Mary!

Sauté one-half stick of the butter, the brown sugar, banana extract, and the cinnamon until they dissolve together. Add the bananas and another one-half stick of butter, and cook until the bananas are tender. Set aside for now, but keep it warm.

Combine the eggs and milk and whisk together. Get a frying pan and heat it up. Put one tablespoon of butter in the pan and melt to coat the bottom of the pan. Now take two slices of bread and put one-quarter of the banana mixture on one slice. You don't have to put on one-quarter of the sauce. There will be plenty of it. Just make sure you spoon out one-fourth of the bananas with some of the sauce.

Cover it with the other slice of bread. Press it down to make a sort of sandwich like serving. It will hold together without you having to push down too hard because the banana mixture will sort of glue

If You Can't Stand the Heat

it. Pick it up and dip the sandwich into the milk and egg wash to coat on both sides. Place it in the pan with the tablespoon of melted butter and cook until golden brown; then flip it over and do the same with the other side. Put it on a plate and sprinkle with some powdered sugar. Repeat until all four pain perdu are finished.

Note: *Pain perdu* means lost bread. My grandparents called it pain perdu. Then my parents just called it lost bread. We called it French toast. I guess that's how we lose things from generation to generation.

Bob's Big Breakfast #1 (Chili Cheese Omelet)

4 eggs
1 cup of whipping cream
2 tablespoons of butter
1 cup of shredded mozzarella cheese
2 cups of Chili (see recipe)
Salt and fresh-ground pepper to taste
1/4 cup of green onion tops (chopped fine)
This recipe is for two servings.

This is a variation of a dish that is served at one of the premiere breakfast places in New Orleans. The Camellia Grill is also absolutely the best place to go late at night if you are hungry. There were many times that we were there after spending the evening frequenting some of the local business establishments. But that's a story for another time.

Using a blender, put in your eggs, whipping cream, and a pinch of salt and fresh-ground pepper. Turn it on high for at least a minute. You're looking for a foamy texture on top of the mix. You are whipping some air into it to hopefully make it lighter.

In a frying or omelet pan, put in a tablespoon of butter. Melt the butter, and then pour in half of the egg and cream mixture. Cook it exactly like you would cook any other omelet. When it starts to bubble up in the middle, check the edges. Lift them up to see if they have started to turn golden brown.

When it has reached that stage all the way across, put half of the cheese on one side of the omelet. Now gently fold the other side over on top of that side. The residual heat will melt the cheese. Slide the omelet off and onto a plate. Cover with half of the chili. Sprinkle on a small amount of green onion tops, and that is it. Repeat to use the second half of your ingredients.

If you need to feed more people than two, it's easy enough to start over and whip up a couple more. Just make sure you have enough chili to cover them.

If You Can't Stand the Heat

If you are one of those folks who have a problem making a perfect omelet, don't despair. Just make sure the egg is cooked through and the cheese is inside. It doesn't have to be pretty. That's why you have the chili, to cover up mistakes!

Note: If this doesn't make you want to come down and have breakfast in New Orleans, then maybe it will make you want to come for lunch or dinner. This dish is just as good at ten o'clock in the morning as it is at ten o'clock at night!

Bob's Big Breakfast #2
(Eggs, Biscuits, and Milk Gravy)

8 eggs
1/2 pound of applewood smoked bacon
4 cups of milk
8 biscuits
2 tablespoons of flour
Salt and fresh-ground pepper to taste

My mother used to make this breakfast for us every once in a while. She would say, "This breakfast will stay with you all day." She was right. Sometimes I think it would stay with you for about three days.

The first thing you do is to make sure you have your biscuits baked and kept warm.

The second thing you do is fry the bacon down until crispy. When done, place on paper towels to drain, and then keep it warm.

Remove all of the oil from the pan except for two tablespoons. Reserve what you pour out to use later. Try to leave as much of the little tasty brown bits of the bacon in the pan as possible as it helps flavor the milk gravy. Put two tablespoons of flour in and mix with the oil. Heat it up and stir a lot. You are trying to make a very light roux. The color should be just barely golden brown.

Now add the milk, salt and fresh-ground pepper, and cook until it starts to thicken up. Try to make it thick enough to easily coat the back of a spoon. This will take awhile, but it's worth it. If it should get too thick, add a little more milk. Now it's time to eat.

Using your reserved leftover bacon drippings, fry two eggs per person. Salt and fresh-ground pepper the eggs and put them on a plate. Break two biscuits in half and cover them with milk gravy. Put a couple of strips of bacon on the side and serve. This serving is for each of the four lucky individuals who are there for breakfast. Just make sure that you are one of the four!

If You Can't Stand the Heat

Crabmeat and Cheese Omelet

1/2 cup of fresh white lump crabmeat (cleaned and picked over for shells)
2 eggs
1/2 cup of whipping cream
1/2 cup of white Monterey Jack cheese (grated)
1/2 teaspoon of flashover seasoning
1 tablespoon of butter
1 cup of Hollandaise Sauce (see recipe)
1/4 cup of tasso (sliced into thin strips)

This is a single serving seriously heavy-duty omelet. It is not for the faint of heart. On second thought, the faint of heart would probably love it too.

Crack your eggs and pour them into a blender. Now add the whipping cream and the FOS. Turn it on and blend it for at least one minute. I like to get a lot of air into the mixture. It seems to cook up fluffier that way.

In an omelet or a frying pan, melt the butter. Once it has melted, put in the tasso and fry it slightly. Remove the tasso, and place on a paper towel for the moment. Now pour the egg and cream mixture into the pan. Just let it cook slowly over a medium-to-low fire. Use a spatula to lift up an edge to see how it's cooking. Keep picking up the edge and tilting the pan to let the uncooked egg portion get under the part that is already cooked. Once it has cooked enough to be done around the edges (a golden brown color), sprinkle on the cheese. Now do the same with the crabmeat.

Using your spatula, fold the omelet over to the other side. It should look like a half moon. Slide it out onto a plate. Now top with the Hollandaise Sauce (see recipe) and then top that with the tasso strips.

Now just sit back and enjoy. Oh, I forgot, I have found that it is a good idea to loosen your belt a bit before you start eating. It will help!

Note: You can cut this in half after you cook it and serve two people, but I fail to see why you would want to do that. Let them get their own.

Eggs Benadou

2 English muffins (toasted)
1 cup of Creamed Spinach (see recipe)
1 cup of artichoke hearts (sliced up)
4 poached eggs (1 for each side of each muffin)
1 cup of Hollandaise Sauce (see recipe)
2 to 3 ounces of tasso (cut into small pieces)
2 tablespoons of butter
1 teaspoon of tarragon vinegar
Pinch of flashover seasoning.

This breakfast item makeover is a little concoction I came up with one day after some people wanted Eggs Benedict and some wanted Eggs Sardou. I thought, why not combine them both and then maybe Cajun the whole thing up just a bit?

Remember that this recipe is for two servings. If you are making this for a few people, just double, triple, or whatever you need to feed them all. The other thing to remember is that you don't want to use marinated artichoke hearts. They are too strong. Try finding the ones that are in brine and rinse them well before you slice them up.

The first thing you need to do is to make sure you have the Creamed Spinach (see recipe) and the Hollandaise Sauce (see recipe) waiting in the wings. This whole thing will be done in just a few minutes, so prepare the spinach and the sauce right before you do the rest.

Once you have those two items warming up in the bullpen, melt the butter in a small pan. Once it's melted, put in the tasso pieces and slightly fry them. Remove them from the pan, leaving the drippings in the pan and putting the tasso aside on a paper towel to drain. Now put the artichoke hearts into the pan and heat them until they are tender. This may take about ten minutes. If you need to add more butter, it's all right to add some. The artichokes will absorb most of it while they are tenderizing. Just keep mixing them with the butter and drippings from the tasso, and when you are done, keep them warm.

Put about one and one-half inches of water into a saucepan. Add one teaspoon of tarragon vinegar to the water. Now heat it up. You don't want it boiling. You just want it at that point where it is just about to simmer.

Take an egg and pour it into a cup. Put the cup close to the water and slowly slide the egg into the water. Do this one at a time for each egg. Cook the egg for about three minutes. When it is done, use a spoon with slots to remove it from the pan and let the water drip off back into the pan.

Have a warm and freshly toasted English muffin ready and on a plate (cut in half). Next, top that with a portion of the artichoke hearts and then a portion of the creamed spinach. Make a little dent in the spinach with the back of a spoon so the poached egg has a place to sit. Otherwise, it may slide off. On top of the spinach, place a poached egg, and on top of that, the hollandaise sauce. Now sprinkle on some tasso on top of it all, and then sprinkle a pinch of FOS over the whole thing.

I usually serve two eggs per person (one whole muffin), but you have to remember as always, these are firemen. Regular people will probably eat just one.

Couple this with a little chicory Café au lait, and it doesn't get much more New Orleans than that!

Desserts

Baked Apples with Ice Cream

4 apples (sweet like red delicious or Rome apples, nothing tart)

1 teaspoon of cinnamon

1/4 cup of golden raisins

1/4 cup of pecans (crushed)

1 cup of Karo dark syrup

1 tablespoon of apple-flavored Cognac

1 tablespoon of caramel cream liquor

4 tabs of butter (1 tablespoon each)

4 scoops of vanilla ice cream

This will put your apple coring skills to work. If you are not good with a paring knife, buy an apple corer. I have this theory that there were only a handful of these made. Everyone just borrows one from a friend when it's needed. You can either buy one of the handful or borrow one from your neighbor.

Core out the center of the apples. Don't go all the way through. Leave the bottom intact. You will be filling it with a liquid and you don't want it to run out. Just make sure you get out all of the seeds and the other inedible parts in the middle of the apple while keeping the bottom intact.

In a small pot, combine the syrup, raisins, pecans, cognac, caramel liquor, and the cinnamon. Heat it up just enough to blend it all together. When this is done, pour equal amounts into each apple. Top each with a tab of butter.

Heat your oven to 350 degrees. Place the apples in a casserole dish and bake them uncovered for forty-five minutes if you want the apple a little firmer. Cook it for an hour if you like it a little softer. You want them to be soft but not mushy. The size of the apple will have a lot to do with how long you cook it. Naturally, the bigger the apple the longer the cooking time.

Take them from the oven and let them sit for a few minutes. You don't want them to be scalding hot. You want them to be just warm enough to eat without burning yourself.

Put one in a serving bowl and top with a scoop of ice cream. Sprinkle just a pinch of cinnamon on top and serve. Repeat. Don't forget to grab one for yourself.

Note: I'm not sure, but I believe that whoever came up with the saying, "an apple a day keeps the doctor away" didn't know that we were going to fill it with sweets and butter and then cover it with ice cream.

Scratch Apple Pie

My wife always made a couple of these pies for the guys at the engine house around the holidays. These things are so fresh and so awesome it's too bad there aren't more holidays!

Crust:
1 1/2 cups of all-purpose flour (plus a bit of additional flour for dusting)
1/4 teaspoon of salt
6 tablespoons of unsalted butter (frozen and cut into tablespoon slices)
2 tablespoons of frozen vegetable shortening
3–4 tablespoons of iced water

In a food processor, combine the flour and the salt. Process for a few seconds, and then add the butter piece by piece. Now add the shortening and process until it resembles a coarse meal. Add the three tablespoons of iced water and continue to process for another thirty seconds. Pinch the dough, and if it doesn't hold together, it is too dry. You will need to add another tablespoon of iced water. Continue to process until the dough turns into a ball.

Divide the dough almost in half, making one piece slightly larger than the other. On waxed paper or a lightly floured surface, roll out the larger piece of dough until it is large enough to cover the inside of a nine-inch pie dish. It will probably be around one-quarter of an inch thick. If the dough should get too sticky, dust lightly with additional flour. Fit the rolled out dough into the pie dish. Roll out the other half of the dough to be used as the top of the pie.

Filling:
2 tablespoons of unsalted butter
2/3 cup of sugar
1/4 teaspoon of salt
1/2 teaspoon of cinnamon

1 tablespoon of vanilla extract
1 tablespoon of finely grated lemon zest
4 medium granny Smith apples (peeled, cored, and sliced into 1/4-inch-thick pieces)
1 tablespoon of lemon juice

If You Can't Stand the Heat

In a large bowl, put together the sugar, salt, cinnamon, vanilla extract, and the zest. Next add the apple slices and coat well. Pour the filling with all of its juices onto the dough that you have in the pie plate and dot with the butter. Now sprinkle the lemon juice all over the top of the filling.

Place the top dough over the pie and crimp the edges with a fork. Using a sharp knife, make a few vent holes in the top crust. Bake for ten minutes at 450 degrees; then reduce the temperature to 350 degrees for thirty-five minutes. Remove from the oven, and let it cool a bit before serving.

Note: To keep apple slices from turning brown while you are preparing the rest of the pie, put the slices into a bowl of water with a little splash of lemon juice. Drain the slices before putting them into the filling mixture.

The dough may be pre-made and refrigerated a day in advance. Just wrap it in plastic wrap so that the dough will not dry out.

Make sure that you have a pan below the pie while baking in the oven. The juices may bubble over, and you'll want something to catch them and prevent them from burning in the bottom of the oven. It's a lot easier to clean a pan than to clean out the black boil over that turns to volcanic rock in the bottom of the oven.

John and Paula's Whipped Pies

20 ounces of crushed pineapple (with juice)
16 ounces of sour cream
8 ounces of cool whip
5.1 ounces of Jell-O instant vanilla pudding mix
2 graham cracker pie shells

Our friends John and Paula would bring this over as a dessert for our Sunday afternoon football game cook-a-thons. It was so good and was supposed to be so easy to make that I asked John for the recipe. I am going to write it down exactly the way he explained it to me…without the expletives.

Mix all of this…stuff…together, and then fill the pie shells. Cover them and chill overnight. This concoction will make two pies.

Note: If you like you can substitute chocolate for vanilla and canned blueberries for pineapple. Try different combinations and see what you can come up with.

If You Can't Stand the Heat

Chambord Macerated Berries and Cake

12 ounces of fresh raspberries
1/4 cup of sugar
1 cup of Chambord
4 slices of pound cake
Whipped cream

This is a quick dessert to put together and a quick one to plate up. I like things that you can put together the day before. That way you will not have to worry about making a dessert while you are cooking everything else.

Place the berries, sugar, and Chambord in a bowl. Mix well, cover, and refrigerate overnight. You want the sugar to dissolve in the alcohol. It really doesn't take overnight, but I like to be sure. A couple of hours will do, but the point is that it is something you can make ahead of time and save yourself some time the next day. You will end up with some tasty berries soaking in a great sauce.

When it is time to serve, place a slice of pound cake in a bowl. Using a slotted spoon, spoon out one-quarter of the berries onto the cake. Repeat with the other slices of cake. The sauce left in the bowl will have a very strong taste. Do not drown the cake with the sauce. It will overwhelm the dish. Just drizzle on enough sauce to complement the dish. You've heard of too much of a good thing. In this case it is absolutely true.

Now spoon on some whipped cream, and you have made heaven on a plate!

Dump Cake

21 ounces of cherry pie filling
20 ounces of crushed pineapple
1 box of cake mix (yellow or white, your choice)
2 ounces of walnuts (crushed up)
1 stick of butter (cut up into tablespoons)

This has to be the simplest dessert on the planet. The name speaks for itself. You basically dump all of the ingredients into a pan and bake it. Foolproof! I can do it blindfolded. I wouldn't recommend trying it that way, but I can. Okay…maybe I cheated a little and peeked, but it's still the easiest recipe on earth.

Get a nine-by-thirteen-inch pan. Dump the pineapple into it. Dump the cherry filling on top of it. Dump the cake mixture on top of that. Pour the walnuts over it. Scatter the butter tabs evenly on top. Place in a 350-degree oven for fifty minutes.

Let it cool for a while before you cut into it. You can either eat it just as is or serve it with a little French vanilla ice cream on top. And if you are going to serve it with the ice cream, be sure to dump it on! Sorry…couldn't resist.

If You Can't Stand the Heat

Apple Bread Pudding with Caramel Cream Sauce

Pudding:
1 tablespoon of butter (for baking dish)
8 cups of day-old French bread (not stale, just day old)
2 cups of whipping cream
1 cup of light brown sugar
1/2 teaspoon of cinnamon
1/4 teaspoon of nutmeg
1 tablespoon of vanilla extract
1/2 cup of walnuts (optional)
3 eggs and one egg yoke
1 small granny Smith apple (peeled, cored, and cut up into small pieces)
1 cup of golden raisins
Apple Cognac (enough to cover raisins)

Sauce:
4 tablespoons of butter (soft)
1 cup of confectioners' sugar
1 cup of condensed milk
1 cup of caramel cream liquor

This is a new twist on an old-fashioned dessert. Twisting the recipe … good. Doing the twist right after you eat this … not so good.

Pudding:

Before you do anything else, put the raisins into a bowl and cover with apple cognac. Let them sit for a couple of hours to plump up. Drain the raisins. And don't waste the cognac. Sip it after dessert.

Use a casserole dish that is nine-by-thirteen, butter the inside, and set aside.

Using a mixer, mix together the eggs, egg yolk, cream, brown sugar, cinnamon, nutmeg, vanilla, apples, and the plumped raisins. I like to add one-half cup of walnuts to the bowl. Some people say that it clashes with the taste of the cognac soaked raisins, and other people think it adds to the flavor. You can decide for yourself if you do or do not want to include the nuts. I mention it now because if you want them in, now is the time to add them.

Once that is done, break your bread up into small pieces. You don't need to cut it up with a knife. Just tear it apart with your fingers. Now put the bread into the bowl with the egg cream mixture, and let the bread soak it up for fifteen minutes. Mix it around a little bit so that all of the bread is soaked. While you are waiting, preheat your oven to 350 degrees.

Place the bread mixture into the buttered casserole dish and spread it out evenly. By this time, all of it should be soaked and has absorbed all of the egg cream mixture. Put it into the oven and cook uncovered for one hour or until you can stick a knife into it and it comes out clean. Remove from the oven and allow it to cool but not get cold. Cut out a serving size for each person and spoon some of the sauce on top.

Sauce:

You can make the sauce ahead of time so it is ready when you are ready to serve.

In a mixer, whip the softened butter and the sugar together. Now slowly add the condensed milk and mix in. Do the same with the caramel cream liquor.

Remove the mixture from the mixing bowl and put it into a saucepan. When you are ready to serve, heat it up until it is smooth and warm.

Note: Don't serve this if you have to go back to work right away. You will probably be plumped up just like the raisins.

Thumbprint Cookies

1 cup of all-purpose flour
1 stick of butter (salted and cut into tablespoon-sized pieces)
1/4 cup of sugar
2 egg yolks
1 teaspoon of vanilla extract
2 pinches of salt
Your favorite jam

My wife made these cookies as a little girl. She said she loved them then, and we all love them now. Give it a try. It's so simple a child can do it. And when they're done, send them out of the room to do their homework, and the cookies will be all yours.

In a mixer, blend all dry ingredients. That would be the sugar, salt, and flour. Add the butter a tablespoon at a time until mixed in. Add the remainder of wet ingredients. That would be the egg yolks and the vanilla. Beat it until it forms a slightly wet dough.

Spray a baking sheet with Pam. Pre-heat the oven to 350 degrees. Roll the dough into one-inch balls, and place on cookie sheet. Use your thumb to make an indent into each cookie. If the dough sticks to you, grease your fingers with butter.

Fill each cookie indentation with your favorite jam (apricot or Concord grape work well). Bake in an oven for twenty-five minutes or until the cookies brown slightly. Let cool.

Note: This cookie makes a sweet, shortbread style cookie. My wife thinks they are great with a glass of milk. That's how she remembers it. I like them after dinner with a glass of wine. Just chalk that decision up to an unusual childhood, and leave it at that!

Peach Granita with Mango Sauce

750 milliliters of peach bellini wine cocktail
2/3 cup of peach puree mix
2 teaspoons of orange zest
Mango sauce:
2 tablespoons of condensed milk
1 cup of mango puree
1 fresh mango (peeled and sliced)

This is a light a refreshing dessert. I know it contains words like *bellini* and *granita*, but who cares? A granita is basically a frozen juice with alcohol (it's New Orleans … you have to put alcohol in the dessert) and some sort of citrus. It never really freezes all the way because of the alcohol in it. That way it's almost like a sorbet or an alcohol snowball if you will. It's easy to make so don't sweat it.

Pour the bellini, the peach puree, and the orange zest into a shallow pan. Whisk together; then put it into the freezer. Every hour, whisk it around a bit. Do this until it is a slushy type of consistency. It should take about four to five hours. In the mean time, make the mango sauce and keep it chilled.

To serve, cut up the fresh and peeled mango into bite-sized pieces. Chill four martini glasses. Put a really big scoop of the granita into one glass. Top with fresh mango, and then top that with some of the sauce that has been mixed together. Repeat with the other glasses, and then hand them out to the adoring crowd. Good to the last slurp!

Note: You can make the granita ahead of time and keep it in the freezer. It will not freeze all the way. I make it the day before so it is done and ready when I want it.

Also, if you have any leftover, put some into a blender with the cut up mangos, the sauce, and a shot of Malibu rum. Blend it together for a really interesting cocktail. Very refreshing in the heat of a New Orleans summer.

Grilled Pineapple Right-Side-Up Cakes

6 fresh pineapple slices (peeled and cut 1/2 inch thick)
1/2 cup of Malibu coconut rum
1/4 cup of pineapple juice
1 tablespoon of brown sugar
1/2 teaspoon of vanilla extract
6 dessert shells (little hollowed out yellow cakes)
Whipped cream

I wonder who it was that first thought of grilling fruit. I really wish I knew because I'd like to thank him. Not only did he come up with something that tastes really great, but he also gave men everywhere another reason to pull out the grill!

Marinate the pineapple by adding the rum, juice, vanilla, and brown sugar to a bowl. Put the pineapples in and mix well. Put it in a Ziploc bag and refrigerate overnight. Do not remove the core of the pineapple. It will be very difficult to grill without that little piece in the middle holding it all together. They tend to fall apart.

When you are ready to eat, fire up the grill and get it good and hot. Remove the pineapple rings from the marinade and place on the grill. Save the marinade. Cook the pineapples until just barely browned and remove to cool. They will be really sweet from their caramelizing. Once they are cool, remove the cores and discard. Cut the pineapple up into bite-sized pieces.

Take the leftover marinade and put it in a small saucepan. On a low fire, reduce by one-third. Allow it to cool. I like to do this the morning of. If I am going to grill that day and I have marinated them overnight, I drain off the marinade and reduce it ahead of time. That way it's already done and cooled by serving time.

Put a single dessert shell into a bowl, and fill with one cut up pineapple ring. Drizzle some of the reduced sauce over it and add a dollop of whipped cream.

Note: If you have the time and care to, toast a little coconut and sprinkle on top of the whipped cream. You can also do this in a completely different way by skipping the cake portion of the program. Just dole out the warm pineapple and warmed sauce on top of vanilla ice cream.

Oreo Heath Ice Cream

General instructions for making ice cream (whatever comes with your ice cream maker)
1 teaspoon of vanilla powder
10 Oreos (crushed)
2–2.8 ounce Heath bars (crushed)

This recipe was given to me by a friend who got it from a friend who got it from his sister-in-law's second cousin three times removed. In other words, I have no idea who started this thing, but it is an awesome ice cream dish. I tweaked it a bit to make it a little different. The strong taste of the vanilla powder does the trick.

I use a Cuisinart Ice Cream maker. The instructions I follow are for making a basic vanilla ice cream. You should use the ice cream recipe that comes with your machine. Since mine makes seven cups, this recipe is for seven cups. Adjust your own accordingly. Also, since it is vanilla ice cream they naturally would use vanilla beans or extract in their recipe. I like to use vanilla powder, but that is up to you.

When I say that the Oreos and Heath Bars should be crushed, I don't mean beyond any reasonable semblance of recognition. I just mean that they should be broken up into small pieces so they blend into the ice cream. I usually put them in a Ziploc bag and break them up with the back of a heavy glass while the bag is wrapped in a towel. No damage to your glass or to the counter top.

When you get down to the last five minutes of freezing time in your ice cream machine, add the Oreos and the Heath Bars. That way they will get mixed in and just make the ice cream into something really different.

If you don't have an ice cream machine, you can use vanilla ice cream from the store. It doesn't come out as well, but it's still pretty good. Just let it get soft; then mix the Oreos and Heath Bars into it; then refreeze.

Note: You have to watch this ice cream very carefully. I made some and put it in the freezer at the firehouse. We had to roll on a fire call, and when I came back, half of it was gone. The guys who covered for us while we were gone said they had no idea where it went. Maybe it just shrank. Can you believe that? Watch it close.

If You Can't Stand the Heat

Butter Pecan Rollo Pretzel Snacks

16 Rollo candies
16 Snyder's of Hanover butter snap pretzels (I get them at Wal-Mart.)
16 pecans
1 tablespoons of butter
A pinch of kosher salt

A friend of ours made these for us one time, and I thought he bought them at some fancy candy store. I never asked him where he got the idea to make them. In any case, I probably couldn't have asked him because my mouth was always full of these things.

In a small frying pan, melt the butter. Now put in the pecans and sprinkle on the salt. Toast them briefly. Just keep them on until the butter slightly browns. You want to get a slight toasting flavor while the butter is being absorbed into the pecans. Allow them to cool. There will be butter that is not absorbed. Just discard it.

Use a non-stick baking tray. I use a silpat (non-stick plastic sheet) on a tray, but any non-stick tray will do. Heat the oven to 300 degrees. Place the pretzels on the tray. Place one Rollo on top of each. Place a pecan on top of each Rollo. Make sure you spread them out. Put the tray into the oven. When the Rollo's soften (about five minutes), remove the tray, and then use a spoon to push them down just slightly. You want the chocolate to penetrate the pretzel until it reaches the bottom of the pretzel and the pecan to stick to the top. After that, put them somewhere that they can cool. Eat.

Note: If you can't find that specific name brand of pretzel, just use one that is shaped like a grid. It is a square pretzel and looks like a one-inch square pretzel checkerboard … without the checkers.

Peach Glace a la Sebastian

1 quart of homemade vanilla bean ice cream
6 fresh peaches (peeled, sliced, and de-stoned)
1 stick of butter
1 cup of light brown sugar
1/2 cup of peach rum
1/4 teaspoon of powdered vanilla
2 ounces of chopped pecans
1 cup of caramel

On a trip to the island of Moorea, my wife and I met and befriended a kid named Sebastian. He was a local who shared some of his fresh vanilla beans with us. They grow everywhere down there, and after we found out that we had a local vanilla bean connection, we immediately came up with this little dessert idea. It's kind of a flashback to Bananas Foster. Or is it Peach Melba? Both? It doesn't matter, its good stuff!

The first thing we did was to make some homemade ice cream with the fresh vanilla beans. We used an ice cream machine and just added the scrapings from the inside of the vanilla bean to the ice cream recipe from the book that came with the machine. Nothing beats the flavor of fresh vanilla in your ice cream, but if you don't want to go through the trouble, just use a good brand of store-bought vanilla bean ice cream.

Heat up a small frying pan and put in the pecans. Cook them for just a short time. Don't burn them! It's easier to do than you might think. Toss the pan a lot and just toast them a bit. Place them in a bowl and set aside for now.

In a large frying pan, melt the butter, and then add the brown sugar. Cook until the sugar is dissolved, and then add the peaches and the vanilla powder. Cook for a minute or two until the peaches soften, and then add the rum. Make sure you take the pan away from the fire when you do this. If you want to look cool and light it up, be my guest. Don't say I didn't warn you. It will take awhile for the

If You Can't Stand the Heat

alcohol to cook out. After that, cook it until it comes to a thickness you like. You can make it a thin sauce or a thick sauce. It's your choice. I personally like it a little thick so it will stick to the ice cream and coat it well.

In a single serving bowl, scoop out some ice cream, and then spoon in some of the hot peaches and sauce over the top of it. Now drizzle on some of the caramel and some of the roasted nuts. Repeat for each person. You should be able to serve eight. Done deal!

Note: If you ever go to the Moorea, say hello to Sebastian for me.

T&J Fudge Brownie Pie

2 sticks of Parkay margarine
1/2 cup of cocoa
1 1/2 cups of flour
2 cups of sugar
4 eggs
1 teaspoon of vanilla extract
1 cup of chopped nuts (pecan, walnuts, etc.)
1 Pillsbury refrigerated piecrust

We were frying turkeys on Thanksgiving. Our friend James brought over this pie as a thank you for frying his. He told me his wife, Tina, made the pie from an old recipe from his mother's family. Well, as usual, everybody was full after the meal, but once they took a small taste of this, it vanished. Maybe they should call it vanishing pie!

Be prepared to make this a day before serving. It really needs to sit up overnight in the fridge to come together.

Using a medium-size saucepan, melt the two sticks of Parkay. When they are melted, add the flour and the cocoa. Take it off of the fire and blend it all together.

After making this a couple of times since, I have learned to just let it sit for about ten minutes to cool off. You don't want it to be too hot when you add the eggs. After a few minutes have gone by for cooling, heat up the oven to 350 degrees.

Now add the sugar, eggs, and the vanilla extract to the saucepan. Mix it all together well with a hand mixer. Next add the nuts, and mix well again. Pour it into the piecrust and slip it into the oven. There will even be a little left over for licking the bowl!

Bake it for forty minutes. The pie will be very gooey in the middle and is best served after being chilled overnight. It will solidify after it is cold. Just put it on a cooling rack until it has cooled off

If You Can't Stand the Heat

enough to put it in the fridge. When it is served, warm it up. It has a better brownie like consistency when it's warmed up.

Note: The first time we ate this we ate it as is, plain (not that there is anything plain about it). The second time (and since) we ate it warmed and served with a scoop of vanilla bean ice cream on top. Tina says to eat it warm with a glass of cold milk. In either case, this pie is simple to make, and like I said before, it has a tendency to vanish without a trace, so make sure you get a slice early.

Glossary

A:

Abita beer: This is a brewing company in Abita Springs, Louisiana. They make many varieties of beer and also make really good root beer.

aioli: An aioli is an emulsified sauce that uses oil, salt, and garlic as a base. Egg is sometimes used to help hold the sauce together. If that is done, it should be called mayonnaise. Mayonnaise should never be called an aioli unless it has garlic in it. For me, it's all too confusing. We (the people who have taught me to cook and I) will say that an aioli is a thin, runny mayo. That's it. If it's thick, its mayo with something added, if it's not, it's an aioli.

al dente: It comes from the Italian meaning "to the tooth." Basically it is pasta that has been cooked to the point of being not too soft and not too hard. If the Three Bears cooked pasta, this would be the baby bear's pasta … just right!

alligator pear: Some people in Louisiana call it an alligator pear. Normally it is called a mirliton. Also known as a *chayote*. It is actually a gourd or squash, but people in Louisiana refer to it as a green vegetable that grows on a vine. It is usually stuffed and cooked and also used in casseroles.

anchovy paste: Anchovies are small fish that are cleaned and canned in oil for consumption. The paste is just the anchovy ground down and put into tubes as a substitute for the canned variety. Among their uses are in salads and on pizzas. I still wonder who it was that first figured out that fish paste would taste good.

andouille: This is a type of Cajun sausage. It is used in cooking gumbos, stews, and even in beans. It is pork that is stuffed in a casing, salted, and smoked with pecan wood and sugar cane. It has a great flavor, and you would use this in place of or in addition to ham. I love it grilled and made into a po' boy sandwich.

Angostura bitters: This is an herbal concoction invented by a German doctor named Siegert. He used this as a medication to help cure stomach disorders. He called it "Amargo Aromatico," which means aromatic bitters. Today it is used in many products such as meats, vegetables, and even in alcoholic drinks. Somebody from New Orleans had to be the one to put it in alcohol. After all, we did invent the cocktail.

applewood smoked bacon: This is a fairly lean bacon that is made from barley-fed pork. It is smoked for twenty to twenty-four hours using apple tree logs. In my opinion, this is the best bacon on the planet.

aromatics: Aromatics can refer to just about anything you put in the cooking pot that adds flavor. In general cases aromatics refer to herbs such as rosemary, thyme, oregano, and garlic. If you ever pinched one of these between your fingers and caught the aroma, you know aromatics.

arrabbiata: This is a Roman pasta dish that contains a red sauce called "arrabbiata." The word comes from the Italian word, which in essence means "angry style." That refers to the fact that there are red peppers in the sauce that give it a little bit of a feisty kick.

au gratin: This comes from the French word *gratin*, which means the scrapings of cheese and bread. Normally it refers to a dish that is baked containing cheese and breadcrumbs. In New Orleans cooking au gratin (aw-graw-tin) usually contains seafood such as shrimp au gratin or crabmeat au gratin. Sometimes people will call scalloped potatoes an au gratin, but it doesn't contain scallops. Confused? Join the club.

B:

back strap: This is the "filet mignon" of a deer. It is the tender part of venison that can be used as filets on the grill, in a Marsala sauce or "paneed" (pon aid).

Balsamic vinegar: This is a flavored vinegar that is dark in color. It comes from Italy and can be used on anything from salads to desserts. Do yourself a favor. If you buy some, get the good stuff. Cheap balsamic is just that … cheap.

Bananas Foster: Brennan's Restaurant in New Orleans created this dish. It's named after a friend of the owner back in the fifties. It is comprised of bananas, rum, sugar, butter, cinnamon, and vanilla ice cream. It is also hands down the best dessert on the planet.

barbeque shrimp: These are shrimp cooked in a butter and a spice sauce. They are not done on the pit. They are cooked either on the stove or in the oven. Large shrimp are used, head on, and produces a sauce that is to die for. French bread is provided with this dish for dipping purposes.

Béchamel Sauce: This is one of the mother sauces. It is a white sauce made from a roux and scalded milk. You can use the sauce like it is or add other things to it to form other sauces. For example, add cheese to a Béchamel Sauce, and you will have a Mornay sauce.

beignet: Pronounced *ben-yea*, it is a ball of dough that is fried. Normally associated with Café Du Monde in New Orleans. They serve fried donuts with confectioners' sugar and coffee. It is also a savory type doughnut that can be filled with seafoods or cheese. If you ever get down to New Orleans, stop at Café Du Monde and try some for yourself.

bisque: A bisque is a classic French soup that is creamy and usually is served with a shellfish such as a crab or a lobster. Crawfish bisque is the making of this type of soup base but with a crawfish dressing stuffed back into the shells and cooked in that soup.

biz: This is a concoction that was named by our friend Miles Wood. It is smoked Mexican peppers fried in olive oil and then ground into a paste. Good on any Mexican food such as chips, tacos, and the like. Also referred to as Miles' Mexican Biz.

blackened: Such as with redfish. It is a meat or fish that is coated with brushed on butter, spices, and cooked on a very hot pan. It will "blacken" the outside, and the inside will remain moist. Most of the time it usually refers to fish, but I have seen it done with chicken and with ground beef. Try a blackened cheeseburger po' boy some time. Yum!

boudin: (boo-dan) Boudin is a rice dressing that is stuffed into casings and cooked. There are basically two kinds of boudin. White boudin is rice, pork, and spices stuffed in a casing. Red boudin is the same thing but also contains pig's blood. After they are cooked, links of boudin are eaten either in the casing or removed from the casing and consumed like a rice dressing.

If You Can't Stand the Heat

boulette: (boo-let) This is a French word that means "small ball" or "dumpling." If you were making crawfish bisque without utilizing the shells, you would make little rolled up balls called boulettes.

bouquet garni: A garni is basically a piece of cheesecloth that is filled with herbs and tied off with a string. You use it in pot dishes where you want to be able to recover the stems from the herbs without searching through the pot once it is cooked. That way you can take out the cheesecloth and throw it away.

bracciole: (bra-jole) Meat cut in such a way as to flatten it out for stuffing with breadcrumbs and cheese. It is then rolled, tied, and pan-fried. It is actually a type of roulade. It is also spelled braciole. The only real distinction that I could find between the two was that *braciole* is an Italian dish of pan-fried meat. *Bracciole* is an American version except that it is stuffed before it is fried. Either version is awesome.

brisket: Brisket is basically the breast meat of the cow. It is usually tough meat because it is from a muscle that is used a lot. It should be cooked with the thick layer of fat on top so the fat will render into the meat and make it tender.

bruschetta: (brew-shetta) A basic bruschetta is a piece of toasted bread that is coated with garlic, olive oil, and salt and fresh-ground pepper. There are many variations, but the normal toppings of choice are cheese, basil, and tomatoes.

buster crabs: Soft-shell crabs are crabs that are molting (shedding their hard shells so they can grow larger), and are taken from the water while their new shells are still soft. That way, you can cook and eat the whole thing. At one time, as far as I can remember, any soft-shell used to be called "buster" because they were literally busting out of their shells. Today, a buster crab is a very small soft-shell crab. Large ones are just soft-shell crabs and really small ones are "buster" crabs. How that change came about is a mystery to me. I can't get the crabs to tell me.

butterfly: To make an incision in order to open up meats and seafood. If you butterfly a shrimp you would cut it down the middle without going all the way through or slightly cut it in order to remove the vein. You might butterfly a steak so it will cook faster.

butter solids: If you melt down butter on a low fire, you will see it separate into liquid and solid. The fats will settle to the bottom. Those are the butter solids. If you remove them you will have clarified butter. Leave them in and they can easily burn, so watch it!

C:

Café au lait: (café ole') This is a dark roast chicory coffee that has warm milk added to it. In French it means "coffee with milk." Try some with some sweet beignets. Good stuff!

Cajun cooking: Although similar to Creole, it was a style of cooking that came from the Acadians who were relocated from Canada to south Louisiana. Actually the British kicked them out of Canada, but that's another story. Acadians eventually became known as Cajuns. They brought their French cooking knowledge with them and applied it to the foodstuffs that were available to them locally.

Cajun Injector: This is the brand name of a product that is used to inject large amounts of seasonings into turkeys, chickens, roasts, etc. After they are injected they are then cooked, and the seasonings will permeate the meat easier than just putting it on the outside. You can inject turkeys, pork roasts, chicken, and even beef. If it can be cooked, a Cajun will inject it to make it taste better.

Calvados: This is French apple brandy. Calvados sauce is made with this brandy.

calzone: This is an Italian word that means "stockings." In cooking it's more like a pizza that is folded in half. Generally you make pizza dough, put fillings only on one side, fold it over, and bake it in the oven. Normally it comes stuffed with marinara sauce, ricotta, and mozzarella cheeses. I like to think of it as an Italian stocking stuffer.

Camellia beans: Camellia is a brand name of beans and peas that are dried and sold in the South.

Cameron's Stovetop Smoker: This is a brand of smoker that you can use indoors. Basically you will load it up with wood shavings (hickory, alder, pecan, etc.) then put on the main dish (chicken, fish, etc.). You use the top of the stove to smoke the meat, and the smoke stays in the smoker instead of going all over the house. There are other brands, but this one is the easiest to find.

If You Can't Stand the Heat

capocolla: This is the name of an expensive Italian salami. It is technically not a ham, though some people refer to it as one. It comes from the "capo" meaning head or the "colla" meaning neck of the pig. If somebody is ordering this ahead of you, follow them home because they are probably making muffulettas.

caprese: A caprese can be a salad, sandwich, or an appetizer. It is usually made from fresh buffalo mozzarella, tomatoes, basil, balsamic vinegar, and olive oil. Best salad ever invented.

cedar plank: This is a piece of dried cedar that is used to impart the flavor of cedar to fish or poultry while it is cooking. This is a plank especially made for cooking. Don't think you're going to go down to the Home Depot and get one. Try a kitchen store or the Internet.

Chambord: This is a French liquor that contains raspberries, blackberries, and cognac. I use it primarily as an after dinner drink or in raspberry deserts.

chayote: Also known as a mirliton or an alligator pear. It is a green vine vegetable that is stuffed or used in casseroles.

chicory coffee: In New Orleans some coffee is made with chicory added. Chicory is the root of the endive plant that is cooked and ground down and roasted. At one time it was used as a coffee substitute. In today's New Orleans it is still added to coffee for a much deeper taste. I used to have this shipped to me from home when I was in the Navy. People thought I had brewed it for days to get it to be so strong and so thick. Someone aboard once referred to it as "Coffee you could write letters with."

chicken demi glace: See demi glace.

chiffonade: It is the cutting of leafy greens and or herbs into thin strips. Usually they are fresh leaves, such as basil, that are rolled and sliced thin for cooking. Not to be confused with julienne, which is doing basically the same thing but with other types of food like carrots or chicken.

Chinese five-spice powder: See five-spice powder.

chipotle in adobo sauce: Chipotles are the jalapenos that have stayed on the vine until the end of the grow-ing season. They have lost most of their moisture content and are picked and then smoked until they dry out completely. Adobo sauce is a meat marinade made primarily of tomatoes, garlic, and spices. You can purchase chipotle in adobo sauce at just about any grocery chain. We use it a lot in Mexican dishes.

Choron sauce: Choron sauce was invented by a Frenchman named Choron … go figure. It is basically a Béarnaise sauce that has tomato puree added. I always thought that maybe he accidentally spilled them together and tasted it then said, "Hey, look what I made!"

chow chow: Chow chow is a type of relish that is normally made up of mostly pickled cabbage or other vegetables. The name comes from the French word *chou*, meaning cabbage. In New Orleans, chow chow is made mostly of yellow mustard and dill pickles with some pickled cauliflower thrown in. How that came to be, as opposed to cabbage, is something I do not know. What I do know is that it is used as a condiment instead of regular mustard on sandwiches and hot dogs. I also use it in deviled eggs.

clarified butter: This is the cooking of butter on a low fire until the milk solids are separated from the butter. Once you pour off the pure clarified butter on the top you can use it when you need to cook but-ter over a higher heat than normal. It's harder to burn that way.

cilantro: Sometimes referred to as Mexican parsley. It looks a lot like parsley when you see it in the store except that if you squeeze a leaf you can immediately tell the difference. It has a strong pungent aroma that is used in many Latin American dishes. Its seeds are coriander, but if you use them to cook with, it will taste totally different than cilantro. And, no, I don't know why. That's just the way it is.

coddled egg: This is the process of cooking an egg in boiling water for a short period of time in order to partially cook it. It is used a lot in making Caesar salads. I always thought that by coddling the egg it would help to kill the bacteria that cause salmonella. Apparently that is not the case, but I'm sure it must help.

If You Can't Stand the Heat

Cordon Bleu: Usually it refers to chicken cordon bleu, which is a chicken breast that is stuffed with ham and cheese then baked or fried. Could also refer to a type of cooking school. Maybe that's where someone first stuffed a chicken breast with ham and cheese. Don't hold me to that; it's just a hunch.

corn milk: After removing the kernels of corn from the cob, if you use the back of a knife to scrape the cobs, a white milky substance will come from the cob. This is referred to as the "milk" of the corncob.

courtbouillion: (coo-be-yawn) This is a traditional Cajun dish that uses a brown roux with tomatoes and spices to make a soup-like dish mainly comprised of redfish. Legend has it that when Jesus fed the masses with fish and loaves of bread, he picked up the fish and left his print on it. That's why to this day all redfish have a spot on their tails.

crab (boiling): When you boil live crabs, you must make sure that they are cold before you put them in the boiling water. If you drop them in like they are, all of the claws will pot off. You must ice them down thoroughly before you put them in. Here it's called "putting the crabs to sleep." It is also sometimes referred to as "stunning" the crab.

crabmeat: You will hear crabmeat referred to as either white or fin meat. The fin and claw meat is darker and in my judgment is not as good as the white lump. Jumbo white lump is the premium and the most expensive. If you are going to use crabmeat as a topper to fish for instance, use white lump. If you are adding crabmeat to a gumbo or the like, use the fin meat. Also, stay away from any crabmeat in a can. Pasteurized cold crabmeat in the can is not something you want to eat on top of your fresh blackened redfish. Fresh is always best.

crawfish (cleaning): (also known as a mudbug) When I was a kid they used to clean the crawfish prior to boiling by "purging" them in salt water. It was supposed to clean out their digestive track. In fact it doesn't do anything except kill the smaller crawfish. These are freshwater creatures. Just rinse them a few times until the water runs clear, and you are good to go.

crawfish (eating): I'm sure you have heard of the term "suck the head, and pinch the tail." This means that when you approach a cooked crawfish you should first twist the tail from the head. Next you squeeze the head while you suck the cooking juices from it. If your crawfish is properly cooked, you should be able to pinch the bottom of the tail and the meat will come right out of the shell. In days gone by it was commonly thought that if you picked up a cooked crawfish with a straight tail, it had died before it was cooked and was not suitable to eat. Sometimes they have a straight tail from being stuck that way in the bag for so long so it is all right to eat the ones with straight tails. Just stay away from the ones that are mushy. These probably died long before they were cooked.

crawfish (freezing): Some folks like to take the leftovers from a crawfish boil and use them in other dishes like etouffee's. To me they are overwhelmed with seasonings and ruin other dishes. If you are going to use leftovers, use them on a salad or in a dish that doesn't require that you add seasoning. If you are going to freeze crawfish tails, boil them in plain water and peel them. Freeze these and also try to save the yellow fat that is in the heads. It adds great flavor to any dish you would make with the tails.

crema: It is a fresh cream similar to sour cream except that it is not as heavy or as sour. It is used as a topping to many dishes.

Crème brulee: This is a dessert made of custard, covered with sugar, and then the sugar is browned with a handheld blowtorch to form a caramel top.

Creole cooking: Creole cooking and Cajun cooking are similar. The difference is that the Cajuns are predominately French in their influence on cooking whereas the Creole is also European in origin, but their influence comes from Spanish, French, and a little Italian. Creole cooking in Louisiana is a little of all of those countries but has some African, American, and Caribbean flavors eventually blended in. They took the basics of European cooking that they knew and adapted it to whatever products were available locally.

Creole tomato: A variety of tomato developed at LSU that grows very well in humid climates. It also is resistant to disease. Has a richer flavor than most other varieties. I personally think it has a certain sweetness to it that no other tomato can compare to.

If You Can't Stand the Heat

crepe: Pronounced "krep" everywhere in the known world except New Orleans. Here it is pronounced, "crape." It is a very thin type of French pancake. It is used in both savory and sweet dishes. Usually it is rolled and stuffed with something either sweet or savory.

crostini: It is just a small piece of toasted bread. It is usually used as a piece of bread to serve an appetizer on or as a piece of bread to dip with.

curry powder: Curry is a spice that is used in India's food preparation. It comes from the Indian word *kadhi*. Curry powder was invented by the British. When they colonized India they devised a dried spice to take the taste of India with them when they returned home.

D:

daube: *Daube* is supposed to be a French word meaning to "braise in wine." It's also supposed to be a Spanish word meaning the same thing. In New Orleans, daube is different from the traditional dishes. Here it is the cooking of a beef roast in a red gravy and serving it over pasta. It is also sometimes cooked and served with slices of hardboiled eggs that have been cooked in the gravy along with the beef.

dead man: If someone tells you to remove the "dead man," he's not telling you to hide a body. The "dead man" are the lungs of a crab. When you clean a crab for use in cooking, you always want to remove these and discard.

debris: Debris in New Orleans doesn't mean the stuff you find all over the streets. It refers to a beef roast that has been cooked down until it completely falls apart. Instead of roast beef slices you have "debris." Served as a po' boy or on fresh-cooked buttered biscuits with coffee. In my humble opinion, Mother's Restaurant serves the best debris in the city.

demi glace: This is a concentrated sauce that is usually of the veal variety. It is a veal stock that has been reduced down for many hours. This gives you a rich brown stock that is mixed with other sauces to give a deeper textured sauce than the one you started with. It is also done with chicken to give you a chicken demi glace.

dirty rice: Dirty rice is a Cajun invention that uses the giblets left over from the chicken. They are ground up, spiced, and cooked. From that point they are mixed with cooked rice. It is served as a side dish with just about anything fried (like chicken).

double broiler: This is two pots that are on top of one another in which the bottom one has water boiling in it. It is used to cook things where a control of heat is needed. You can take it away or put it back on the heat as needed.

dressed: When ordering a po' boy sandwich you might be asked if you want it dressed. They doesn't mean you are going to put clothes on it. If you say yes you will have a sandwich covered with lettuce, tomato, mayo, and pickles.

Dutch oven: We use two different kinds of Dutch ovens here. One is the traditional oven often called a "black iron pot." The other is a newer version, which is an iron pot that has an enamel surface on the interior. Both have tight fitting lids. The traditional pot is cast iron and has to be seasoned before you use it the first time. This pot will never see water for cleaning. It is cleaned by wiping it out thoroughly and then oiling the surface to prevent rust. The longer you use it the better pot it becomes. I have known people who have had pots handed down from generation to generation. The second is a cast iron pot that has been covered by enamel. It can be cleaned in a dishwasher. Both conduct heat very well and are used to cook gumbos, stews, and many varieties of dishes.

E:

Eggs Benedict: There are way too many stories as to how this dish was created. Let it suffice to say that it is an English muffin topped with ham, a poached egg, and hollandaise sauce. Period.

Eggs Sardou: No controversy here as to where this dish got its name. It was named after a French dramatist who frequented New Orleans. I guess he visited Antoine's enough that they named the dish after him. It consists of the bottom of an artichoke, a poached egg, some creamed spinach, and of course hollandaise sauce.

emmental cheese: Emmental is basically a mild variety of real Swiss cheese. I say real Swiss cheese because other countries produce emmental and call it that, but it is not the original emmental that was founded in Bern, Switzerland.

erky lurky: See urky lurky. It is spelled both ways.

Espagnole Sauce: This is one of the mother sauces. *Espagnole* is French for "Spanish." Makes sense to me. The story goes that the French king at the time had Spanish cooks. They wanted to make the French brown sauce more Spanish so they added Spanish tomatoes thus ending up with Espagnole Sauce.

etouffee: (a-two-fay) The word is translated into the word "smother." I suppose that is because you cover the dish while cooking it. It is similar to a gumbo except that most etouffees are made with a roux made from flour and butter. Since it is a light colored roux, the butter doesn't have time to burn as it would if you would try to make a dark roux. Normally it is made with crawfish or shrimp. It is red in color due to the fat in the crawfish. If it is made with shrimp, tomato paste is sometimes added. That will also make it red in color. You can also use tomato paste if cooking with crawfish but purists would frown upon it.

F:

Farina flour: See "OO" flour.

file: Pronounced fee-lay, this is the ground up leaves of the sassafras tree that are used in gumbos as a flavor enhancer or a thickener. Before vegetables were available year round file was used when okra was out of season to thicken gumbos and stews.

fish: When you buy fish they should not smell like fish. They should have no smell at all. Look in their eyes and see if they are shiny. Fish with milky or discolored eyes are to be passed over. Some places will put out fresh fish, and then when they go unsold after a day or two they will filet them and present them as fresh. That's why you always want to sniff the fish. No fish smell means fresh fish.

fish sauce: Fish sauce is a condiment used in Asian cooking. It comes from fermented fish mixed with various spices.

five-spice powder: This is a powder that is used in Chinese cooking. It has five different flavors mixed together. Salty, sweet, sour, savory and then bitter.

flank steak: Flank is a cut of beef from the belly of the cow. It is usually a pretty tough piece of meat. The best way of preparing this is a London broil. Even though it has nothing to do with London, it is still called a London broil. When it is cooked, it should be cut against the grain and on a bias or it will be nearly impossible to chew. If you cook it correctly, it makes one of the best sandwiches ever.

flauta: Comes from the Spanish word for flute. In cooking it is a tortilla that is rolled and has a filling.

FOS: Any recipe in this book that has FOS in it refers to flashover seasoning. There is a recipe for it in the beginning of the book. I have been mixing my own spice since I can remember. I named it after a firehouse term "flashover."

French bread: French bread would look somewhat familiar to someone outside of New Orleans if they compared it to a type of bread on which you would serve a sub or a hoagie. Looks are deceiving because they are totally different. New Orleans French bread is light in weight and soft and airy on the inside. It is also very crispy on the outside. I understand that it gets that way because of the high humidity and maybe even that it is being made below sea level. Either way it is great bread to eat without getting a mouth full of dough that you might get from the baseball bat types of French bread I have had elsewhere in the country. You can actually taste what is inside of the sandwich.

French toast: Known in New Orleans as lost bread or Pain Perdu. It is sliced bread that is dipped in egg and milk and then fried in a pan with a little butter. It is usually served for breakfast with powdered sugar, syrup, jelly, or just about any topping you want.

If You Can't Stand the Heat

G:

glace: It comes from an old French word meaning "to freeze." Also means to glaze or ice something.

Goya rice: Goya is just the name brand of rice that is sold in many Latin countries. They make many products primarily sought after in the Latin market. I use Goya rice when I make Mexican rice. I like authentic.

grape seed oil: This is oil that is squeezed from grapes and is used in cooking. One of its great features is that you can use it on very high heats without it burning. It is also good as a salad oil. Who knew that grapes had oil?

granita: A granita is a partially frozen dessert that comes from Italy. When we talk about granitas here it is usually partially frozen because it contains alcohol. Imagine that! I use it to put on top of fresh fruit in desserts. It's usually frozen somewhere between a slushy and chipped ice.

green onion: A green onion in New Orleans is commonly referred to as a shallot although it is not. A green onion is really a scallion. They are long and green with a white bulb on the end. They are normally used as a mild onion that is chopped and added to gumbos and other dishes at the end of the cooking process.

grillades: It's difficult to tell the origin of the word *grillades*. In any case it's supposed to mean thin slices of meat that have been braised in their own juices along with tomatoes and vegetables. It is usually served with grits or, better yet, cheese grits.

gumbo: Gumbo is an African word meaning okra. It is a thick type of stew or soup made with seafood and or meats. It is comprised of a roux, stock, and the trinity followed by the main feature of seafood, meat, or even just herbs. Gumbos are as varied as you could possibly imagine. Everyone has his or her mama's recipe or his or her grandmother's recipe. You can go to ten different restaurants that serve gumbo, and they will all taste different. So when you make your own, it will be your own.

gumbo crabs: When making a seafood gumbo, crabs are often added. I like to use the lightest crabs I can find. They contain the smallest amount of crabmeat, but the crab flavor can still be extracted from them. We call a light (weight wise) crab a "kite."

H:

Hoisin sauce: In Chinese the word means "seafood" even though there is no seafood in the sauce. It is a Chinese dipping sauce made from sweet potatoes.

Hollandaise sauce: One of the mother sauces. It is a combination of egg yolks, butter, spices, and lemon that are emulsified into a sauce. It is used in such dishes as eggs Benedict. The only thing it wouldn't taste good on is another sauce.

holy trinity: Also referred to as the trinity. This is the use of chopped onion, celery, and bell pepper as a vegetable base when cooking. It is just like the mirepoix used in French cooking, but bell peppers are substituted for carrots.

hot capocolla: See capocolla.

I:

injector: See Cajun Injector.

immersion blender: This is a handy little kitchen devise that acts as a hand-held mini-blender. They are usually about a foot long and have little propeller blades on the bottom. If you have something that is in a pot and needs to be blended, especially something hot, you would use this. It cleans up easily as opposed to a regular blender. A quick rinse, and you're done.

If You Can't Stand the Heat

J:

jambalaya: Jambalaya (jam-ba-lie-ah) comes from the French word "jambon" meaning ham and an African word "ya" meaning rice. It comes to the table in two different ways. Both are basically meat and or seafood cooked with vegetables in a rich stock. The Creole version (red jambalaya) has tomatoes in it where the Cajun version (brown jambalaya) does not. The Cajun style gets its color from the browning of the meat on the bottom of the pot before adding the veggies. What they have in common is that both dishes are cooked and then rice is added to the pot, covered, and allowed to cook without stirring or removing the lid. The rice cooks and absorbs all of the stock then mixes with the veggies, meats, seafood, and spices.

Jasmine rice: Jasmine rice is a type of Thai rice with the scent of the jasmine flower. It is used primarily in Asian cuisine. Once again, I use it for Fried Rice (see recipe). Authentic!

julienne: To julienne is to cut food up into long and thin strips. Similar to a chiffonade, but that is usually referring to herbs or greens that are rolled and cut whereas julienne can be any cut up food such as carrots or even chicken.

K:

Karo Syrup: Brand name of a company that manufactures corn syrup. It comes in different colors, but the most popular one (and the one I use in cooking) is the dark syrup. Until it was invented, people brought their jug to the grocer and filled it with syrup from a barrel. The Karo name is something that is supposed to have come from the wife, whose name was Caroline, of the man who invented it. There are other theories, but I like that one best.

Kitchen Bouquet: This is a sauce that is used to add seasoning and browning. My mom always used it to make gravies darker and to add the flavoring that comes from Kitchen Bouquet to foods, usually chicken.

Kirshwasser: Kirshwasser is German liquor that is not sweet even though it is made of cherries. Sometimes it is referred to only as Kirsch. Great stuff for desserts.

Kosher salt: This is a coarse salt that is different from normal table salt. Table salt adds iodine thus, iodized salt. Kosher salt is used in a lot of cooking especially in the gourmet world. It is only referred to as kosher salt in North America. In other parts of the planet it is called coarse salt. Because its grains are so coarse it doesn't dissolve as easily when coated on meats and stays on the surface. Therefore, it helps draw the blood from meats without making them salty, thus making the meat kosher. If you followed all of that, you get a gold star.

L:

lagniappe: It comes from the Spanish word *la napa*, which means, "something added." This eventually became the word *lagniappe*, which in New Orleans is translated into "a little something extra." If you went out to a restaurant and ordered a hamburger and the fries were thrown in for free, we would say that the fries were lagniappe.

liquid smoke: Liquid smoke is a bottled flavoring that when added to food will give it a smoky taste. It is very strong so very little goes a long way.

lo mein: This is a Chinese dish with noodles cooked together with either meat or seafood along with vegetables.

London broil: See flank steak.

lost bread: In New Orleans lost bread is another way of saying French Toast. It's also referred to as Pain Perdu. My grandparents used to make French toast out of day-old French bread slices and called it Pain Perdu. My parents called it lost bread. We call it French toast.

M:

macerate: This is a process by which you would soak something in a liquid to soften it. In the case of cooking, it usually refers to the soaking of fruit in alcohol. When you macerate raspberries, you would

If You Can't Stand the Heat

soak them in a raspberry liquor so they would soften and release their own sugars. Just make sure you save enough liquor for the berries and don't drink enough to macerate yourself.

mandoline: Not to be confused with a musical instrument called a mandolin. This is a kitchen implement that is used to slice things. For instance, if you were going to thinly slice a veggie or a piece of fruit, you might use a mandoline (man-dough-lean). Just make sure you use the holder that comes with it; otherwise, you may lose a fingertip.

maque choux: Maque choux, which is pronounced mock-shoe, is a dish that contains corn and tomatoes. It's a combination that came from French and Native American influences in Louisiana.

Marsala: Marsala wine, like port, is a fortified wine that is normally used in cooking. If you cook it down until it thickens, add butter and onions, it becomes a Marsala sauce.

mirepoix: In Louisiana we use a vegetable base called the trinity. That would be onions, celery, and bell pepper. In classic French cooking they use a mirepoix. That would be a base of onions, celery, and carrots.

mirliton: Elsewhere in the cooking world a mirliton is a pastry covered with almonds. In Louisiana a mirliton is a green vegetable that grows on a vine. Also known as a chayote or alligator pear. In New Orleans we grow them and then stuff them. We also use them in casseroles.

Mornay Sauce: Even though it sounds really fancy, a Mornay sauce is just a Béchamel sauce that has cheese added to it.

Mother Sauces: There are five sauces that are called mother sauces. They are béchamel, Espagnole, hollandaise, tomato, and veloute. These sauces can be used on their own. The reason for the mother sauce label is that you can use any of them as a base to create many more sauces.

mortadella: This is an Italian salami that has little white flecks of ground pork fat in it. They used to grind the pork fat with a mortar and pestle thus mortadella.

MSG: The long version is monosodium glutamate. This is a sodium product that is used as an additive to foods for enhancing the flavor of that food.

mudbug: Just another word used to refer to crawfish. They grow in fresh water under the mud thus, mudbug.

muffuletta: Pronounced (muff-al-letta) or (moof-a-lotta). Tomato, tomata. Who cares? Just get down to Central Grocery on Decatur Street and have one. Theirs is the best because they invented the thing. It is a sandwich made with Sicilian bread. It contains Italian meats and cheeses, but the thing that makes it great is the olive salad. It is heated to melt the cheeses and unless you have a bottomless pit for a stomach, you can't eat a whole one. They are meant to be shared.

N:

Neufchatel cheese: This is a soft, dry white French cheese. The American version is like a cream cheese and is used sometimes as a substitute for cream cheese.

Nueske's: This is a company that produces great smoked meats and gifts. When I need some applewood smoked bacon or a smoked duck breast and can't find it at a store, I order from Nueske's.

O:

olive salad: An olive salad is not what one would normally think of as a conventional salad. It comes in a jar and is comprised of olives, garlic, carrots, cauliflower, and olive oil that have been mixed and marinated with vinegar. It is used inside of a muffuletta sandwich. Sometimes we just spread it on hot bread and chow down. That's what firemen do!

"OO" flour: An Italian wheat flour that is very fine. Used to make pasta and dough. Also called farina flour.

orzo: In Italian it means "barley." But to the average person it is pasta that is made in the shape of rice. I use it when I want the flavor of pasta without all of the volume.

If You Can't Stand the Heat

oyster liquor: This is always used in reference to the juice that comes out of the shucked shell of the oyster. When it is shucked, the oyster has a slightly salty liquid that the oyster is surrounded by. As the oyster is cut from the shell for cooking it is put into a container along with the juice. That is the oyster liquor. It is used in cooking along with the oyster or by itself to add some oyster flavor to a dish.

Oyster sauce: This is a thick brown sauce made of oysters that is used in many Chinese and Thai dishes. Hey, it's not just a Cajun thing; Asians like oysters too!

P:

Pain Perdu: Also known in New Orleans as lost bread or elsewhere called French Toast. The direct translation to English is Lost Bread. Most of the time it gets lost in my stomach.

pancetta: This is an Italian pork product that has been salt cured. It is dried for months but not smoked. Think of it as Italian bacon without the smokehouse flavor.

panko: Panko is a Japanese breadcrumb that is made from dried bread that does not include the crust. It is white in color and makes a really crusty outside coating when used in the frying of whatever you happen to be frying.

paneed: In Louisiana cooking it is pronounced, "pon aid." This means to pound down meats until they are thin and then dredge them in some kind of coating. After that they are fried in oil. Paneed veal, paneed chicken, etc. In French it means "to coat with breadcrumbs."

Parmigiano-Reggiano: This is often called the king of cheeses. After aging for a year, the taste and aroma are wonderful. It comes from Parma, Italy. It is used in a wide variety of dishes or simply eaten on its own. For my money it is hands down the best cheese ever invented.

pasta (salting): Always add salt to the water when you are cooking pasta for the very simple reason that it will be the only time you get to put any spice into the pasta.

Paul Prudhomme: He is a chef from Opelousas, Louisiana, that has one of the best restaurants in the world. It is K-Paul's in the French Quarter. He also has a line of spices and has written many cookbooks on Louisiana dishes.

peanut oil: Peanut oil is naturally made from peanuts. It is a clean tasting oil that has a high smoke point. I prefer it when frying anything because it will withstand higher temperatures than some other oils without burning. Just be prepared to look deep into your wallet because it is expensive...but so worth it.

Pecorino Romano cheese: This is a sharp Italian cheese that is made of goat's milk. The word "pecora" is Italian for goat. It is a sharp salty cheese that is used in many Italian dishes.

peel: We're not talking about a banana peel here. The peel I am referring to is a long-handled paddle that has a large, flat, wide tip and is used in baking. I'm sure you have seen it used to slide pizzas in and out of the oven.

pesto: The name comes from an Italian word that means "to crush." It was started in Genoa, Italy. It is a sauce made from fresh basil leaves, garlic, cheese, pine nuts, and oil. Recently I have seen people make pesto with cilantro and even with mint. They are for specialty dishes. I guess they use the word *pesto* because it looks like the original.

pickle meat: In some places they use the term salt pork. It's not quite the same as what we here in New Orleans call pickle meat. It's used in red beans and to give flavor to greens. It is a pork butt that has been pickled. You can find it readily at any neighborhood grocery in New Orleans.

Pickapeppa Sauce: Pickapeppa comes in small bottles. It is derived from a combination of different fruits and sugars. It was invented in Jamaica and is known as the Jamaican ketchup. Its uses are varied and found in many dishes around the globe.

picking a crab: If someone asks you if you know how to pick a crab, they are not asking you for an opinion in a crab beauty contest. This refers to taking a crab apart and picking out all of the crabmeat to use in cooking. It also refers to (my favorite) picking out all of the meat just to eat it.

If You Can't Stand the Heat

pirogue: (pee-rouge) It comes from a Spanish word *pirague*, meaning "dugout canoe." It is a flat bottom boat used in Louisiana primarily because it can go through very shallow water. Out on the bayous, you can see many Cajuns using this type of boat to check their crawfish traps.

pith: This is the very nasty-tasting white layer that is below the zest on citrus fruit.

pizza paddle: Normally called a peel. It is used to put a pizza into an oven and remove it from the oven.

pizza stone: This is a ceramic or clay stone that is used to mimic the effects of a pizza oven while cooking at home. You heat it up in the oven and slide a homemade pizza onto the stone. It evenly distributes the heat throughout the pizza. Also used to make calzones and breads.

plum sauce: A condiment that is made of plums and other ingredients that is used in Asian cooking. It is a type of sweet and sour sauce used for dipping egg rolls and other fried items.

po' boy: (or poorboy) Nobody, and I mean nobody, really knows where the term comes from. There seems to be as many origins for this word as there are types of gumbo. I tend to go with the one that uses the words "pour boire." That's French for "for drink." It was a sandwich brought home to make peace or as a peace offering. Supposedly, when men came home after tying one on, they would bring home an offering of peace in the form of an oyster sandwich. That was eventually Americanized into po' boy. I like this story the best because to this day you can go down to Acme Oyster House and get an oyster po' boy called the peacemaker. In other parts of the country it would be a type of hoagie or a sub. There is also a story that during a strike, inexpensive sandwiches were made to feed those "poor boys." Maybe that one is closer to the truth, but I like the first one better.

prosciutto: The Italian word for ham. This meat is dry cured and not cooked. We use it to cook with in many dishes as a flavor additive.

Q:

queso: Mexican word for cheese. Mexican cheese melts well.

R:

ramekin: A ramekin is a small round dish that can withstand high temperatures. You use them to cook individual portions of food in high heat ovens.

ravioli: Word is that it comes from the Italian word *riavvolgere*, which means, "to wrap." Not sure if it's true, but it doesn't matter. It is basically two layers of pasta that are put together and stuffed. I like to stuff them into my mouth. But that's just me.

remoulade: Some will say that there are a few different types of remoulade. The classic is white whereas the Cajun version is red. There may be some that are rust colored or even almost orange. The classic white version is French in origin. The original was served with meat. In Louisiana we use remoulade mainly with seafood (shrimp remoulade). They are all basically the same. Just about all of them contain mayo and Creole mustard. From there it varies in ingredients. Onions, garlic, lemon, Tabasco, and other things can be added. The color differences come from either adding ketchup or paprika. The more you put in of either, the redder it gets. I think it is the best sauce ever invented. I use it on salads, seafood...all kinds of things. If people wouldn't think it was strange I'd probably bathe in it.

roasted garlic: This is a method of changing the taste and texture of garlic by covering it in olive oil and baking it in the oven. It will make the pods soft, make them sweeter, and allow you to use them to make dishes that you otherwise couldn't with plain garlic. If for instance, you wanted to make garlic butter this would allow you to use softened garlic that would easily blend and mix with the butter.

rope: Refers to the "slime" that comes from cooking okra. When you cook okra with an acid (such as a tomato) it will help break down that "rope" and to some extent eliminate it. In Louisiana you might hear someone say, "Cook all of the rope out of the okra."

roulade: A roulade is something that has been cut thin so you can stuff it. It is then rolled and either eaten or cooked to be eaten. Some people call it a braciole, but in actuality a braciole is a roulade, but a roulade isn't necessarily a braciole. A California roll in a sushi bar is also a type of roulade. If you followed all of that, explain it to me, will you?

If You Can't Stand the Heat

roux: There are many different kinds of roux. Basically it is comprised of flour and oil. It is the base for gumbos and gravies. Some are made with flour and vegetable oil. Some are made with olive oil and some with butter instead of oil. It all depends on what you are cooking.

In this book you will notice that I stress using room temperature stocks when adding them to a roux. Some people will disagree with this. They will tell you it needs to be hot. I just find that it is much easier to avert disaster if you use room temperature stock. If you want to try adding hot stock to your roux, be my guest. Just don't blame me if you have to start over.

S:

San Marzano tomato: These are similar to a Roma tomato only sweeter in taste than your average plum tomato. They grow in a region where the soil is partially volcanic ash. This is supposed to filter the growing process of the tomato and make it a highly sought after tomato by many cooks. To simplify, I use them because they taste better. That's it.

sauté: Comes from the French word *sauter*, which means to jump or flip. If you put some oil in a shallow pan and slowly fry something down, as in onions, your are sautéing. You have to turn whatever you are sautéing often. You have seen chefs flip food in a sauté pan. That is "sautering" or sautéing.

scallion: In New Orleans, a scallion is referred to as a shallot although technically it is not. Technically they are green onions. They are long and green with a white bulb on the end. If you come to New Orleans and ask for a scallion, you might get a funny look. Be prepared.

sea salt: Salt that is processed by evaporating the water out of seawater. I use it when I need salt to prepare any dish with seafood as a base. Put it back where it came from, that's my motto.

Semolina "OO" flour: See "OO" flour.

sesame oil: Sesame oil is made, as I'm sure you can guess, out of sesame seeds. It has a high heat point, which makes it very popular in Asian cuisine.

shallot: A shallot is a small type of onion that tastes much sweeter than a normal onion. They don't grow like typical onions, which grow one at a time. Shallots grow in clusters. In New Orleans, if you say shallot, it usually refers to a green onion. Elsewhere, a green onion is called a scallion.

shrimp (buying): The old saying is that if you can smell them, don't buy them. Also, if you see any of that rusty color through the head, don't buy them. They should be clear to the eye and kept cold.

shrimp (count): When you hear someone say the shrimp are a twenty-six to thirty, they are referring to the amount of shrimp to a pound. Fifteen to twenty, twenty-one to twenty-five, and so on. Ten count shrimp are great for barbequed shrimp. You might also hear someone refer to mixed shrimp. If you buy them at the dock, they are not sorted by size and will have small, medium, and large mixed together.

shrimp (deveining): When you buy fresh shrimp they will have a black line down their back. It is part of their digestive track. You want to butterfly them and remove the "vein" before you cook them.

shrimp (freezing): Never freeze shrimp with the heads on. Not only will it ruin the shrimp, the sharp barbs will poke holes in your Ziploc bags and the water will spill out. Some people believe that it's all right to freeze them with the heads on for a short period of time. I don't subscribe to that theory. Freeze them without the heads. Use the heads to make shrimp stock then freeze the stock.

silpat: A silpat is a silicon-based mat that is used in cooking instead of parchment paper. It's flexible like paper but cleans very easily. They come in a variety of sizes and I use them whenever I have to bake pastries in the oven. Nothing sticks to them so the food comes off easier than if you use a pan or dish.

soft-shell crabs: Crabs will molt or shed their shells to continue to grow. Once they have lost their hard shell, it takes awhile for their new shell to harden. At the time of the molting they are harvested, and you are able to eat the entire crab because of the soft shell. You can also do the same with crawfish. They molt too.

sopressata: This is a type of Italian salami. You will know it when you see it because it has little black flecks of peppercorns in the meat when it is sliced.

If You Can't Stand the Heat

Sriracha: This is a Thai sauce that is found in the United States. It is made of chilies and garlic and will add a lot of zip to any dish. The original Thai version of this has more of a watery smooth texture whereas the U.S. version is thicker. Both of them are pretty hot!

"suck the head and pinch the tail": When eating boiled crawfish you start by pinching the tail away from the head. There is a lot of really spicy juice in the head. In order to get the meat from the tail you pinch it and if cooked properly, the tail meat will fall out. So the correct way to attack boiled crawfish is to "suck the head and pinch the tail."

T:

tapenade: A tapanade is a spread that is put on top of bread that is usually made with olives. Normally it is a mixture of olives and other things and is put atop crispy breads for an appetizer. I have also seen it done with fruits. There are now whole bars set up for this. A tapanade bar. Next thing you know we'll have bruschetta bars. Not a bad idea.

tasso: You can think of tasso as a Cajun ham. It's a pork butt that has been spiced and smoked. You can't make a ham sandwich out of it (although that might not be too bad come to think about it), but it is used as a meat additive in cooking things from gravies to cream sauces. It will give whatever dish you are making a certain smokiness and also give it a little kick. Maybe even a push and a shove.

Thai chili sauce: It is a sweet sauce that can be used straight from the bottle as a spicy dip or added to foods while they are cooking to give it an extra sweet and spicy kick.

tilapia: This is a fish that is sometimes referred to here in New Orleans as a "Mexican Redfish." I'm not sure how they ended up with that distinction because they are neither Mexican nor are they redfish. I think it is probably because they were used a lot, along with drum, as a substitute when redfish became popular to "blacken." People almost wiped out the species, so substitutes were needed to give time to the redfish to replenish their population. Tilapia can live in fresh, brackish, and salt water. They grow large and are a good, solid, and tasty fish. They grow fast and are often farmed for this reason. They are found practically everywhere on the planet and are omnivores.

Tony Chachere's: Tony was a Cajun cook from Opelousas, Louisiana. He started a company that makes spices, marinades, and the like that are found in grocery stores across the country. Tony Chachere's Creole seasoning is very popular and used by many here in Louisiana. If I run out of FOS, I use Tony's as a substitute.

trinity: Also referred to as the holy trinity. Refers to the use of chopped onion, celery, and bell peppers as a vegetable base when cooking. Similar to the mirepoix used in French cooking but using bell pepper instead of carrots.

U:

Urky Lurky: This was invented in a New Orleans firehouse and was called this because the cook supposedly used whatever happened to be lurking around the fridge after the last shift had left. It contains pasta, olives, garlic, olive oil, and meats. Sometimes vegetables are also included. If it is made with seafood, it is Urky. If it contained meats instead, it's spelled with an E as in Erky. Don't ask me why because I don't know. I don't think anybody does. You can generally add anything you want to it and it's going to be lurky. Whatever is hanging around!

V:

Veal demi glace: See demi glace.

Veloute sauce: This is one of the mother sauces. In French cooking it means "velvet." You combine a reduced stock with a roux and cook it until it is velvety smooth.

venison: Venison refers to deer meat.

Vidalia onion: A Vidalia is a sweet onion that was originally grown in Vidalia, Georgia. Its taste makes it ideal for cooking in certain dishes where you want a slightly sweeter taste then a regular onion. Try making some Vidalia fried onion rings sometime. Good!

 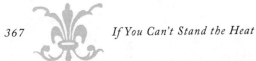 *If You Can't Stand the Heat*

W:

wasabi: This is a Japanese root plant that, when processed, is used in cooking. It is a kind of a Japanese horseradish. It is used in sushi, and we use it to mix into sauces to give them a little more zip. Use it sparingly, or you will be blowing smoke rings without using a cigar. Also comes in a powder form.

wonton: Wontons are little sheets of dough that are stuffed with a filling, fried or steamed, and then eaten with a dip. Wonton wrappers are the part of the wonton that you would purchase in order to fill them. When filled and folded, fried or steamed, we call them "pot stickers." You can also cut them up and fry them by themselves. I like to eat them just like that or put fried wontons into soups. Versatile little suckers, aren't they?

Z:

Zatarain's Liquid Crab Boil: Zatarain's is a company that produces many of the spices and condiments that we use in cooking here in New Orleans. The liquid crab boil is a highly concentrated blend of spices that is used when boiling crabs, shrimp, or crawfish. No self-respecting New Orleanian would be caught dead without some in his or her pantry.

Zatarain's Crab Boil Complete: This product comes in a large plastic container. It has all of the ingredients required to cook boiled seafood without the need to add anything else.

Zatarain's Fish Fry: Another product from Zatarain's that is used for a coating when frying seafood and vegetables. Similar to cornmeal, but finer and better tasting.

Zatarain's Pro-Boil: The same as Zatarain's Crab Boil Complete except with even more concentrated flavors and kick.

zest: Zest is the outer part of a citrus fruit that is removed by grating it off. It is used in cooking to impart extra or strong flavor of that particular citrus fruit (orange, lemon, etc.).

INDEX

If You Can't Stand the Heat

If You Can't Stand the Heat